Post-Disaster Reconstruction

Post-Disaster Reconstruction

Lessons from Aceh

Edited by
Matthew Clarke, Ismet Fanany and Sue Kenny

publishing for a sustainable future

London • Washington, DC

First published in 2010 by Earthscan

Earthscan Ltd, Dunstan House, 14a St Cross Street, London EC1N 8XA, UK
Earthscan LLC, 1616 P Street, NW, Washington, DC 20036, USA
Earthscan publishes in association with the International Institute for Environment and Development

For more information on Earthscan publications, see www.earthscan.co.uk or write to earthinfo@earthscan.co.uk

ISBN: 978-1-84407-879-0 hardback

Typeset by 4word Ltd, Bristol, UK
Cover design by Susanne Harris

A catalogue record for this book is available from the British Library

Library of Congress Cataloging-in-Publication Data

Post-disaster reconstruction : lessons from Aceh / edited by Matthew Clarke, Ismet Fanany and Sue Kenny.
     p. cm.
  Includes bibliographical references and index.
  ISBN 978-1-84407-879-0 (hardback)
  1. Indian Ocean Tsunami, 2004. 2. Tsunami damage–Indonesia–Aceh. 3. Tsunami relief–Indonesia–Aceh. 4. Disaster relief–Indonesia–Aceh. I. Clarke, Matthew. II. Fanany, Ismet, 1952- III. Kenny, Susan, 1946-
  HV603 2004 .I44 P67 2010
  363.34'9480959811–dc22
                                   2009053717

At Earthscan we strive to minimize our environmental impacts and carbon footprint through reducing waste, recycling and offsetting our CO_2 emissions, including those created through publication of this book. For more details of our environmental policy, see www.earthscan.co.uk.

Printed and bound in the UK by The Cromwell Press Group. The paper used is FSC certified.

Mixed Sources
Product group from well-managed forests and other controlled sources
www.fsc.org Cert no. TT-COC-2082
© 1996 Forest Stewardship Council
FSC

*To the courage and determination of the survivors of
the earthquake and tsunami that hit Aceh on
26 December 2004*

Contents

Conclusion

List of Figures and Tables

Chapter 6

Figures

Tables

Silence can be Deafening and Emptiness can be Blinding[1]

When the Indian Ocean tsunami hit, on 26 December 2004, I was in Melbourne, Australia. The news that first day was that various places in the region had suffered some destruction and loss of life. However, as further reports came in, the numbers of casualties grew by the hour as the true extent and severity of the disaster became clear.

Aceh was barely mentioned during those first hours. I later learned that this was because communication out of Aceh was near impossible, and there were almost no reporters there at the time, owing to the armed conflict between the Free Aceh Movement (Gerakan Aceh Merdeka, GAM) and the Indonesian government. This conflict had severely restricted access by outsiders for a number of years. Very soon, however, Aceh dominated the news concerning the tsunami, as it became apparent that it was the hardest hit.

I returned to Jakarta on 1 January 2005 and it was only then that I began to have an inkling of the magnitude of what had happened in Aceh. As was the case for most people at the time, I had no idea how bad the situation really was, even though I had learned that thousands of people had been killed in Aceh and that many more were missing or otherwise unaccounted for. I was unable to reach any of the many friends I have in the region, but this fact, in itself, did not bother me unduly, since telephone connections often fail following natural disasters. However, I did wonder about them, and if any of them or their families had died.

Yenny Wahid, the Director of the Wahid Institute, where I serve as Executive Director, had just returned from Aceh. She had gone there the day after the tsunami, and she spoke of destruction, human tragedy and death, on a scale which was like nothing I had ever heard before. There was little time in which to visualize the situation or think about her story, however, as she instructed a small team, of which I was part, to prepare and assemble as many relief supplies as possible. Former President Abdurrahman Wahid, also known as Gus Dur, joined the team. We were to leave for Aceh within days. I had never imagined that I was about to participate in the world's largest relief effort ever undertaken in peacetime, involving so many people from so many countries, and so many millions of dollars. Governments all over the world pledged large amounts of money, and NGOs arrived unannounced in Aceh en masse to offer help and their experience. Thousands of individuals volunteered their time and energy and donated money. Military forces from several countries were sent to Aceh by their governments to lend their equipment and personnel. It was a remarkable response that reflected the severity of the disaster.

This is my story of the disaster. Since this is a book about the reconstruction of Aceh, it is appropriate that we should begin with the damage, destruction and loss. It was these effects that reconstruction efforts have tried to address. It was the purpose of the massive relief effort that the damage should be repaired, the destruction rebuilt, and the loss replaced. The reality, however, proved less straightforward.

As my aircraft approached Iskandar Muda airport in Banda Aceh, I could see from the window that I was coming to a strange place, quite unlike its former self, that I had visited many times before. This once familiar place now seemed very unfamiliar. The airport was surrounded by hundreds of tents that had changed the landscape completely. I saw large cargo planes and military helicopters from other nations. The arrival hall was full of people from different parts of the world. The faces of the people I saw and met were strange to me, and all wore an unsettled expression of dread mixed with curiosity. I did not yet understand the full effect of the tsunami, and had no idea what I was about to see.

On the way from the airport to the city, I encountered two things that left a lasting impression on me and that, from then on, provided a frame of reference in understanding the effects of the tsunami. The first was the smell of death. Before I had seen the first corpse (of many that I came across during that short five-day visit), I was struck by the stench of rotting human flesh that was present everywhere. It was strangely powerful. The smell that day in Banda Aceh made me wonder how many bodies there were, as the smell was so strong, yet at first not a single body was visible. Smells can leave a lasting impact that is never forgotten.

The second thing I encountered was the first visual evidence of life lost, a mass grave. Gus Dur asked the driver to stop and everybody got out. We went to the grave and said a prayer, led by Gus Dur. What I saw then gave me my first indication of the extent of the disaster in terms of loss of life. It showed in no uncertain terms that this was no ordinary disaster. Clearly we were in the midst of an unusual situation that demanded an unusual response. The mass grave, with no indication of who the dead were, symbolized a finality that I found both strange and saddening. I had been told from the time I was very little the importance of remembering and paying respect to family members who had died, by visiting their graves, for example. But as I was saying my prayer next to the mass grave that day, I knew that no family members of those who were buried there would ever come to visit.

For the rest of the journey to Banda Aceh, silence reigned in the car. It was as if everybody was having a private conversation with themselves. I was thinking about the smell, and the mass grave: the visible and invisible signs of the tsunami's devastation. During my short stay in Aceh, I was to see much more visible damage, destruction and loss, and would also perceive much that was invisible.

I, like the other team members, spent all my waking time in Aceh travelling in and around Banda Aceh, including the most affected areas on and near the beaches. One of the most striking sights in all these places was the mess and scattered wreckage. I had never seen so much! The whole area was covered by it. It restricted people's movements and hindered emergency work. By the time I was there, the debris that had blocked most of the main roads had been cleared aside and was piled high. In some areas, the walls of debris were up to five metres high. Another striking aspect was what the wreckage consisted of. All sorts of things littered the place: leaves and branches; plastic items; parts of buildings, cars and trucks; cloth and clothing; all in large quantities, thrown about in an unsightly manner as if hurled by an angry, insane giant.

The effect of the huge amount and variety of debris was further emphasized by the fact that many objects had ended up in the most unlikely places: twisted cars in rice fields; a whole boat on part of the ground floor of a house whose top floor had been torn off; fronds from a coconut palm in a roofless living room; and so on. The whole place was chaotic. Things were in places they were not supposed to be, and things that one expected to be in a particular place were somewhere else.

I never thought that the impact of seeing objects where they were not supposed to be, or of not seeing things where they were expected, could be so great. This was particularly the case when I went to an area near the beach, where rows of houses once stood. The houses had all gone. There was no sign that even a single house had ever stood there, let alone rows of them. Even the land where those houses had been was gone – it was now ocean! There was nothing there, except the water moving slowly and rhythmically, as gentle and benign as the waves at any swimming beach. I stared at the water where there had once been houses. I had visited one of them several times. People talk about silence that is deafening; that day I learned that emptiness can be blinding.

But perhaps what moved me most in terms of what I could see around me was the dead bodies. There were so many of them, all over the place, mixed with all the debris. And this was already the second week of hard work by so many people who had come to help. The dead bodies were lying in all sorts of positions and conditions. They were swelling. Most were without any clothes. I could not bear to watch, as they were collected and buried in mass graves using tractors and other types of heavy machines. The people doing this attempted to do so in a dignified manner, but I found it hard to accept that the dead had to be collected and buried in this way.

And then there was the smell of rotting human flesh again. It was present all the time, everywhere I went. But if the smell was not bad enough, what I witnessed next was even more harrowing. It concerned the surviving victims of the tsunami. By then, most of them were already in temporary emergency accommodation, such as tents. After running around frantically for a couple of days, studying the physical destruction and handing out supplies to victims, I began to look at the faces of the survivors. These included children who had lost their parents, parents who had lost their children, husbands or wives who had lost their spouse, boys and girls who had lost their siblings, men and women who had lost their friends or neighbours or someone else. In short, practically every survivor had lost someone. And all of them had lost the physical elements of their life.

Several things that were notable by their absence struck me as soon as I tried to talk to the survivors. In children, I noticed the absence of a desire to play. Many of them simply sat, looking sad and confused. I remember talking to other volunteer workers about the children's lack of interest in games. We tried to get them some toys, such as soccer balls, but this made little impression. It was as if what they had experienced had been so massive that it had erased any other impulses they might have felt at normal times.

In adults, I noticed silence. They would sit or lie down, their faces empty of expression. They looked, without seeing anything. Their blank stares reflected an emptiness of soul. Just as the first smell of rotting human flesh I encountered in the car from the airport on the day I arrived had told me something about the loss of life from the tsunami, so the children's lack of desire to play, and the adults' blank stares, indicated to me incredible suffering, part of which was caused by the damage, destruction and loss I had witnessed, and part by the manner in which it had occurred. Some of them may have had some inkling of the future uncertainty that would no doubt follow. All were reluctant to face the future, and were frightened of what might come next.

It was not what these survivors said, but rather what they did not say, that meant much. No one spoke about feelings. Some of what they did say, however, indicated the complete helplessness felt by many. This partly explained the silence and the blank stares. They said, for example, that the disaster had been the wrath of God because they had not been good enough Muslims. It occurred to me that, to people with such a strong view of God, there must be nothing more frightening than His wrath.

Another thought that came to mind in the face of their silence and blank stares was the faith-shattering effect of the tsunami. Muslims believe that Allah is supremely merciful and loving. In addition, they also believe that Allah is all-forgiving, and will absolve those who repent. The tsunami had occurred just days after the end of the fasting month of Ramadhan, at the end of which Muslims believe they are freed of their past sins. The whole month of fasting is supposed to erase all wrongdoing. Under this conception, the tsunami, as an expression of the wrath of God, had occurred during a period of purity from sin.

I did not know, and still don't, to what extent this explained the survivors' condition that I witnessed. I do know that this idea became one of the most common themes of sermons at the mosques, when they addressed the tsunami and its aftermath. I also know that some of my friends and acquaintances in Aceh have become more religious, outwardly at least. They now practise the five daily prayers more regularly, go to the mosque more often, and, in the case of women, are more observant of Islamic dress requirements, such as the wearing of headscarves.

What I also realized at the end of my five-day visit to Aceh was that the tsunami had inflicted two types of disaster on the Acehnese. One was physical destruction: the death of family members and friends, destruction of houses and other property, damage to infrastructure, loss of businesses, and so on. The second was destruction of the soul: shattered faith, lost hope, a crippling sense of helplessness, and a loss of certainty about how the world works. I left Aceh with the belief that the two were equal in their severity. I took away a concern that the reconstruction and rehabilitation efforts, with all the good intentions and sincerity that accompanied them, might fail to recognize the nature and extent of the second type of destruction. If this proved to be the case, it would mean that this psychological destruction would not receive much attention. The efforts to help the people of Aceh, therefore, would overlook an important aspect of community life, and this would affect significantly the outcome of the hard work of so many.

It is probably true that reconstructing physical destruction is an easier problem to deal with than reconstructing damaged psyches. Physical destruction can be quantified more easily. It is possible to calculate how many square kilometres of area require cleaning up, how many kilometres of road and how many bridges have been destroyed, how many houses, schools, and mosques have been washed away, and how many stores, fishing boats and other businesses damaged. These all received urgent attention, the availability of money, manpower, and expertise being virtually all that was required to restore the environment.

A natural disaster is only a disaster because it affects the life of human beings. A landslide, for example, is not a disaster when it occurs in an unpopulated area, no matter how large the slide is. But if it buries houses and causes material damage and loss of life, it becomes a disaster. This, of course, is the reason why the 2004 Indian Ocean tsunami is considered one of the worst natural disasters in history. The number of people who lost their lives was among the highest on record. This tsunami also has the distinction of being the single natural disaster that affected more countries than any other.

If the affect on human beings is the determinant of whether a phenomenon is a disaster or not, it follows that the second type of destruction discussed above, the destruction of the psyche, should also receive equal attention. While the loss of life and damage to property contribute significantly to psychological devastation, other factors play a role as well. The belief system of the victims, for example, might contribute. Their world view may not take into account the possibility of a happening of the magnitude experienced in Aceh and they may be poorly equipped to imagine, much less deal with, the result. If physical safety is associated with moral conduct, as it was for some of the victims of the tsunami in Aceh, the absence of that security might completely undermine the most basic of their beliefs.

Understandably and predictably, the reconstruction work in Aceh has largely addressed the first type of destruction rather than the second. Reports of the reconstruction are full of statistics about what had to be built, repaired or replaced, and to what extent this was completed during the period of time in question. Success has generally been measured in terms of the rebuilding of physical structures. It is understandable that many donors and organizations prefer to participate in this kind of reconstruction. They are required to report to those who provide their funding, and their terms of operation are usually limited. They expect to achieve concrete results in a limited period of time.

The second type of reconstruction does not lend itself to tight scheduling and clear reporting. For this reason, while it is obvious that the victims of the tsunami in Aceh require more than reconstruction of the physical environment, only the replacement of tangible items is measurable. It was understood, for example, that facilitating religious networking would provide emotional and spiritual support, and efforts in this area were measured, among other things, by the rebuilding of mosques. The mosque, however, is only a small part of religious infrastructure. The loss of the individuals who managed and ran activities at mosques is more important. These people possessed the religious knowledge and insight to offer spiritual guidance and emotional structure to survivors who would have to build new lives. They would have been able to provide this help without a mosque or any other items, if required. A mosque without them, however, is of limited use. Religious knowledge and the ability to provide meaningful counsel cannot be quantified.

The reconstruction and rehabilitation work in post-tsunami Aceh has taught the world many things. They have been a reminder of how devastating natural disasters can be. They have pointed up the aspects of natural disaster that are easily dealt with. But they also suggest that we know little about psychological reconstruction, especially how to accomplish this in ways that will conform to and be accepted within the particular world view of the victims. In this, every community is unique, and we must be aware that what has been lost represents generations of accumulated sociocultural wisdom. Money and goodwill, no matter how well intentioned, cannot quickly restore a culture; perhaps only time can do that. Moreover, we have also learned that reconstruction means different things to different people.

Ahmad Suaedy

Notes

1   The editors would like to thank Dr Rebecca Fanany for her assistance in the translation of this chapter, which was submitted in Indonesian.

List of Acronyms

ACARP	Aceh Community Assistance Research Project
AGAM	Angkatan GAM (GAM Forces)
AMM	Aceh Monitoring Mission
ASNLF	Aceh/Sumatra National Liberation Front
ATRT	Asian Tsunami Response Team
AusAID	Australian Agency for International Development
Bappenas	*Badan Perencanaaan dan Pembangunan Nasional* (National Development Planning Agency)
BPK	*Badan Pemeriksaan Keuangan* (Financial Auditing Agency)
BPP	*Biro Pemberdayaan Perempuan* (Bureau for Women's Empowerment)
BRA	*Badan Reintegrasi-Damai Aceh* (Aceh Reintegration-Peace Agency)
BRR	*Badan Rehabilitasi dan Rekonstuksi* (Recontruction and Rehabilitation Agency)
CE	Common Era (AD)
CGI	Consultative Group on Indonesia
CIGS	Community Infrastructure Grants Scheme
CoHA	Cessation of Hostilities Agreement
DII	Darul Islam Indonesia rebellion
DIPA	*Daftar Isian Proyek Anggaran* (List of Budgeted Projects)
DOM	*Daerah Operasi Militer* (Military Operations Area)
DPR	Indonesian legislature
FPI	*Front Pembela Islam* (Islamic Defenders Front)
GAM	*Gerakan Aceh Merdeka* (Free Aceh Movement)
IFEES	Islamic Foundation for Ecology and Environmental Sciences
IICORR	International Islamic Christian Organization for Reconciliation and Reconstruction
IIRO	International Islamic Relief Organization

IMF	International Monetary Fund
KDP	World Bank-Government of Indonesia *Kecamatan* Development Programme
KHI	*Kompilasi Hukum Islam* (Compendium of Islamic Law)
KPA	*Komite Peralihan Aceh* (Aceh Transition Authority)
KPK	*Komisi Pemberantasan Korupsi* (Commission for the Elimination of Corruption)
KSK	*kepala satuan kerja* (heads of work units)
LAPIS	Learning Assistance Programme for Islamic Schools (AusAid programme)
LKMD	*Lembaga Ketahanan Masyarakat Desa* (Village Community Resilience Council)
LMD	*Lembaga Musyawarah Desa* (Village Assembly)
LNG	liquid natural gas
LoGA	Law on Governing Aceh (Law no 11/2006)
LRC	Lampuuk Recovery Centre
MER-C	Medical Emergency Relief Charity, Saudi-funded charitable organization in Aceh
MMI	*Majelis Mujahadin Indonesia* (Indonesian Mujahidin Council)
MoU	Memorandum of Understanding
MPR	People's Consultative Assembly
MPU	*Majelis Permusyawaratan Ulama* (Consultative Council of Ulama)
MUI	*Majelis Ulama Indonesia* (Indonesia Ulama Council)
Musrembang	*Musyawarah Rencana Pembangunan* (Consultative Meeting on Development Planning)
NAD	*Nanggroe Aceh Darussalam* (Peaceful State of Aceh)
NBA	*Negara Bahagian Aceh* (Federated State of Aceh)
NGO	Non-governmental organization
PBP	Bakornas (National Coordinating Board for Disaster Management)
PPP	United Development Party
PRRI	Permesta rebellion
SAK	*Satuan Anti Korupsi* (Anti-Corruption Unit)
Satkorlak	*Satuan Koordinasi Pelaksana* (Operational Coordinating Units)
SBY	(President) Susilo Bambang Yudhoyono
SIRA	*Sentral Informasi Referendum Aceh* (university student-led referendum movement, Aceh Referendum Information Centre)
TDF	The Development Forum

TNA	*Tentera Nasional Aceh* (Aceh National Army – more commonly known as AGAM)
TNI	*Tentara Nasional Indonesia* (Indonesian military)
UNDP	United Nations Development Programme
USAID	US Agency for International Development
WH	*Wilayatul Hisbah* (Vice Squad/moral police)
WWF	World Wildlife Fund

INTRODUCTION

Deconstructing Aceh's Reconstruction

*Sue Kenny, Matthew Clarke, Ismet Fanany
and Damien Kingsbury*

Introduction

On Sunday 26 December 2004, just a minute or so before 8.00am local time, an earthquake measuring 9.0 on the Richter scale occurred 30km below sea level at 3.307°N 95.947°E. The earthquake lasted for ten minutes and was the world's fourth largest earthquake since 1900, with the fault rupture extending over a length of 1200km at the junction of the Eurasian and Indo-Australian plates. The descending Indo-Australian plate pulled down the Eurasian plate and then released its edge, which rebounded, lifting the ocean floor with it. The resulting tsunami directly affected 11 countries, killing up to 300,000 people and displacing over one million more. The closest land mass to the epicentre was the province of Aceh, or Nanggroe Aceh Darussalam, the northern part of the Indonesian island of Sumatra. Aceh experienced the full force of the tsunami.

Within 45 minutes of the earthquake, the tsunami reached land at the capital of Aceh, Banda Aceh. The force of the tsunami caused immediate destruction and death. Sweeping all before its path, the rising ocean razed natural and human-made structures. Within minutes, over 800km of coast was flattened. No warning systems were in place, and local populations were caught completely unprepared for the tsunami, which ranged in height between three and 12 metres throughout the coastal region. The loss of human life and damage to the natural habitat was enormous. It is estimated that 130,000 people in Aceh were killed (some reports estimated 170,000 deaths) – three times as many women as men – and another 500,000 people were displaced (UNDP, 2006). In addition to the human devastation, the physical geography was changed, with much of the land being dragged into the sea, and shorelines displaced hundreds of metres inland. Dwellings and the physical infrastructure were destroyed. More than 250,000 houses were totally or partially damaged. Community infrastructure such as drinking water supplies, facilities for handling wastewater, refuse disposal, drainage, roads, schools, clinics, meeting halls and mosques were damaged.

Over half a million cubic metres of debris, including timber, bricks and mud, replaced houses, roads and farmlands, disrupting accessibility and most aspects of daily life. The UNDP estimated the cost of recovery in Aceh to be US$5 billion – almost equal to its entire annual GDP. The Indonesian government declared the earthquake- and tsunami-affected parts of Nanggroe Aceh Darussalam to constitute a disaster area, and appointed the National Coordinating Board for Disaster Management (BAKORNAS PBP) to implement the emergency response. In addition, the international community also responded to this emergency.

The scale of the devastation and ensuing human suffering prompted an unparalleled outpouring of global sympathy, leading to unprecedented donor commitments of over US$13 billion to assist the reconstruction effort (World Bank, 2007; Telford et al, 2006). Support was received from 133 countries, and over 16,000 foreign military troops provided additional support in what was one of the largest non-military missions for over 50 years (BRR, 2006). The level of financial support that was pledged and the promises made by international agencies raised global expectations of an effective and speedy recovery. The scale of the destruction created so-called *greenfield sites* for reconstruction, providing unmatched opportunities for holistic reconstruction practices. The international community, including bilateral donor governments, multilateral development agencies such as the World Bank and the United Nations Development Programme (UNDP) and international non-government organizations (NGOs), could apply the lessons learnt from previous humanitarian interventions. If a positive could be found in the disaster wrought by the tsunami, it was that the lives of survivors would be significantly improved through intelligent international assistance. Within days, an international relief effort was in operation, with over 60 international NGOs providing assistance (growing to more than 200 within weeks) alongside many Indonesian NGOs which were also providing assistance. Short-term relief efforts soon evolved into longer-term reconstruction and development activities.

Indonesia's President declared an end to the Aceh emergency response phase at the end of March 2005, and the National Development Planning Agency (BAPPENAS) assumed responsibility for developing a rehabilitation and reconstruction plan for Aceh (and also Nias, which experienced a separate earthquake on 28 March 2005). A master plan for rehabilitation and reconstruction was set in law in April, 2005 by Presidential decree. The following day the President announced the establishment of the Agency of the Rehabilitation and Reconstruction for the Region and Community of Aceh and Nias (BRR), whose task it was to coordinate the reconstruction effort to ensure that a 'reliable, dignified, prosperous and democratic Aceh

and Nias' was established (BRR, 2007; www.e-aceh-nias.org/about_brr/
profile.aspx).

Sufficient time has now passed to begin assessing the effectiveness of the
response and subsequent reconstruction efforts following this disaster.
While there is a developing body of literature on the failures and successes
of the reconstruction process, the existing evaluations tend to be either
official reports concerning matters of donor funding expenditure, infrastructure and material development and general statistical analyses, or
reports and articles written and produced by NGOs themselves that discuss
their own specific programmes. For example, the World Bank has prepared
many reports on reconstruction expenditure. It has estimated that 58 per
cent of the allocations had been dispersed by June 2007, with significant
disbursements still required, particularly in the housing and transport
sectors (World Bank, 2007). The Indonesian government has been concerned that, notwithstanding the huge allocation of funds to housing, there
remains significant unmet need for housing, with a shortage of 20,000
houses in November 2007 and most housing projects ceasing in April 2008
(Embassy of the Republic of Indonesia, 2007). (For reports written by
NGOs themselves, see Oxfam International, 2006; UNDP, 2006; Caritas
Australia, 2005; Brennan and Rimba, 2005; Doocy et al, 2006). These
evaluations demonstrate how perspectives on the success or otherwise of
the reconstruction efforts are largely dependent upon who is providing the
assessment and the criteria used.

Rather than focus on the bald (and often inconsistent) statistically based
overviews of aid delivered, this volume explores different experiences
and assessments of the post-tsunami reconstruction of Aceh from the perspective of different players. The book reflects on the settings of Aceh
reconstruction; the roles and experiences of different players in the reconstruction; what, according to different viewpoints, went right or wrong,
and why; and what can be learned from the different experiences and perceptions and future challenges for Aceh.

A brief history of Aceh

While people have long inhabited northern Sumatra, Aceh's recorded
human history dates to around the 1st century CE, monsoonal winds and
Aceh's prime trading position ensuring it had early contact with the rest of
the then known world. Roman and Indian pottery from this period has been
found, while spices from the archipelago which probably transited through
Aceh were known in ancient Rome. Indian traders, who were known to have
visited from at least the 5th century, brought to Aceh both Hinduism and

later Buddhism, and the first organized states. Chinese traders also knew of Aceh as a stopover on their way to India (McKinnon, 2006).

According to the Liang Annals (502–556), Chinese traders referred to an area within Aceh as the Buddhist state of Po-Li (Stein, 1907), and Perlak (possibly another name for Po-Li) was probably established as a trading port by the 9th century, given that the Sailendra Dynasty in Java was flourishing at this time and that it conducted international trade, and Indian and Arabic texts from around the 9th century mention this area as a part of their trading routes. Montana (1997) notes that there is evidence to show the existence of an Islamic community at Nissam and Lamuri from the beginning of the 12th century, while the Acehnese region of Samudra-Pase was recognized as having a Muslim ruler, Sultan Malik al-Salih, by the late 13th century (Djajadiningrat, 1958). Over the next 600 years the kingdoms of the region, including Samudra[1] (later Pasai, or Pase) and Pidie, combined with Aceh Besar to form Aceh. As Seigel noted, since this time: 'The history of Atjeh[2] is told largely in terms of Islam and trade' (Siegel, 1969: 4). Aceh's focus on trade gave it an outward-looking aspect, towards India, the Arab states and the Ottoman Empire, rather than focusing inwards towards the archipelago (Reid, 2006; McKinnon, 2006).

Although established as a Hindu and later a Buddhist region, as a result of Indian trade, Islam established itself in Aceh comparatively early in the history of the South-East Asia region. Islam first entered the Indonesian archipelago, along with Arabic and Indian traders, through Aceh sometime after 800 CE. It is part of the mythologizing of Aceh's past that the first Islamic kingdom, Perlak, was established within the region of Aceh in the year 804. As Islam's starting point in the archipelago, and the last point of departure for the Haj, Aceh was named by Arab traders as 'Mecca's Verandah' (*Serambi Mekkah*). It was from Aceh that Islam spread to the rest of the archipelago, from around the 13th century.

While Samudera-Pasai existed as Aceh's precursor state, the unification of Aceh was not achieved until after 1521, following the Acehnese defeat of Javanese forces that had occupied the region in the 14th century. Acehnese domination of its near region continued over the following years, but soon came into conflict with the Portuguese. Portugal's capture, in 1511, of the vital trading port of Malacca, introduced *kafir* (infidels) into this Islamic region and, moreover, introduced a new rival to Aceh's expanding military power. Notably, with Islamic trade increasingly avoiding Portuguese-controlled Malacca, Aceh's trading position was boosted. Acehnese forces unsuccessfully attacked Malacca, in 1537, 1547, 1568, 1573 and 1575, at this time consolidating links with the Ottoman Empire. Notwithstanding the lack of success against Malacca, Aceh was more successful in occupying Perlak on the Malayan Peninsula, in 1575.

Although facing numerous internal and external challenges, Aceh's greatest period came under its 12th sultan, Iskandar Muda ('Young Alexander') (born 1583, ruled 1607–1636). Iskandar Muda's conquests included much of northern Sumatra, the defeat of a Portuguese fleet at Bintan in 1614, and the occupation of Pahang, Kedah and Perak on the Malayan Peninsula. At this time, Aceh became a major centre of Islamic learning in the region, as well as a departure point for pilgrims attending the Haj. However, a major expedition against the Portuguese at Malacca in 1629 was a disaster, with the loss of several hundred ships and almost 20,000 men, marking the final point of Aceh's expansion.

While Aceh never regained the power it had under Iskandar Muda, the state consolidated and by the early 19th century was again an important and powerful regional trading state, dominating the pepper trade, with numerous international links and formal recognition by other trading states, including Britain, the United States and the Ottoman Empire. Aceh's regional status, however, was increasingly threatened by the expanding Dutch Empire, which sought to control regional trade. In 1824, Britain and Holland agreed to divide the Malay world into spheres of control, leaving Aceh within the Dutch sphere, and in 1871 Britain dropped its opposition to Dutch control of Aceh. Two years later, the Dutch invaded and although initially success- fully repelled, the following year managed to occupy most of the coastal area (however, not without heavy Dutch losses and, for some time, only a pre- carious foothold). It was not until 1912 that the Acehnese leadership was finally killed or captured and Aceh finally brought under Dutch control, and even then there continued to be sporadic attacks against the Dutch, contin- uing until the Japanese invasion of 1942. In 1945 Indonesia declared its independence, which was strongly supported in Aceh, notably by sending troops against the Dutch in North Sumatra, but seemingly on the under- standing that, reflecting local aspirations, it would lead to independence or a high degree of local autonomy within a loose federal structure.

Indonesia came into being in 1949, adopting a federalist model, poten- tially allowing considerable scope for self-determination on the part of its constituent states. However, when Indonesia was unilaterally reconstituted as a unitary state in 1950, Aceh's quasi-autonomous status was lost and, in the following year, Aceh was subsumed into North Sumatra. Declining to accept this loss of autonomy, in 1953, Aceh's governor Teungku Daud Beureueh declared Aceh's independence from Indonesia, initially joining with the Darul Islam Indonesia (DII) rebellion, declaring the Federated State of Aceh (Negara Bahagian Aceh – NBA), and later starting the PRRI- Permesta rebellion as a means of securing this claim.[3]

In a bid to resolve Aceh's separatist aspirations, a nominal 'special administrative' status was granted in 1959 (accepted in 1963). Beyond relative autonomy in religious, educational and cultural matters, this turned out to have little meaning in practice.

In the period following the rise of Indonesia's New Order government and its increased emphasis on international partnerships in mineral exploitation, Aceh found itself subject to economic domination by interests primarily located in Jakarta, with a consequent loss of potential wealth accruing to Jakarta. In particular, exploration in 1972 indicated the presence of extensive liquid natural gas (LNG) deposits off the coast of Aceh, and in 1973 the Indonesian government signed a sales contract for the export of this LNG (Purnomo 2003) which almost completely excluded Acehnese economic interests, provoking significant local resentment. This resentment was manifested in the resurrection of the idea of Acehnese independence among a relatively small number of Acehnese intellectuals. To put substance to this claim, on 4 December 1976, Teungku Hasan di Tiro proclaimed Aceh an independent state.

The history of the conflict since 1976 is generally located in three phases. The first phase occurred between 1976 and 1989, during which about 600 GAM (Free Aceh Movement) recruits were trained in Libya. In response to an increased GAM military effort, the military undertook a counter-insurgency operation, known as the 'Military Operations Area' (DOM – Daerah Operasi Militer) until 1998. In this second phase (the period from 1989 until 1998), it has been variously estimated that between 10,000 and 26,000 people were killed in Aceh.[4] There were brief reversals of Indonesia's official military policy on Aceh, such as the withdrawal of Kopassus (special forces) troops in 1998 and the formal lifting of military operations, but, perhaps more importantly, different strategies directed by Jakarta following the fall of President Suharto in May 1998. This situation was reversed with a new military operation in 1999, which was notable for its massacres of civilians (see Tapol, 2000a; 2000b). The third phase is generally said to have started with the military again being reigned in, with a signing of a 'humanitarian ceasefire' on 12 May 2000, and again for three months from June 2000. It was around this time that Aceh's 'civil society' movement reached the height of its influence, peaking with the march of several hundred thousand people in Banda Aceh[5] on 8 November 1999, and a rally in November the following year.[6] By 2001, the TNI increased troop numbers in Aceh to more than 30,000, while leading generals overwhelmingly rejected President Abdurrahman Wahid's peace efforts and again pushed for a full-scale military 'resolution' to the insurgency.

On 19 January 2001, a seven-month-old ceasefire was extended for another month, following all-party talks in Switzerland, and Aceh was made a 'special administrative region', which in theory gave it a greater level of local autonomy beyond that granted to sub-provincial regions under the

2001 autonomy legislation.[7] However, in practical terms, that status has counted for very little. By early 2001, GAM was estimated to control around 60 per cent of all of Aceh, and had assumed local responsibility for government services such as education, health care and infrastructure.[8]

In January 2002 the introduction of special autonomous status was announced, including the implementation of Islamic shariah law and greater revenue-sharing of Aceh's natural resources. However, as Shulze has noted, 'the special autonomy ... has not really been implemented' (Shulze, 2004: 55). In December 2002, GAM and the Government of Indonesia signed a 'Cessation of Hostilities Agreement' (CoHA), which was beset with difficulties over competing views and was undermined in particular by the use of TNI-backed militias (Aspinall and Crouch, 2003). The TNI pressed for an end to the ceasefire, which it engineered at the final meeting in Tokyo on 19 May 2003, and the resumption of full-scale hostilities.

On 19 May 2003, the Indonesian military launched its largest military operation since the invasion of East Timor in December 1975. The return to full-scale military activity followed the collapse of the talks in Tokyo (CoHA, 2002).[9] The CoHA had ostensibly been to allow the opportunity to discuss a negotiated settlement to the conflict. But the Indonesian government's insistence at the end of the talks that GAM disarm – effectively to surrender – and accept 'special autonomy' for Aceh under the name of Nanggroe Aceh Darussalam (NAD – Peaceful State of Aceh) was rejected by GAM, which provided the pretext for the TNI's renewed military operations.[10] Over the next two months, under a state of martial law, the force of 32,000 soldiers and paramilitary police sent in readiness for the seemingly inevitable end of the CoHA was increased to just under 60,000,[11] and widespread fighting and social dislocation resumed.

The shape of the war in Aceh changed in formal terms 12 months later, but conflict continued unabated until the tsunami that devastated Aceh on 26 December 2004. Even then, and despite GAM declaring a unilateral ceasefire, the TNI quickly resumed their military campaign. In late January 2005, GAM's leadership met with Indonesian representatives under the auspices of the Crisis Management Initiative in Helsinki to discuss a possible resolution to the conflict. Talks continued until July, when an agreement between the parties was initialled, allowing its formal signing on 15 August 2005. Key elements of the agreement were the Indonesian government's willingness to reduce military and police numbers by around half, to allocate 70 per cent of income from natural resources to be used by the Acehnese government, and to allow the creation of local political parties to contest local elections, finally giving substance to earlier offers of autonomy. In December 2006, Aceh held elections for the positions of governor and district heads (*bupati*), which were overwhelmingly won by GAM candidates.

Since then, Aceh has increasingly stabilized, its economy has grown quickly and it appears to be re-establishing itself, in a range of ways, as an important location in the archipelago.

Aid donors and aid recipients in Aceh

The tsunami brought an unprecedented gathering of donor organizations to Aceh and other locations throughout South and Southeast Asia. It has been suggested that the magnitude of the disaster, including the fact that significant numbers of Westerners were involved and events were extensively covered on television, had a great deal to do with the level of aid offered to tsunami-affected areas, and that television coverage was instrumental in many funding decisions (Cosgrave, 2006; Korf, 2007). As has been the case in other contexts in recent years, the combination of media exposure, personal association, and natural interest in catastrophe generated an enormous public response, which led in many cases to donation to relief organizations by individuals who were not previously interested in such concerns. In Australia, for example, the relative familiarity of the public with resort areas in Indonesia and Thailand meant that many people had a conception of what the disaster-affected areas and their populations were like. This led to an unprecedented level of attention being paid to the event in the media, with a large part of this attention focusing on Aceh, as one of the most severely affected areas.

Despite the desire of the public to contribute to reconstruction following the tsunami, and the race between aid organizations to begin disbursement in the region, the delivery and implementation of aid was marked by delays and problems (Telford et al, 2006). Aid donors, it has been suggested, did not, in many cases, elicit the participation of aid recipients, and failed to recognize the need for disaster survivors to take responsibility for their own welfare (Cosgrave, 2006). This meant that aid recipients felt they were in a position of having to accept much needed funds or assistance and also the plans of the donor organization for the use of money and expertise. This was a significant feature of the experience of the residents of Lampuuk, and will be discussed further below.

It has also been noted that funding decisions often had little to do with needs assessment in tsunami-affected areas. Rather, political considerations in the donors' countries of origin were often significant in allocating aid. The intended recipients were rarely consulted (Cosgrave, 2006). This state of affairs likely related to the international media coverage of the disaster, and tended to reflect the interest and concern around the world for the victims of the tsunami but resulted, according to some observers, in some affected areas being overlooked and some aid packages being inadequate for their intended purpose (see, for example, ActionAid, 2006). In Aceh, in particular, this was a significant source of concern among tsunami survivors, which led to social conflict and frustration among many aid recipients (Korf, 2007). One observer has even argued that the flood of tsunami aid served to humiliate survivors, supposing them to be passive recipients of the generosity of others after having been 'pure' victims of a force of nature. While the aid offered to survivors appeared to be an asymmetric gift, many donors seemed to expect reciprocation in the form of gratitude for their efforts and generosity (Korf, 2005).

The hospitality of the residents of tsunami-affected areas toward foreign organizations and individuals involved in the aid process has been commented on as well. The praise heaped upon stricken communities, calling them selfless in their offering of unconditional generosity (see, for example, Clark, 2005), stands in contrast to comparable but negative criticisms of donors. While there can be no doubt that the aid process following the 2004 tsunami encompassed a range of successes and failures, it is important to maintain an appropriately balanced perspective. Donors were neither self-serving and hungry for praise while seeking to satisfy their domestic political needs, nor selfless angels of mercy intent on helping victims at any cost. Aid recipients, on the other hand, were not guileless innocents grateful for any gesture of assistance, nor were they mercenary operators hoping to extract as much as possible from naïve donors.

If any lessons are to be learned from the aid experience following the Indian Ocean tsunami, aid donors and recipients must be viewed more rationally and, as far as possible, separately from preconceived ideas about the nature of both parties. A great deal has been written about the ideological nature of the aid process (see, for example, Young, 1997; Diprose, 2002; Howitt, 2002; Popke, 2003; Barnett, 2005), but this is of limited use in the field, in making operational decisions about the disbursement of funds and the implementation of programmes. What is important, however, is to consider the experiences of donors and recipients as they appeared to the parties involved, in the hope that this may be of use in designing future aid interaction that is more consistent with the needs of both, and that better fulfills its intended function. It is in this context that an examination of the specific nature of aid donation following the tsunami will be most useful.

The Indian Ocean tsunami led to very high levels of personal donation in countries around the world. In this case, aid came from governments and other institutional donors but also, significantly, from individuals concerned about the aftermath of the disaster. This personal donation was necessarily through aid organizations of one kind or another. The actual aid was then disbursed through what has been called a brokering process (Korf, 2007).

The aid brokers in this case included government agencies, bilateral and multilateral aid agencies, private charities, NGOs and individuals from the recipient country as well as from the donor nations. The post-tsunami recovery was also unique, in that the media functioned as an aid broker, as noted above, through extensive coverage that shaped public opinion around the world (Post, 2006).

Donors, whether individual or institutional, must rely on organizations, as brokers, to disburse aid in the manner which was intended. Following the tsunami, there was unprecedented pressure on aid organizations and exposure of their practices due to the extremely high levels of media coverage that went along with the huge amount of aid money available. Private donors (as opposed to governmental agencies), in particular, tended to expect results they could see in a short period of time (Korf, 2006). The media rapidly took up the role as documenter of the aid process, providing the public with a full range of pictures showing new houses and municipal buildings, roads and infrastructure, smiling villagers, and so forth.

The high level of media coverage of the tsunami aftermath made for a kind of competition among aid donors, who found themselves vying for publicity (Cosgrave, 2006). They had to fight for a place in media reportage and also to show their constituents that they were administering donated funds in the manner intended. The photos and documentation of the recovery effort in places like Lampuuk became an expression of gratitude for assistance received that was transmitted to the public in the West (Korf, 2007). This situation, it has been claimed, led to the observed pressure for aid organizations to pay more attention to domestic political concerns than to local need (Cosgrave, 2006).

Some observers suggest that this led to an undermining of the aim of aid and resulted in a great deal of bad feeling on the part of recipients (Cosgrave, 2006; Korf, 2007). It should be noted, in this context, that the extreme nature of the tsunami and the widespread devastation it caused combined with the high level of media coverage created a context where perceptions on the part of both donors and recipients were magnified. The aid brokers, for example, felt a need to find attractive, marketable targets for their donations. These targets tend to be understood as deserving of assistance and hence represent a satisfactory expression of gratitude for donations to the public who have contributed to relief efforts. Tsunami victims, however, frequently felt that worthy projects that were important to them were being overlooked, often for reasons that were not clear. These emotional displays of aid implementation have been viewed as posturing on the part of aid organizations and brokers (Nanthikesan, 2005), complete with a 'handing over' of the gift to beneficiaries who respond with gratitude (Korf, 2007). It is also possible to view the selective nature of aid targets as a manifestation of aid organizations' desire to keep themselves in business with continuing donations and publicity, particularly in light of the competition many of these organizations experienced after the tsunami.

Nonetheless, the desire of donors to see that their contributions were making a difference and were resulting in improved conditions for the tsunami survivors they had undertaken to assist was understandable. Celebrities and public figures of all kinds made well-publicized visits to tsunami-affected areas, including former US presidents George Bush and Bill Clinton, USAID Administrator Andrew Natsios, Icelandic singer Bjork, *American Idol* runner-up Clay Aiken, daughter of Malaysia's prime minister Nori Abdullah, and Malaysian movie star Michelle Yeoh. This kind of visit has been cynically referred to as 'tsunami tourism', a term that also includes trips made by ordinary people who hoped to see the tsunami-affected areas and feel that they were helping by contributing to the local economy.

Notable amid this environment of goodwill and cooperative aid was the widely reported dissatisfaction felt by aid recipients. A number of reports on the aid disbursement effort cited a lack of communication felt by recipients and what they viewed as a lack of consultation (ActionAid, 2006; Eye on Aceh, 2006; Korf, 2005; Cosgrave, 2006). These reviews further note that some residents of Aceh felt excluded from the reconstruction process and ended up as passive observers, while aid organizations made decisions for them (see, for example, Eye on Aceh, 2006). While little has been written concerning the internal decision-making processes of aid organizations in relation to funding for post-tsunami reconstruction, it is almost inevitable that the drivers of organizations' behaviour will differ from the goals of the residents who are to be aid recipients. Nonetheless, recipient satisfaction remains an important aim of aid organizations in general (Centre for Peace Building International, 2006), meaning that the impressions of aid recipients are worthy of consideration and potentially valuable in providing information about this aspect of the aid process.

Understanding perceptions of 'reconstruction'

While there is considerable use of the term 'reconstruction' in the analysis of the development of post-tsunami Aceh, the meaning of 'reconstruction' is rarely specified or analysed. There are three different ideas of reconstruction, which often overlap: first, reconstruction as immediate relief to ensure that lives are saved; second, as restoration, rehabilitation and recovery to return survivors' lives to 'normal'; and finally, rebuilding and renewal, often discussed in the context of 'building back better'. It has been the international agencies who have been most keen to ensure that reconstruction 'builds back better'. In the immediate aftermath of the tsunami, the Acehnese people wanted to 'return to normal'. Yet as time progressed, they also wanted 'better' lives, including sustainable livelihoods in a secure and peaceful Aceh. Of course, returning to a previous situation is never possible in any case, because it is important to consider the impact of time. The passing of time from the point of origin to the point of reconstruction means that it is not possible to recreate the starting point. Rather than moving along a circle, the impact of time produces a result similar to that of a corkscrew. A full rotation of a corkscrew does not return one to the point of origin, but rather a corresponding, but distinct, point further away. In the case of Aceh, the dramatic physical, social and economic changes, including the tremendous loss of life brought by the tsunami, meant that Acehnese life could never be returned to a state that existed prior to the tsunami. Thus the reconstruction of Aceh has required the construction of new concepts of 'normal'. The path to new concepts of normal in Aceh has been a difficult one, full of tensions between efforts to strengthen real or imagined past customs and beliefs, such as the tension between strengthening commitment to sharia law on one hand, and reclaiming women's rights through celebration of Acehnese traditional heroines and supporting the more radical new women's groups on the other. A new concept of 'normal' also underpins the acceptance of peace in Aceh and the integration of ex-combatants into the Acehnese economy.

In addition to the differences in the processes that have been understood as reconstruction, the object of reconstruction has varied. Immediately after the tsunami, emergency food, clean drinking water, medical aid and shelter were the top priorities. For many commentators, the primary object of reconstruction has been the physical infrastructure, including housing, roads, mosques, hospitals, schools, and meeting halls in affected areas. One of the criticisms of the reconstruction effort by the Acehnese is that as long as international agencies focus on buildings, they often forget about equipping buildings for effective and on-going use. For example, libraries were built, but had no staff or books. Too many schools were built with too few students and teaching resources. Houses were built without access to sewerage and electricity. The Acehnese argue that the focus on the physical infrastructure can be explained by its visibility to foreign donors. It is a way of proving to donors that agencies were 'doing something'.

Less visible, but equally important, is the reconstruction of the governance infrastructure. This involves both the restoration of the governance systems in villages and the rebuilding of an administrative and regulatory framework, with political and legal systems in place, and people with the capacity to operate these systems. In the tsunami-affected areas, villages lost people in leadership positions, who needed to be replaced and supported to take on the new and often daunting tasks of restoration and renewal. In the regional capital, Banda Aceh, administrative structures had to be rebuilt with new personnel. New political and legal systems needed to be put in place, especially after the Helsinki Peace Agreement in 2005 and the subsequent granting of relative autonomy. Linked to the Peace Agreement has been the necessary reconstruction of relationships between ex-combatants and their supporters, on one hand, and the military and other anti-GAM forces on the other. These non-tangible forms of reconstruction are absolutely vital for the future of Aceh. Indeed, understanding the perceptions of the reconstruction requires an analysis that goes beyond the response to the destruction brought about by the tsunami, although the tsunami has been the catalyst for far-reaching change to the lives of the people of Aceh.

From the perspective of many Acehnese, perhaps the most important object of reconstruction has been the rebuilding of their livelihoods. Immediately after the tsunami, many Acehnese participated in the Cash for Work programmes, that gave them small amounts of cash to support themselves and their families. Within months, a number of livelihood programmes had been established to provide micro credit and small grants and loans to families, mainly to restart their small businesses, such as a wayside stall or a *becak* (motorcycle) taxi. This form of reconstruction involves both restoring and improving (through better equipment for example) small business enterprises.

Much of the discussion of Aceh's reconstruction focuses on the role of Western aid and development agencies and NGOs as if they were the key, or even the only players. It is important to understand the key roles that other groups, and especially the Acehnese people themselves, have played throughout the reconstruction. Many commentators have reflected on the way in which so many of the survivors swung into action, where neighbours and families provided shelter for each other. Their efforts were reinforced with the arrival of the Acehnese diaspora. Indeed, for all the talk of capacity-building of the Acehnese, it was many of the international agencies, who despite all their goodwill and promises, were those who needed their capacities to deliver aid to be 'built'. Local NGOs have also played a significant role in liaising with villages and as brokers for aid programmes. Indonesians from throughout the archipelago arrived to help, particularly in the first six months. Last but not least, the Indonesian authorities contributed significantly to the reconstruction, especially once they had established the Agency of the Rehabilitation and Reconstruction for the Region and Community of Aceh and Nias (BRR) in the first half of 2005, to coordinate the reconstruction processes. Somewhat surprisingly, to many foreign observers, given that a state of civil emergency had been in place in

Aceh since May 2004 (replacing martial law), the Indonesian government allowed foreign aid workers into the region, albeit on a restricted basis at first, and with threats to expel any organizations that defied the restrictions. However as time passed, a good working relationship between international NGOs, the Indonesian government, the regional government, and perhaps most importantly the BRR, was established.

Thus it is clear that reconstruction is not a one-dimensional process, and this is the approach taken in this book. Reconstruction refers to all of the dimensions of reconstruction mentioned above. Thus the story of the reconstruction of Aceh is one of many approaches, players and intentions, resulting in different experiences, perceptions and tensions. It is thus a story of contradictions, for example between what was expected and what occurred, between asset and deficit approaches, between internally and externally driven interventions and between positive and negative assessments.

Volume contents

The reconstruction of Aceh has been one of the largest single-site responses to a natural disaster in human history. However, there has yet to be a study that seeks to understand this reconstruction effort in different contexts and from the perspectives of the different agents: communities, political actors, government authorities, representatives of religious groups, Indonesian NGOs and international NGOs. This book seeks to rectify this lacunae, and as such, it will have significance for international aid and community development policy-making, disaster planning and management and the complex dynamics involved in the monumental task of rebuilding after major disasters. This volume will also provide a comprehensive account of the key actors involved in the Aceh reconstruction process.

This book is broken into two main sections: Section One discusses the context of reconstruction in Aceh and the concept of participatory practice; while Section Two presents various case studies illustrating the complexities, strengths and weaknesses of the reconstruction efforts in Aceh.

Chapter 2 by Michelle Ann Miller discusses the role of Islamic law (sharia) in the post-tsunami Aceh reconstruction effort. This chapter aims to understand how sharia is conceptualized by the key NGO and civil societal actors in Aceh, and how their development priorities and programmes have been influenced accordingly. The central argument is that Muslim and non-Muslim NGOs and institutions in Aceh have tended to view capacity-building in vastly different terms, as demonstrated by their divergent development goals and activities. Further, it is argued that while the implementation of Islamic law could potentially play a constructive role in the rebuilding of Aceh (for example, by settling legal disputes about land ownership, guardianship, marriage status for widows and Islamic micro-finance), yet so far it has led to greater community disenfranchisement than empowerment. These arguments are developed by examining four broad groups in Aceh according to their different attitudes about sharia. These are: 1) Islamist groups that explicitly promote Islamic law; 2) NGOs that implicitly support sharia by providing funding and other forms of humanitarian assistance to Acehnese religious institutions; 3) secular and non-Muslim faith-based NGOs that seek to accommodate the cultural and religious needs of the Acehnese people but do not necessarily support Islamic law; and 4) NGOs and humanitarian workers who view sharia with suspicion and concern. To illustrate the complexity of attitudes about Islamic law, the chapter further divides this fourth category of detractors of sharia into a) rationalists, who mainly see reconstruction in material terms and who view Islamic law as an obstacle to the development process, and b) orientalists, or NGOs who view the Acehnese people on the basis of their Islamic identity and who tend to associate sharia with prescriptive anti-libertarian belief systems.

In Chapter 3 Damien Kingsbury notes the ways in which Aceh's political evolution set the backdrop for the post-tsunami reconstruction. He explores how the political environment of Aceh has undergone a profound redevelopment in the period following the tsunami. Given the normative qualities associated with such alteration, Acch's political change could be understood as a political reconstruction especially compared with the province's previous political under-development. Aceh's recent political history had been one of Jakarta-appointed governors working with the military, in effect as an administration of occupation within a conflict environment, with all the corruption and abrogation of civil and political rights that this type of administration implies. The removal of Aceh's last Jakarta-appointed administrator and the more conciliatory rule of his temporary successor marked an important shift in Aceh's political life. The signing of the Helsinki Peace Agreement in 2005 ended the province's 29-year-old separatist conflict, significantly reduced the military and police presence, and disarmed the Free Aceh Movement (GAM). Perhaps more importantly, it also allowed for the creation of local political parties and the elections of a new governor and district officials, marking a further and more profound development in Aceh's political reconstruction. In addition to this were the internal changes to Aceh's political environment. The outgoing temporary governor ensured that the provincial administration employed or re-employed staff identified with the previously illegal Free Aceh Movement, thus Acehnizing the civil administration. Parallel to this, Aceh civil society groups and NGOs re-emerged as active and vocal political participants, while new political parties and like formations contested with existing parties in what was widely embraced as a largely free political environment. This chapter provides an overview of Aceh's recent political evolution, and in particular focuses on how non-GAM political and civil organizations came to embrace, own and help shape a new autonomous political environment.

Chapter 4 by Sue Kenny begins with a discussion of the ascendancy of ideas of local participation in development discourse and practice. It then investigates how far participatory approaches have been evident in the reconstruction of Aceh. Four different forms of participation are considered. These are participation as *manipulation, consultation, partnership* and *ownership*. The evidence provided by both primary and secondary sources indicates a variety of degrees of commitment to participatory approaches. External agencies paid little attention to participation of survivors at the beginning of the relief phase, yet ironically, immediately after the tsunami, many of the survivors took control, demonstrating their capacities to undertake partnership as 'ownership'. By the beginning of 2006 most aid agencies understood the importance of local participation, although it was mostly in the form of consultation, and for some agencies participation was an effective form of manipulation. There were also examples of participation as a (limited) form of community development-based ownership. What this analysis suggests is that even where there is a commitment to participation of local people in post-disaster reconstruction, there are many constraints and challenges. This chapter identifies these constraints and many challenges and suggests some ways of progressing the participatory agenda.

The first of three case studies in Section Two is presented by Ismet Fanany in Chapter 5. This chapter discusses the model of constructive engagement between aid deliverers and recipients using the example of Lampuuk. Organizations, both government and private, rushed to the disaster area trying to help and bringing with them people, expertise, experience, and a lot of money. The destruction was so severe that it was difficult even to figure out where to start helping the survivors. There was a great deal of variation in the approaches used by organizations in delivering the aid. At one extreme, an organization simply gave money to affected villages. It assumed the people knew best what they wanted and needed. At the opposite extreme, survivors were told what they needed and how this would be delivered. The organization in question not only decided what kind of houses people should have, for example, but also where they should be built, even when this did not coincide with people's preferences. There were many criticisms of the two approaches. The first approach encouraged people to use the money for consumptive rather than productive purposes, lacked sustainability, caused disputes between villagers, and was susceptible to corruption. In the second approach, the absence of the recipients' participation often led to disastrous results, with people refusing to live in houses that had been completed, for example. There were many approaches in between the two extremes, however. A balance between participation of the recipients and decision-making by aid deliverers worked best. The issue was how recipients could be engaged. Fieldwork in this area suggests that the construction of roads and houses in this village gave residents great satisfaction.

Chapter 6 by Craig Thorburn reports on the impact of the tsunami of local governance structures in 18 villages. Comprehensive surveys were undertaken in these villages to discern the impact of the tsunami. Three main issues became apparent across these different villages: governance, livelihoods, and village infrastructure and housing. While the experiences of each of the surveyed villages were different, there were a number of commonalities and patterns with clear lessons that could be extracted. Moreover, despite the often critical tone of many of the interviewees and focus groups, people were pleased overall with their situation, and hopeful of future prospects. This was largely because of the good local leadership, and of inclusive, transparent decision-making processes which many of these villages had experienced prior to and after the tsunami.

Matthew Clarke and Suellen Murray consider the perspective of Western NGO works and their perceptions of the reconstruction efforts in Aceh in Chapter 7. This chapter reports on the experiences of 21 non-relief staff deployed to tsunami-affected areas by an international NGO and is therefore based upon their own perspectives. It distils a number of lessons for improving the capacity of NGO staff to respond to large-scale complex humanitarian emergencies by drawing from the experiences of these interviewed staff. The study identifies three main issues that affected the capacity of interviewed staff to respond effectively to the tsunami: governance at relief operation sites; infrastructure and implementation of systems; and selection of deployed staff and their preparation and support. While the size of the tsunami was unprecedented in terms of geographical spread and devastation, the issues reported by the interviewed staff (governance, systems and preparation) are relevant to any large-scale complex humanitarian emergency and therefore are relevant to any NGO undertaking relief operations. It is argued that the experiences of these staff are not peculiar to this international NGO. Therefore, the lessons distilled from these qualitative interviews will be relevant to other NGOs with relief operations. Based on these lessons, a number of general recommendations are provided in order to improve the capacity of NGO staff to respond to future emergencies. Given the prominent role NGOs have in implementing relief interventions (on behalf of bilateral and multilateral donors as well as using their own publicly raised funds) it is incumbent on these organizations to consistently seek to improve the capacity of their own staff to respond effectively to complex humanitarian emergencies.

The volume's eighth chapter, by Fuad Mardhatillah, considers the experiences and role of the Badan Rehabilitasi dan Rekonstuksi (BRR) during the post-tsunami reconstruction. Decades of social strife followed by natural disaster have scarred the community and contributed to a general pessimism, reflected in its thinking, world view, and behaviour. While most Acehnese recognize the need for a new start, it is often difficult to leave the ways of the past and to forget old scores, even if these old ways are incompatible with a new beginning leading to a better future. Dilemma and contradiction are manifested everywhere, and Aceh remains a region of high social tension. Not surprisingly, rehabilitation and reconstruction efforts in the region have been affected by this social context. This chapter will present a reflection on the formal processes of rehabilitation and reconstruction of Aceh and will describe the challenges faced by BRR in carrying out its post-tsunami programmes, now that its term has passed.

Chapter 9 by Annemarie Samuels considers the non-physical reconstruction of neighbourhoods in the capital of Aceh – Banda Aceh. Returning to the capital city three years after the tsunami, Samuels argues that local people are the main actors in remaking their society and are completing a reconstruction process that has no definite end. Through presenting personal stories, this chapter argues that the efforts that 'affected people' themselves undertake to remake their society are the most crucial part of the reconstruction process; and that without them any form of reconstruction is not possible. While the rebuilding of houses and neighbourhoods has been an impressive construction effort, these buildings are less important than the rebuilding of social ties and social relationships that their inhabitants are also experiencing. This final case study therefore explore some of the longer-term, everyday aspects of grass-roots reconstruction in Banda Aceh that have continued well past the final opening ceremony of these new housing estates and long after the final buildings have been completed and handed over to their new residents.

While this volume has considered the reconstruction of Aceh following the Indian Ocean tsunami, there are numerous lessons that can be drawn that are applicable to responses to future complex humanitarian emergencies. Matthew Clarke and Sue Kenny highlight 11 lessons in Chapter 10 that should be understood by the international community to ensure that future responses to disasters are more effective and efficient. These lessons range from the importance of recognizing the non-physical destruction that complex humanitarian emergencies cause, to the importance of drawing on the inherent strengths of surviving communities to understanding that reconstruction does not mean returning to an 'identical' past.

The final chapter is an Afterword by Ismet Fanany. In this chapter, consideration is given to the invisible landscape – or the private and personal impact of the tsunami on the Achenese. The physical reconstruction of Aceh has taken precedence, but great damage was also inflicted upon the hearts and minds of the local people. This imperfectly understood fact has barely been addressed. This Afterword notes the limitations of the physical reconstruction in this regard.

Conclusion

This is an important volume in terms of understanding Aceh's reconstruction for a number of reasons. Firstly, this is the first volume that brings together different perspectives on the reconstruction of post-tsunami Aceh. Secondly, it is also a study of informal capacity-building in post-tsunami, post-conflict Aceh that takes an in-depth look at both Acehnese and non-Acehnese understandings of development and capacity-building and the high level of disconnect between them. Further, this book is the first study to position the post-tsunami reconstruction effort within Aceh's multi-layered historical, cultural, socio-political and religious contexts.

References

ActionAid (2006) *Tsunami Response: A Human Rights Assessment*, London, ActionAid

Alfian, I. (2003) 'Aceh and the Holy War (Prang Sabil)', in Reid, A. ed. *Verandah of Violence: Background to the Aceh Problem*, Singapore, Singapore University Press

Anderson, C., Mehden, F., and Young, C. (1967) *Issues of Political Development*, Englewood Cliffs, NJ, Prentice Hall

ASNLF (2002) *The Stavanger Declaration*, Acheh-Sumatra National Liberation Front, Stavanger, Norway, 21 July 2002

Aspinall, E. and Crouch, H. (2003) *The Aceh Peace Process: Why It Failed*, East-West Center, Washington. Policy Studies 1

Ba'asyir, A. B. (2000) 'Sistem Kaderisasi Mujahidin Dalam Mewujudkan Masyarakat Islam', address to *Kongres Mujahidin I Indonesia*, 5–7 August 2000, Yogyakarta. www.geocities.com/kongresmujahidin/ (note: Ba'asyir's name is spelled Ba'syar' in this document)

Badan Rehabilitasi dan Rekonstuksi or Recontruction and Rehabilitation Agency (BRR) (2006) *Profil - Pembentukan BRR*, www.e-acehnias.org/about_brr/profile.aspx 6 November 2007

Baraja, A. Q. (2000) 'Kebangkitan dan Keruntuhan Khilafah', address to *Kongres Mujahidin I Indonesia*, 5–7 August 2000, Yogyakarta. www.geocities.com/kongresmujahidin/

Barnett, C. (2005) 'Ways of Relating: Hospitality and the Acknowledgement of Otherness', *Progress in Human Geography*, vol 29, no 1, pp5–21

Barton, G. (2002) *Abdurrahman Wahid, Muslim Democrat, Indonesian President: A View from the Inside*, Sydney, UNSW Press

Brennan, Richard J., and Kamaruddin Rimba (2005) 'Rapid health assessment in Aceh Jaya District, Indonesia, following the December 26 tsunami', *Emergency Medicine Australasia*, vol 17, no 4, pp341–350

Centre for Peace Building International (2006) Lessons of Recovery Assistance after the 2004 Tsunami: Summary Report from International Symposium, 5 May

Clark, N. (2005) 'Disaster and Generosity', *Geographical Journal*, vol 171, pp284–386

Embassy of the Republic of Indonesia, (2007) 'Aceh Rebuilding Nearly Complete: Officials' Bulletin Berita, Canberra, www.kbri-canberra.org.au/brief/2007/11/112807–8.htm

Eye on Aceh (2006) *People's Agenda? Post-Tsunami Aid in Aceh*, Eye on Aceh/Aid Watch, www.acheh-eye.org/data_files/english_format/ngo/ngo_eoa/ngo_eoa_2006_02_00.pdf

Caritas Australia (2005) 'Caritas Australia's Response to the Indian Ocean Disaster, 26 December, 2004', www.caritas.org.au/emergencies/asiaEarthquake/materials/20050422-Caritas%20Australia%20-%20CaritasTsunami%20Report.pdf, 22 April 2005, 14pp

CoHA (2002) Cessation of Hostilities Agreement, signed by Dr Zaini Abdullah on behalf of ASNLF, and Wiryono Sastrohandoyo on behalf of the Government of the Republic of Indonesia, Geneva, 9 December 2002

Cosgrave, J. (2007) Synthesis Report: Expanded Summary. Joint Evaluation of the international response to the Indian Ocean tsunami, London, Tsunami Evaluation Coalition

Dagi, I. (2001) 'Human Rights and Democratization: Turkish Politics in the European Context', *Journal of Southern Europe and Black Sea Studies*, vol 1, Issue 3

Diprose, R. (2002) *Corporeal Generosity: on Giving with Nietzsche, Merleau-Ponty, and Levinas*, Albany, NY, SUNY Press

Di Tiro, H. (1984) *The Price of Freedom: The Unfinished Diary by Hasan di Tiro*, Ontario, The Open Press

Djajadiningrat, H. (1958) 'Islam in Indonesia', in Morgan, K. ed, *Islam – The Straight Path: Islam Interpreted by Muslims*, New York, The Ronald Press Company

Djuli, N. (2005) *Acheh, Nationalism and Islam*, Centre for Citizenship and Human Rights, Occasional Papers, Melbourne, Deakin University

Doocy, S., Gabriel, M., Collins, S., Robinson, C. and Stevenson, P. (2006) 'Implementing cash for work programmes in post-tsunami Aceh: experiences and lessons learned', *Disasters, The Journal of Disaster Studies, Policy and Management*, vol 30, no 3, pp277–296

Fealy, G. and Platzdasch, G. (2003) 'The Masyumi Legacy: Between Islamist Idealism and Political Exigency', *The Dynamics of Political Islam in Indonesia* a conference organized by the Melbourne Indonesia Consortium, Melbourne University, 11–12 July

GAM 13.7.2005 'GAM'S Commitment to Democracy', Norsborg, Sweden, State of Acheh Ministry of Information

GAM 14.7.2005 'Regarding GoI Proposal For Political Parties for Acheh', Norsborg, Sweden, State of Acheh Ministry of Information

GAM 15.7.2005 'Clarity Needed to Reach Peace Agreement', Norsborg, Sweden, State of Acheh Ministry of Information

Harsono, A. (2001) 'Aceh Secession Hobbled by Internal Strife', *The American Reporter*, 14 February (2001)

Howitt, R. (2002) 'Scale and the Other: Levinas and Geography', *Geoforum*, vol 33, pp299–313

Hulst, W. (1991) (trans: ASNLF). 'From Now On, It Is Not Just Free Acheh But Free Sumatra!', *NRC Handelsblad*, 1 June

ICG (2003) *Jema'ah Islamiyah in South East Asia: Damaged but Still Dangerous*, Jakarta and Brussels, 26 August

Jones, S. (2003) Testimony of Sidney Jones, Indonesia Project Director, International Crisis Group, before the Subcommittee on East Asia and the Pacific House Committee International Relations Committee, US House of Representatives, Washington, 10 June

Kell, T. (1995) *The Roots of Acehnese Rebellion*, Ithaca, NY, Cornell Modern Indonesia Project

Khilafa Online (2004) www.khilafah.e-syariah.net/ accessed 11 August

Kingsbury, D. (2006) *Peace in Aceh: A Personal Account of the Aceh Peace Process*, Jakarta, Equinox

Kinzer, S. (2001) *Crescent and Star: Turkey Between Two Worlds*, Farrar, New York, Straus and Giroux

Korf, B. (2005) 'Sri Lanka: The Tsunami After the Tsunami', *International Development Planning Review*, vol 27, no 3, ppi-vii

Korf, B. (2006) 'Disaster, Generosity, and the Other', *Geographical Journal*, vol 172, pp245–247

Korf, B. (2007) 'Antinomies of Generosity: Moral Geographies and Post-Tsunami Aid in Southeast Asia', *Geoforum*, vol 38, pp366–378

Lewis, B. (2002) *The Emergence of Modern Turkey*, by Bernard Lewis, Oxford, Oxford University Press

Loeb, E. (1974) (1935) *Sumatra: Its History and People*, London, Oxford University Press

Madjid, N. (1997) *Tidak Ada Negara Islam: surat-surat politikNurcholish Madjid Mohamad Roem*, Jakarta, Djambatan

Marsden, W. (1975) (1811) *The History of Sumatra*, 3rd edn, Kuala Lumpur, Oxford University Press

McKinnon, E. (2006) 'Indian and Indonesian Elements in Early North Sumatra', in Reid, A. ed. *Verandah of Violence: Background to the Aceh Problem*, Singapore, Singapore University Press

Montana, S. (1997) *Nouvelles donnees sur les royaumes de Lamuri et Barat*, Association Archipel, France

MoU (2005) Memorandum of Understanding between the Government of the Republic of Indonesia and the Free Aceh Movement, 15 August

Nanthikesan, S. (2005) 'Post Tsunami Posturing', *Lines Magazine*, vol 3, no 4, www.lines-magazine.org/Art_Feb05/Editorial_Nanthi.htm

Nazaruddin S. (1985) *The Republican Revolt*, Singapore, Institute of Southeast Asian Studies

Oxfam International (2006) 'The Tsunami Two Years On: Land Rights in Aceh', www.oxfam.org.uk/what_we_do/issues/conflict_disasters/downloads/bn_tsunami_twoyears.pdf, 7 December 2006, 11pp

Popke, E. J. (2003) 'Poststructuralist Ethics: Subjectivity, Responsibility and the Space of Community', *Progress in Human Geography*, vol 27, no 3, pp298–316

Post, U. (2006) 'Attention Deficit: Disasters and the Media', *Magazine for Development and Cooperation*, vol 46, no 1) www.inwent.org/E+Z/content/Archive-eng/index.html/

Reid, A. (1969) *The Contest for North Sumatra: Atjeh, the Netherlands and Britain, 1858–1898* Kuala Lumpur, Oxford University Press

Reid, A. (1979) *The Blood of the People: Revolution and the End of Traditional Rule in Northern Sumatra*, Kuala Lumpur, Oxford University Press

Reid, A. (2004) 'Indonesia, Aceh and the modern nation-state', speech to National Integration and Regionalism in Indonesia and Malaysia conference, University of New South Wales at the Australian Defence Force Academy, Canberra, 26–28 November 2002

Reid, A. (2006) 'Aceh's View of its Place in the World, 1500–1873', in Reid, A. ed. *Verandah of Violence: Background to the Aceh Problem*, Singapore, Singapore University Press

Saeed, A. (2003) *Islam and Political Legitimacy in Asia*, London, RoutledgeCurzon

Saeed, A. (2006) *Interpreting the Qur'an: Towards a Contemporary Approach*, London, Routledge

Saeed, A. forthcoming. 'Citizenship in the West and "being Muslim": Western Muslim Responses', in Mansouri, F. ed. *Islam, Human Security, and Xenophobia*, London, Cambridge Scholars Press

Saeed, A. and Johns, A. (2004) 'Nurcholish Madjid and Contextualised Understanding of the Qur'an', in Suha Taji-Farouki (ed.). *Modern Muslim Intellectuals and the Qur'an*, Oxford, Oxford University Press

Sardar, Z. (2004) 'Searching for secular Islam', *New Humanist*, 6 September

Sen. A. (1999) *Development as Freedom*, Oxford, Oxford University Press

Siapno, J. (2002) *Gender, Islam, Nationalism and the State in Acheh: The Paradox of Power, Co-option and Resistance*, London, RouledgeCurzon

Siegel, J. (1969) *The Rope of God*, Berkeley and Los Angeles, University of California Press

Sjamsuddin, N. (1985) *The Republican Revolt: A Study of the Acehnese Rebellion*, Singapore, Institute of Southeast Asian Studies

Stein, M. (1907) *Ancient Khotan*, vol 1

Sulaiman, I. (2006) 'From Autonomy to Periphery. A Critical Evaluation of the Acehnese Nationalist Movement', in Reid, A. ed. *Verandah of Violence: Background to the Aceh Problem*, Singapore, Singapore University Press

Tapol (2000a) *Bantaqiah trial: an examination of the indictment by TAPOL*, TAPOL Report, 25 April 2000

Tapol (2000b) *A Reign of Terror: Human Rights Violations in Aceh 1998 – 2000*, Tapol, March 2000

Telford, J., Cosgrave, J. and Houghton, R. (2006) 'Joint Evaluation of the international response to the Indian Ocean tsunami: Synthesis Report', London, Tsunami Evaluation Coalition

United Nations Development Program (2006) 'Survivors of the Tsunami: One Year Later', www.undp.org/tsunami/UNDP-Tsunamireport-final.pdf, 24pp

World Bank (2007) 'Aceh Reconstruction Expenditure Update', siteresources. worldbank.org/.../

Young, I. M. (1997) *Intersecting Voices*, Princeton, NJ, Princeton University Press
Zurcher, E. (2004) *Turkey: A Modern History* (revised edition), New York, I.B.Tauris

Notes

1   After which the island of Sumatra is named.
2   This is not a typographical error; following the spelling revision in 1972, the sound previously represented by 'tj' is now represented by 'c'.
3   While DII was not a separatist rebellion, many Acehnese, including the ASNLF (Aceh/Sumatra National Liberation Front), claim that Aceh's participation in it was for the purposes of securing either independence, or a high degree of local autonomy, which is borne out by the declaration of the NBA in 1955. The main period of rebellion ended in 1957, although some rebels held out until 1959 and others until 1963, with the ending of Darul Islam.
4   The variation in figures derives from a range of public and private sources. 10,000 is the most usually quoted number, including by some NGOs and most of the media. GAM claims that 26,000 people were killed during this period. However, there do not appear to be any reliable statistics about this matter.
5   Various news reports said that up to a million people converged on Banda Aceh from around the territory.
6   This subsequent rally was smaller, with a few hundred thousand present, as a consequence of military and police intimidation, road blocks and killings to prevent it from taking place.
7   The primary difference is that Aceh (and Papua) were allowed to retain the province as the primary site of local administration, whereas elsewhere regional autonomy was devolved to the sub-provincial level.
8   This responsibility tested the resources of the ANSLF/GAM, which was not equipped to progress from revolutionary activity to functional self-government.
9   Aspinall and Crouch (2002) claim this was a consequence of GAM and the Indonesian government not being able to compromise on their respective positions of accepting Special Autonomy and complete independence. This is incorrect. GAM actually accepted the final Indonesian proposal on a political resolution to allow the CoHA to continue, but this was followed by a further demand that GAM surrender. It was at this point that GAM refused and the talks broke down.
10   There had been two previous agreements to reduce conflict in Aceh, both of which comprehensively failed, primarily as a consequence of TNI (or ABRI) intransigence.
11   This assessment was undertaken by Matt Davies, based on open source information, in August 2003. Davies' assessment counted TNI and Polri by unit, and provided totals for each of the services involved in Aceh.

SECTION ONE

THE CONTEXT OF RECONSTRUCTION

2

The Role of Islamic Law (Sharia) in Post-Tsunami Reconstruction

Michelle Ann Miller

Introduction

Few issues have generated as much controversy as Islamic law (sharia) in post-tsunami, post-conflict Aceh. Many of the international aid agencies involved in the large-scale reconstruction and rehabilitation effort have viewed sharia with suspicion and concern. Others have implicitly or explicitly supported the expanding application of Islamic law, by providing funding and other forms of humanitarian assistance to Acehnese religious institutions and organizations. Acch's evolving Islamic legal system has also been the subject of heated national debate. As the only Indonesian province authorized to implement Islamic law in its entirety, Aceh has been viewed by Islamist groups as a model for the rest of the country, but by certain moderate Muslim and non-Muslim organizations as a potential threat to Indonesia's pluralist foundations.

The divisions between proponents and detractors of Islamic law have fuelled debate about whether sharia has a constructive role to play in the reconstruction of Aceh. There have been questions about whether Islamic law, as it has so far been interpreted and implemented, has assisted or impeded the large-scale reconstruction and rehabilitation effort. How has it affected the development priorities and programmes of international donors and aid agencies? Has it served as a panacea for social disunity and conflict, as the Indonesian government and Islamic leaders and scholars (*ulama*) intended, or has it created new destabilizing tensions within Aceh and in its relations with the outside world?

This chapter considers these questions from the viewpoints of the key stakeholders involved in Aceh's reconstruction; namely, the international and foreign humanitarian agencies at work in Aceh, Indonesian government officials, *ulama*, former Free Aceh Movement (*Gerakan Aceh Merdeka*, GAM) rebels and Acehnese NGOs and civil society organizations. It begins with a brief background of Islamic law in Aceh. The perspectives and attitudes of the main governmental and non-governmental stakeholders about the role of sharia in the reconstruction process are then canvassed, as well as the points of correspondence and contention between them. Finally, the implementation of Islamic law is briefly examined within Aceh's post-tsunami, post-conflict policy environment to ascertain its role in the rebuilding of Aceh.

The central conclusion of the analysis is that while Islamic law could potentially play a constructive role in Aceh's efforts to rebuild itself, by emphasizing social welfare and justice, it has so far reinforced unequal power hierarchies, rather than promoting the formation of a more egalitarian society. In this, the 'constructive role' of sharia is considered in terms of the extent to which it has empowered Acehnese communities to regain control over their own lives. Further, it is argued that Islamic law, as it has been interpreted and applied in Aceh, appears to have been primarily concerned with morality as an end in itself, rather than with the Islamic principles of social justice and welfare as means to a greater end. This narrow focus has in turn contributed towards the growth of a kind of moral vigilantism, making it difficult for the public to hold to account those legally responsible for enforcing sharia, while at the same time enabling opportunistic Islamist groups to take the law into their own hands.

Background

Formally called Nanggroe Aceh Darussalam (lit; State of Aceh, Abode of Peace), Aceh has a reputation as the most devoutly Islamic region of Indonesia. Also known as *Serambi Mekkah* (Verandah of Mecca), the almost entirely Muslim region[1] was the first entry point for Islam into the Indonesian archipelago, via Indian and Arabic traders in the 8th century CE.[2] Over the centuries, Acehnese culture, customary law (*adat*) and identity have been heavily imbued with Islamic principles and practices, as embodied in the Acehnese saying, *adat ngon hukom lagee zat ngon sifeuet* ('the relationship between *adat* and (Islamic) law is like our essence with our character').[3]

Acehnese claims to a distinctive identity, however, have never been based solely on Islam. Though Acehnese uprisings against Indonesian rule were influenced strongly by Islamic conceptions of social justice and *jihad* (holy war), they largely stemmed from grievances over external interference and neglect. Acehnese involvement in the *Darul Islam* (House of Islam) rebellion of the 1950s and early 1960s resulted mainly from regionalist anger over Aceh's incorporation into North Sumatra, and eventually subsided after Jakarta reinstated the province of Aceh and conferred in principle *Daerah Istimewa* (Special Region) status to the Acehnese people in the fields of religion (Islamic law), education and *adat*.[4] Aceh's first separatist insurgency, which was launched in 1976 by the Free Aceh Movement (GAM), shared some common grievances with the *Darul Islam* rebels, such as regional resentment over the New Order regime's centralizing state policies, which gradually rendered meaningless Aceh's *Daerah Istimewa* status. Unlike the *Darul Islam* insurgents, however, who sought to establish an autonomous Aceh province within an Islamic Indonesian state, GAM 're-declared' the 'free and independent Sovereign State' of 'Acheh-Sumatra' with the aim of severing all ties with the 'foreign regime of Jakarta and the alien people of the island of Java'.[5] Although virtually all GAM rebels were Muslims, the independence movement was explicitly nationalist in nature, basing its claims to territorial sovereignty on the construct of a distinctive Acehnese ethnic, linguistic, cultural, historical and geographically specific identity. GAM never sought to establish ties with Islamic movements elsewhere, and rejected Indonesian government offers to implement sharia in Aceh. For GAM, such offers were aimed at dividing Acehnese society and discrediting their cause in the eyes of the international community, 'to make us look like Afghanistan'.[6]

Though the fundamental issue that separated GAM and the Indonesian government for almost 30 years until both sides signed a peace agreement in Helsinki in August 2005 was competing nationalisms, and not religion (Islam), many in Jakarta believed that Islamic law could help to resolve the Aceh conflict. This belief became increasingly central to Indonesian government thinking following the collapse of the New Order regime in 1998, when politicians and legislators in Jakarta began to look towards decentralization, or regional autonomy, as the most democratic way of containing destabilizing centrifugal forces and were prepared to recognize a 'special' place for separatist regions like Aceh within Indonesia's unitary state. It was this rationale that informed the development of Law no 44/1999 on the 'Special Status of the Special Province of Aceh', which granted Aceh the right to implement Islamic law and to organize its own religious, customary law and educational affairs. The law also envisaged the creation of an independent *ulama* council with the same status and decision-making powers as Aceh's provincial parliament.[7] Based on the three key tenets of the *Darul Islam* settlement, Law no 44/1999 reflected the dominant view in Jakarta that the contemporary conflict had stemmed from the New Order's failure to honour Aceh's special autonomous status. Related to this belief was the idea that Acehnese support for GAM would gradually decline if Acehnese *ulama* were restored to their pre-New Order position of socio-political influence. Among nationalist Islamist groups and organizations, which tended to portray Aceh as a symbol of the New Order's perceived injustices against

Muslims, there were also growing calls to implement sharia in Aceh as part of their broader goal to introduce Islamic law in other parts of Indonesia.[8]

Whereas Aceh's *Darul Islam* insurgents would have welcomed the opportunity to implement sharia, the structure and expectations of Acehnese society had undergone major changes since the 1960s.[9] Acehnese *ulama*, like religious leaders elsewhere in Indonesia, had been emasculated under the New Order, and what little influence they retained had been through their incorporation into its institutional framework. In Aceh, *ulama* who joined the state-sponsored MUI (*Majelis Ulama Indonesia*, Indonesia Ulama Council) had been co-opted into the Indonesian military's territorial campaign against GAM during Suharto's final decade in power, when Aceh had effectively been turned into a Military Operations Area (*Daerah Operasi Militer*, DOM).[10] Rural-based *ulama* who did not join the MUI or other state-sanctioned institutions were either arrested, or confined to an educational role in their Islamic boarding schools (*dayah*). After Suharto's resignation, MUI *ulama* in particular were unable to achieve significant political influence as many Acehnese people, whose daily experience of Indonesian authority was violence, 'preferred to listen to students and NGOs than to government officials and *ulama*'.[11] Law no 44/1999 was also passed weeks after the East Timorese people had successfully voted to secede from Indonesia, in a United Nations monitored referendum. For many Acehnese, who were angered by Jakarta's ambivalence about past and ongoing human rights violations committed by Indonesian security forces personnel, the most tangible embodiment of democracy was Aceh's own university student-led referendum movement (*Sentral Informasi Referendum Aceh*, SIRA), with its rallying call to decide Aceh's political status via popular ballot. The precariousness of Indonesian authority in Aceh was underscored in November 1999, when about 500,000 of Aceh's 4.2 million people gathered at the Baiturrahman mosque in Banda Aceh to demand a referendum on Acehnese independence. Even Acehnese *ulama*, who stood to benefit most from Islamic law, were divided between the minority of pro-integration urban-based MUI *ulama* and the rural-based Islamic boarding school *ulama*, who warned that 'the *dayah ulama* are ready to face the consequences' if the students' referendum demand was not met.[12]

It was within this context that the successive governments of Abdurrahman Wahid and Megawati Sukarnoputri adopted a dual-track Aceh policy approach that involved acquiescing to military pressure for more intensive counterinsurgency operations against GAM on one hand (as shown, for example, by the sharp annual increase in Aceh's civilian death toll between 1999 and 2004),[13] while searching for a political solution to the conflict on the other hand. This latter approach took the form of a limited peace process with GAM and a more comprehensive 'special autonomy' package pursuant to Law no 18/2001, which changed Aceh's name to Nanggroe Aceh Darussalam (NAD) and granted the province greater self-government in three core areas: (1) a greater share of its natural resource wealth, (2) the right to hold direct democratic local elections, and (3) authority to establish its own Islamic court system (called *Mahkamah Syari'at*).[14] Law no 18/2001 was hardly implemented, however, amidst Aceh's deteriorating security situation, war-damaged infrastructure and unpopular political leadership, widely seen as corrupt. What limited advances were made under the new special autonomy arrangement were in the field of Islamic law, largely because of the political assertiveness of a newly formed MPU (*Majelis Permusyawaratan Ulama*, Consultative Council of Ulama) and a government sharia agency (*Dinas Syariat Islam*), which were established in July and August 2001 respectively and acted quickly to 'socialize' Islamic law among the local population.[15] The MPU and sharia agency were also actively involved in drafting a slate of regional regulations (*qanun*) on Islamic law in accordance with Law no 18/2001 in preparation for the establishment of the *Mahkamah Syari'at*.

Although these sharia *qanun* and the *Mahkamah Syari'at* were introduced before the December 2004 tsunami, it was only in the aftermath of the natural disaster that Islamic law took on a life of its own. There were at least four reasons for this.

First, a basic Islamic legal framework had already been established in the form of a series of sharia *qanun* and gubernatorial decrees that were passed by Aceh's provincial parliament between 2002 and 2004. These *qanun* were by no means comprehensive, covering as they did only rudimentary guidelines on the structure and functions of sharia courts, the implementation of Islamic law in the areas of faith (*aqidah*), devotion (*ibadah*) and the greatness/magnificence of Islamic teachings (*Syi'ar Islam*). The *qanun* also included specific penalties in the form of imprisonment, fines and public canings for moral violations of Islamic law, such as the sale and consumption of alcohol (*khamar*), gambling (*maisir*) and illicit relations between men and women (*khalwat*).[16] Aceh's Islamic legal framework was further reinforced by the introduction in July 2006 of a Law on Governing Aceh (Law no 11/2006, LoGA), which included three chapters on sharia: 'Syari'at Islam and its Implementation' (Chapter XVII), the 'Syari'yah Court' (Chapter XVIII) and the 'Ulama Consultative Assembly' (Chapter XIX). The LoGA required all Muslims domiciled in Aceh to follow Islamic law, all individuals in Aceh to respect sharia, and outlined the authority of Aceh's sharia courts in the fields of civil, family and criminal law.[17] While Indonesian legislators predicted that Aceh's Islamic legal system would take 'more than one hundred years'[18] to complete, the existence of these laws and by-laws, combined with the sharia courts and a newly established vice squad, the *Wilayatul Hisbah* (lit; Control Team), meant that Islamic law could be enforced, albeit initially in a limited form.

Second, Aceh's religious bureaucracy became increasingly assertive in expanding its own authority after the tsunami.[19] In particular, Aceh's sharia agency and the *Wilayatul Hisbah* (WH), which shared the same headquarters in Banda Aceh, became more zealous in their efforts to monitor the implementation of Islamic law. When the green-and-white uniformed WH was first established in 2004, it only operated in and around Banda Aceh.[20] By late 2006, however, the so-called 'moral police' had established a province-wide presence and had become far more vigilant in defending public morality. In the first half of 2007 alone, the WH handled 397 cases involving alleged violations of sharia, compared with 373 cases for all of 2006.[21] Aceh's religious administration believed that Islamic law needed to be implemented in order for Acehnese society to recover from the conflict and tsunami, and that its past failure to uphold sharia had contributed towards Aceh's contemporary problems. The WH's existence and expansion, however, was contingent on the presence of social maladies. As such, its vigilantism could not be divorced from its expansionary tendencies and desire to attract more state power and funding.[22]

Third, Aceh's religious bureaucracy was able to assert its authority to the extent that it did because Aceh's political landscape changed dramatically after the tsunami.[23] Although the province remained under civil emergency rule for more than seven months after the tsunami, and intensive fighting between GAM and Indonesia's security forces continued in the countryside, GAM's political leadership and the Indonesian government decided to use the unique opportunity presented by the tsunami to search for a negotiated peace.[24] GAM remained basically opposed to sharia, but agreed to focus on the more substantive issue of Aceh's political status within Indonesia in a series of peace talks with Indonesian government representatives that were mediated in Helsinki by the former Finnish president, Maarti Ahtisaari, and his Crisis Management Initiative non-governmental organization. After these talks culminated in the signing of an historic peace agreement between both sides on 15 August 2005, GAM became more circumspect in their public criticism of Islamic law. One important concession by Jakarta through the Helsinki peace process was its decision to allow the Acehnese to hold direct democratic local elections, and the former rebels were conscious of the fact that sharia was a highly sensitive political issue that could affect their own election campaign. According to a senior GAM representative, 'If we win [the election] we will put an end to sharia. But we have to be careful about how we approach this matter because most Acehnese people accept it.'[25]

Fourth, the accelerated expansion of Islamic law after the tsunami was made possible by a shift in public opinion. The great majority of Acehnese people tried to make sense of, and cope with the natural disaster through religion. As the Christian[26] NGO World Vision observed, all of their Acehnese interviewees believed that 'the culture of Islam is an excellent antidote to fear and grieving'.[27] Somewhat differently, Médecins Sans Frontières found in their psychological evaluation of tsunami victims in Banda Aceh that 'Without exception, the people we spoke with during the assessment understood the tsunami as a punishment or a warning from Allah for being "immoral".'[28] Related to this popular belief that the tsunami was divine punishment for the collective sins committed by the Acehnese people was the idea that strict adherence to sharia was necessary to prevent another disaster.[29] This message was often repeated by *ulama* during Friday prayers, either to advance their own conservative agenda, or to defend Acehnese culture and values against the massive influx of foreign, non-Muslim aid workers and volunteers into Aceh, or both. For instance, during the first Friday prayers after the tsunami, the General Secretary of the Indonesian *Ulama* Council (MUI), Din Syamsuddin, told some 2000 worshippers at Banda Aceh's Baiturrahman Mosque that they might have been the cause of the disaster. 'Allah will not love us without also testing our love for Him … Maybe this disaster was because we have forgotten Him and His teachings and failed to implement shariah law,' said Din Syamsuddin.[30] In a more widely publicized case, sharia judge H. Marluddin A. Jalil was applauded at a conference in the North Aceh capital of Lhokseumawe for saying that 'The tsunami was because of the sins of the people of Aceh' and 'The Holy Koran says that if women are good then the country is good.'[31] Other religious leaders implausibly suggested that the tsunami was caused by the immoral conduct of women, because far more women died than men, and, unlike many men who wore shorts, more women were found naked because their sarongs were ripped off by the waves.[32] The survival of mosques in Banda Aceh and the nearby fishing village of Lampuuk was also widely interpreted by sharia advocates as testimony of Allah's intervention in the disaster, and a warning to the Acehnese to become better Muslims. Although national and international NGOs have since sought to dispel these superstitious explanations and to assuage the sense of guilt felt by many Acehnese, by erecting roadside banners and providing tsunami/earthquake education programmes,[33] such messages have continued to be promoted in mosques throughout Aceh.

Little wonder, then, that sharia was accepted uncritically by many Acehnese who sought solace in Islam and Friday prayers in the weeks and months after the tsunami. While few Acehnese criticized Islamic law itself, however, certain groups and individuals expressed concerns about its interpretation and application in Aceh. These tensions between advocates and detractors of Aceh's Islamic legal system are complicated and multi-layered, but a simplified version is presented in the following pages in order to assist our understanding of how sharia has been understood by the main stakeholders in Aceh as the province struggles to rebuild itself after the tsunami and after almost three decades of armed conflict.

Attitudes to Islamic law

How the key players in the reconstruction process have viewed Islamic law has varied considerably between different groups and organizations, and to a lesser extent, within them. There are already signs that the attitudes of foreign and international donors, Indonesian government officials, *ulama*, GAM and Acehnese NGOs to sharia have affected their capacity to relate to one another, which in turn has implications for their normative commitment to a more coordinated aid effort. As the accelerated expansion of Islamic law in post-tsunami, post-conflict Aceh currently shows no signs of slowing down or stagnating, it is likely to influence future forms of engagement between foreign and Indonesian donors and their Acehnese partners, as well as on their development priorities and activities in the region.

There has been a visible shift in the collective approach taken by the international development community towards sharia in Aceh. Divisions between foreign donors and aid agencies about the relevance of Islamic law to the reconstruction effort, that were quite pronounced immediately after the tsunami, have lessened considerably. This is largely because most of the foreign NGOs and aid agencies that openly criticized Islamic law were either asked to leave Aceh or left voluntarily, and those that remained passively accepted its inevitability or supported it. After the tsunami, the most vociferous critics of sharia were North American Christian missionary organizations.[34] Most of these proselytizing groups left within three months of their arrival, in part because of the lack of willing converts among Aceh's almost entirely Muslim population, in part because of threats by Islamist groups, and in part because of Indonesian government pressure. In the most public case, the North American Virginia-based Christian WorldHelp organization attempted in January 2005 to relocate 300 tsunami orphans from Banda Aceh to a Christian orphanage in Jakarta.[35] Drawing parallels between their own work and that of Mother Teresa, who placed Hindu children in Catholic orphanages in Calcutta, WorldHelp stated on its website that it would 'plant Christian principles as early as possible' in the minds of the Acehnese Muslim orphans.[36] The Indonesian government, confronted by outraged Islamic organizations, quickly intervened and banned all tsunami orphans from leaving Aceh on the grounds that the disaster had increased the risk of child trafficking.[37] As a result, WorldHelp 'immediately stopped all fundraising efforts' for Acehnese tsunami victims and removed aid appeals from its website.[38]

Of the foreign NGOs that remained in Aceh, the great majority refrained from publicly condemning Islamic law. Even the handful of Christian organizations that continued to work there did not openly evangelize, but tried to quietly promote their faith through their programmes. For example, the Michigan-based Christian International Aid organization aimed to 'demonstrate Christ's love' to the Acehnese people, but emphasized the need to be 'appropriate in how we do it' by building medical training facilities in Banda Aceh.[39] While such faith-based organizations did not support sharia, they were conscious of the potentially inflammatory consequences of criticizing Islam and how this could undermine their credibility, activities and community relationships with their Acehnese stakeholders. As Dudley Woodberry of the Fuller Theological Seminary explained: 'Most people are thinking that Christian witness involves both word and deed, so they are seeing this as a holy ministry,' but in tsunami-affected areas where they are not allowed to evangelize, 'it basically has to be the ministry of deed.'[40]

Some other foreign development agencies have advocated a potentially constructive role for Islamic law in the reconstruction process. For instance, the Birmingham-based Islamic Foundation for Ecology and Environmental Sciences (IFEES) and the World Wildlife Fund (WWF) worked together after the tsunami to promote environmental protection and sustainability from an Islamic perspective.[41] Within this approach it was thought that 'Islamic values should be adapted during the reconstruction and rehabilitation process in Aceh to strengthen and safeguard Aceh's environment against future threats as well as to ensure that Acehnese people are considered in all decision-making processes.'[42] Implicit in this approach were two interrelated assumptions, that: a) sharia was widely accepted by the Acehnese people, and b) local communities were more likely to participate actively in development processes if foreign development programmes and discourses were positioned within an Islamic framework. These assumptions were also reflected in a joint report by the Indonesian government's National Development Planning Agency (*Badan Perencanaan dan Pembangunan Nasional,* Bappenas) and the Consultative Group on Indonesia (CGI), a consortium of 21 bilateral donor countries (including the USA, France, Germany and Japan) and 11 multilateral creditors, such as the World Bank, the IMF and the Asia Development Bank.[43] The CGI and Bappenas described their 'guiding principle' in Aceh's reconstruction as follows:

> *All assistance towards rebuilding the lives, confidence and dignity of
> the Acehnese must take into consideration the fact that Islam is the
> primary cultural force in the province. Communities in Aceh are
> centred around* meunasah, *a community mosque; approximately
> 200,000 of 950,000 students in Aceh attend Islamic schools, one of
> two major universities in Banda Aceh was an Islamic university. As
> such, engaging mass-based Islamic organisations with networks and
> branches down to the village level … is essential to ensure that pro-
> grams for rehabilitation and reconstruction are designed in a
> people-centred and participatory manner.*[44]

The CGI-Bappenas report went on to add, however, that while all reconstruction efforts must comply with Aceh's special autonomy status,
including its right to implement Islamic law, the concept of sharia itself
remained 'vaguely defined', with the result that 'while on the one hand, it is
important to consider the fact that syariah is the law of the land, it is also
equally important to understand that the Acehnese themselves were still
engaged in a lively debate over what constitutes syariah.'[45] Because of this
ongoing debate, the CGI-Bappenas report urged all parties involved in
Aceh reconstruction to maintain a policy of strict neutrality regarding
Islamic law.[46]

There were at least three problems with this policy of 'neutrality'. The
first was that the CGI-Bappenas report departed from its own normatively
neutral position by assuming the cultural primacy of Islam in the reconstruction effort, despite its acknowledgement that less than one-third of
Acehnese students (200,000 of 950,000) attended Islamic schools and only
one of Banda Aceh's two main universities, the Ar-Raniry State Islamic
Institute (*Institut Agama Islam Negara*, IAIN) was officially Islamic. The
second problem was that the international development community's
neutrality was arguably reprehensible in cases where the *Wilayatul Hisbah*,
which had a reputation for 'arrogance' and 'thuggery' in their dealings with
the civilian population,[47] overstepped their authority and violated international human rights instruments. The European Union (EU), which led the
Aceh Monitoring Mission (AMM) that was mandated with 'monitoring and
supporting the peace process'[48] in Aceh, was criticized harshly by some outside observers for adopting a double standard of defending the European
Convention on Human Rights, on one hand, while refusing to interfere in
cases where the WH humiliated and degraded alleged sharia violators without offering proper judicial recourse, on the other. Although the EU
released a paper in December 2006 outlining its concerns about restrictions
on religious freedom in Aceh, inequitable judicial access, corporal punishment, discrimination based on gender and lack of respect for privacy, the

AMM maintained that the sharia issue needed 'to be kept in perspective' because the 'main thing is there is peace'.[49] The EU and the AMM believed their neutrality regarding Islamic law was necessary to avoid being accused of meddling in Aceh's internal affairs and of taking sides in the uncertain peace process. In adopting a non-position on Islamic law in Aceh, however, the EU and the AMM were seen by some as being complicit in violations of the Acehnese people's civil and political rights to freedom of religion and expression.[50]

The third problem with this 'neutral' policy was that while the Indonesian government's Bappenas agency and CGI donor countries and their aid agencies in Aceh argued that they simply wanted to help, some were politically motivated. Since its first unilateral offer of Islamic law to Aceh in 1999, the Indonesian government had encouraged the Acehnese people to accept sharia. CGI donor countries that declared their neutrality in relation to sharia were also sometimes believed to be otherwise by other foreign and Indonesian NGOs. For example, the USA and the US Agency for International Development (USAID), were seen by conservative Acehnese and Indonesian Muslims as being anti-Islam, or 'Islamophobes', with a hidden agenda to 'Christianize' or 'Americanize' the Acehnese people.[51] This theory was typically promoted by Islamist groups whose political motivation was to increase their own power and influence through sharia. Like some conspiracy theories, however, there was an element of truth in this claim. Since the September 11, 2001 terrorist attacks on the USA, USAID had changed its Indonesia policy from primarily funding reform-minded civil society organizations, as a means of strengthening Indonesia's democratization process, towards sponsoring more than 30 Indonesian moderate Muslim organizations as potential bulwarks against religious orthodoxy. After the tsunami, the US government made little secret of its strategic interests in delivering aid to the world's most populous Muslim nation. The US Secretary of State, Colin Powell, described the USA's humanitarian assistance to Aceh as proof that 'America is not an anti-Islam, anti-Muslim nation.' More candidly, the US Senator Sam Brownback argued that the tsunami was 'a foreign policy moment'.[52] As one former political counsel at the US embassy in Jakarta cynically put it: 'Now we're trying to bribe organizations, including Islamic organizations, to win them to our side.'[53] America's closest ally in the region, Australia (another CGI donor country), had equally strong strategic interests in containing Islamic extremism, especially after the 2002 Bali bombings and the 2003 Marriott Hotel bomb blast in Jakarta. In post-tsunami Aceh, therefore, geopolitical interests and security considerations certainly factored into the reconstruction priorities of USAID and its Australian counterpart, the Australian Agency for International Development (AusAID), as shown by the interventions by both donor countries into Islamic education (for example, through AusAID's Learning Assistance Program for Islamic Schools programme, LAPIS).[54]

Some foreign Islamic NGOs were also believed to have used the opportunity presented by the tsunami for religious or political gain. Two of Saudi Arabia's largest charity organizations, the International Islamic Relief Organization (IIRO), which had links to the Al-Qaeda terrorist network, and its affiliated World Assembly of Muslim Youth, were accused by US government agencies of using humanitarian assistance as a vehicle for disseminating radical Wahhabist (a scripturalist interpretation of Sunni Islam) ideas and for spreading Saudi foreign policy.[55] While the IIRO's charity work in Indonesia had previously been benign, and in Aceh had included rebuilding homes and other basic infrastructure, its post-tsunami religious activities (such as funding Islamic organizations and rebuilding mosques) were viewed by some as part of its characteristic 'religious imperative that comes hand-in-hand with aid.'[56] An earlier *US News and World Report* had also described the IIRO's charitable activities as being invariably accompanied by 'a blizzard of Wahhabist literature', which, in its most extreme form, included preaching 'mistrust of infidels, branding of rival sects as apostates, and emphasis on violent *jihad*' that 'laid the groundwork for terrorist groups around the world'.[57] Another Saudi-funded charitable organization in Aceh, the Medical Emergency Relief Charity (MER-C), which had 12 other Indonesian offices, mostly in the country's sectarian conflict areas, had also previously produced two *jihad* fundraising videos and was rumoured to have taken advantage of the post-tsunami situation to further its radical cause.[58]

Beyond this mutual mistrust between foreign donors and their Muslim and non-Muslim aid agencies, the complicating dynamic of individual biases about Islamic law must be factored into the post-tsunami reconstruction equation. If Western, non-Muslim NGOs have not been especially candid in voicing their concerns about sharia, then the same could not be said for individual foreign development workers. Despite the burgeoning body of literature on post-tsunami reconstruction in Aceh, there has so far been a lack of reflective empirical research about this disconnect between the officially neutral nomenclature used by Western NGOs and donor agencies and the personal biases of some of their staff. More in-depth research is needed into how individual humanitarian and development workers view sharia, especially given the centrality of foreign assistance to the reconstruction process, the increasingly conservative Islamic environment within which foreign NGO employees must function, and what this means in terms of their capacity to constructively engage with the Acehnese Islamic groups and organizations they seek to embrace.

What limited information is currently available on this subject suggests a tendency by foreign NGO workers to view Islamic law in negative terms. As the head of Aceh's Rehabilitation and Reconstruction (BRR) Agency, Kuntoro Mangkusubroto, explained: 'Security has been the most frequent question asked by foreigners. But the application of sharia has also been of concern to them.'[59] Many foreigners have viewed Islamic law as an obstacle to the reconstruction effort, which they have mainly conceptualized in terms of material improvements such as rebuilding the provincial infrastructure, providing technical skills, generating employment, and so on. Some Western development workers have viewed sharia's defenders as dogmatic ideologues whose rigid adherence to an esoteric worldview has impeded rational decision-making and strategic development planning.[60] Such 'rational' attitudes about Islamic law have tended to be reinforced by the different language spoken by sharia advocates, whose understanding of 'development' and 'capacity-building' has included a dominant emphasis on spiritual growth and Islamic education, rather than on material development. In this, there has been an element of 'othering' the Acehnese people by foreign development workers on the basis of their Islamic identity, including misunderstandings about what this identity entails, and the association of Islamic law with anti-libertarian, explicitly prescriptive and radical belief systems. For instance, while the US military was generally praised for its rapid delivery of humanitarian assistance after the tsunami, some North American military aid personnel who went straight to Aceh from Iraq reportedly felt uncomfortable in another predominantly Muslim region, having themselves been 'past targets of Islamic fundamentalists'.[61] As a result, their 'interpersonal interactions between independent groups and the local Acehnese appeared to be strained'.[62] 'Creeping fears related to issues such as terrorist attacks on Westerners'[63] have also been articulated by foreign development workers on the Private Sector Development (PSD) Blog site, a joint initiative of the World Bank and International Finance Corporation (IFC). In one sense, the PSD Blog site has usefully illustrated this disconnect between the official position taken by institutions and the attitudes of staff employed to carry out their objectives. The World Bank and IFC have formally remained neutral about Aceh's Islamic legal system, but the PSD Blog authors, all of whom are World Bank Group members, have been overwhelmingly critical. Interestingly, the most common complaint about sharia among PSD bloggers has related to lifestyle limitations, and their need to escape to Weh Island near Banda Aceh, where there has been a 'complete seeming disregard by both local and expats for Aceh's shariah law' and where 'unmarried couples sharing cottages and women in bikinis sunning themselves is an open and familiar sight, as is the open consumption of beer and spirits ... and staff all sporting dreadlocks are happy to provide joints as an off-the-menu specialty.'[64]

Such 'immoral' attitudes and behaviours have been used by conservative Indonesian and Acehnese Muslims and radical Islamist groups as justification for their agenda to implement Islamic law in full. Post-tsunami Aceh has been a magnet for fundamentalists of all religious denominations, who have viewed the devastated province as fertile terrain for proselytizing and recruiting new members. Unlike the fundamentalist Christian missionary organizations, however, many of the radical Islamist groups that flocked to Aceh after the tsunami were Muslim militia who had previously been recruited, armed and trained by Indonesia's armed forces for incorporation into their counterinsurgency campaign against GAM. After the tsunami, these militia proxies were especially alarmed by the potentially corrosive impact of Western aid workers, journalists and armed forces personnel on the moral fabric of Acehnese society, and more broadly, on Indonesia at large. Conceptualizing *jihad* in Indonesian nationalist terms, they aimed to defend Indonesia's moral integrity and cohesiveness against the infidel (*kafir*) intruders.[65]

Three Muslim militias that established a high public profile in Aceh soon after the tsunami were the Islamic Defenders Front (*Front Pembela Islam*, FPI), Laskar Mujahidin and the Indonesian Mujahidin Council (*Majelis Mujahadin Indonesia*, MMI). The FPI, which was best known for its attacks on Jakarta nightclubs, bars and brothels during the Muslim fasting month of Ramadhan,[66] sent 250 militia to Aceh and announced plans to shuttle in another 800 of its members on Indonesian military warships.[67] Although FPI's Vice-Chairman and leader of its Aceh mission, Hilmy Bakar Almascaty, claimed that his team had simply come 'to help', he warned that 'If anyone who comes here does not respect the Shariah law, traditions and constitution, we must give them a warning and then we must attack.'[68] Hilmy further urged Aceh's military commander, General Endang Suwarya, 'to keep the US separate' from other humanitarian agencies, arguing that 'if you come here and take women and try and Westernise them, this is a problem for me'.[69] The Indonesian military-backed Laskar Mujahidin, which also sent 250 militia to Banda Aceh (50 of whom were flown in on Indonesian military planes), were equally anti-American and set up four base camps marked by English-language signs reading 'Islamic Law Enforcement' near the airport and around foreign aid agencies.[70] Though Laskar Mujahidin claimed the purpose of their Aceh mission was 'to help our Muslim brothers',[71] they were linked to the militant Islamic Jemaah Islamiyah organization led by the radical Muslim cleric Abu Bakar Bashir. So was Majelis Mujahadin Indonesia (MMI), which was founded by Abu Bakar in August 2000 as a coalition of Islamist groups that aimed to turn

Indonesia into an Islamic state. After the tsunami, the MMI sent 206 militia to Aceh,[72] 19 of whom were subsequently expelled from the province by the Indonesian Air Force after setting up a command post at Banda Aceh's Iskandar Muda Air Force base.[73]

Despite their divisive language and unsettling effect on Western aid agencies, these Muslim militia gained a certain degree of respect among Aceh's civilian population for their tireless collection and burial of thousands of rotting corpses. Muslim burials were something that non-Muslim NGOs could not provide; their primary focus was on offering humanitarian assistance to tsunami survivors, not on performing last rites for the deceased. For Acehnese Muslims, however, Islamic burials were an important ritual in coming to terms with the deaths of their loved ones.[74] As one village leader explained:

> *During the conflict, MMI were our enemies. But after the tsunami they worked here for three months. They never rested. When they found a corpse, they shouted 'Allah Akbar' ['God is Great'] and prayed for their souls. We knew why they were really here, but we thanked them because they helped us.*[75]

According to this village leader, the 'real' reason why MMI and other Muslim militias came to Aceh was to impose their narrow interpretation of Islam on the Acehnese people. Indeed, the militias aimed to defend sharia and Acehnese morality against Western immorality at least as much as they sought to assist tsunami victims. In addition to providing Muslim burials, MMI staged proselytizing rallies (*dakwah*), offered 'spiritual guidance', announced plans to adopt and educate 10,000 Acehnese orphans and distributed 'prayer kits' containing copies of the Koran and prayer mats.[76] Laskar Mujahadeen and the FPI performed similar duties, but FPI were by far the most vocal about their other agenda to 'chase down any Christian group that does anything beyond offering aid'.[77]

Not all Acehnese appreciated the Muslim militias' 'help'. GAM's exiled political leadership in Sweden issued a statement announcing that the 'FPI and MMI are not welcome in Aceh and have never been supported by the Acehnese people,' and that their 'counterproductive' and 'terroristic' activities 'contradict the teachings of Islam'.[78] For GAM, the Islamic militias, like sharia, were an unwanted 'gift' from Jakarta that aimed to create new horizontal socio-political cleavages based on 'SARA' (*Suku, Agama, Ras, Antargolongan*: Ethnic, Religion, Race and Inter-Group).[79] The day after Aceh's first direct gubernatorial elections on 11 December 2006, which delivered a clear victory to GAM candidate Irwandi Yusuf (with 38.57 per cent of the vote[80]), the new governor clarified his position on Islamic law:

> *The problem is that sharia law was imposed on us by the central government in Jakarta ... For us, sharia is less about punishment and more about how to improve the well-being of the people.*[81]

Irwandi Yusuf was careful not to reject sharia as such, but he vowed to stop its repressive expansion under his watch, because 'Sharia law was created not to get humans into trouble but to form an Islamic community.'[82] Other GAM spokesmen also maintained that the Acehnese did not want Islamic law from 'outside forces, because Syariat Islam is already the flesh and blood of the Acehnese nation.'[83] In other words, GAM believed that sharia in Aceh should be based on personal communication with Allah, or God's law, as opposed to man's law, which they claimed had turned Islam into a political commodity.

Similar views have been expressed by human rights NGOs and Acehnese women's organizations, which have argued that Islamic law enforcement in Aceh has discriminated against already marginalized societal elements, mostly women and the poor. For many human rights NGOs, the most objectionable aspect of sharia in Aceh is that human rights issues – which are especially salient in Aceh given its history of violent conflict – are missing from the province's Islamic legal framework. Reflecting a common opinion in human rights NGO circles, Charmain Mohamed of Human Rights Watch argued that 'there can be no lasting peace in Aceh without accountability for human rights violations'.[84] The humanitarian NGO, International Islamic Christian Organization for Reconciliation and Reconstruction (IICORR) also pointed out that the 'extreme interpretation' of sharia in Aceh is incompatible with, and alien to, previous understandings of Islamic law by Acehnese people, and that its failure to provide redress for past human rights violations and corruption has had negative social consequences.[85] A London-based Acehnese human rights activist has similarly argued that in focusing on moral minutiae, Aceh's conservative religious administration has missed the point that sharia should strive for social justice and welfare:

> *In contrast to their self-proclaimed agenda of defending Islam, in reality today's conservatives are actually diminishing Islam, reducing it to small things that are inadequate or irrelevant in the face of the challenges of modern life or development. Ask the conservatives questions that reach beyond their favorite topics of gambling, alcohol and head scarves, for example about how their interpretation of religion can promote or support the reconstruction of Aceh, or Aceh's political and economic development and they are unable to answer.*[86]

It is true that until now, Aceh's religious administration has been unable to adequately account for its overarching emphasis on public morality, and why it has avoided addressing Aceh's social and economic problems, which are substantial. The head of Aceh's sharia agency, Alyasa Abubakar, has argued that Islamic law has a positive role to play in the reconstruction process because it 'helps to create a conducive atmosphere for the economy, prosperity and justice in Aceh', but he has not elaborated on how this can be achieved, beyond stating that 'people can work with peace of mind'.[87] The sharia agency director has remained equally non-committal about growing public demands for an *anti-korupsi qanun* to punish corrupt government officials, dismissing the issue as a non-priority on the grounds that 'there is already national legislation on corruption'.[88]

While Acehnese women's NGOs have generally refrained from condemning Islamic law itself, some have objected to their exclusion from the development of sharia *qanun*, and have expressed their frustration that the expansion of Aceh's Islamic legal system has included a concurrent increase in acts of violence against them. The International Crisis Group reported that 'Women complain that they are disproportionately the targets of WH raids, with far more operations against them for not wearing *jilbabs* [Islamic headscarves] than against men for not attending Friday prayer.'[89] Women's NGOs such as Flower Aceh and the Acehnese Women's Empowerment Group have argued that the predominantly male WH (which in 2006 comprised 70 men and five women)[90] has been aggressively enforcing the wearing of headscarves and other minor moral issues, at the expense of their protection. Reflecting a common perception among Acehnese feminist groups and also among former GAM rebels, one female Indonesian journalist in Aceh blamed the discriminatory targeting of women under sharia on 'Arab cultural imperialism', arguing that the repressive behaviour of the WH was 'not necessary at all, since what happened in Aceh is Arabization, not Islamization',[91] or the importation of Arab cultural norms and values, as opposed to the Islamic religion.

It is worth noting that Acehnese feminist NGOs that have criticized Islamic law have been marginalized in Aceh and have mainly appealed to foreign audiences. Since October 1999, when Aceh's first sharia by-law (Regional Regulation no 451.1/21249) was introduced (ordering the province's 119 policewomen to wear brown veils to 'serve as role models for Muslim teachings in Aceh'[92]), women have found it increasingly difficult to speak openly about the *jilbab* issue, for fear of being labelled 'un-Islamic' or 'secular'. According to an Acehnese NGO, the focus on women's morality by Aceh's religious bureaucracy has ignited two new horizontal conflicts: between men and women, and between women and women.[93] This is because Aceh's male-dominated Islamic administration has dictated the direction and form of sharia, and the expansion of Islamic law has created growing space for the voices of conservative women's organizations to be heard. The most prominent of these women's groups, the Bureau for Women's Empowerment (*Biro Pemberdayaan Perempuan*, BPP), has sent mixed messages about gender equality to the women they claim to represent by encouraging women to challenge traditional gender stereotypes on the one hand, while on the other, warning them not to 'forget their role as determined by God as women' or their husband's 'right to lead their wives and to fulfil their wives biological, sociological, psychological and economic rights.'[94] This has generally been the approach taken by post-Suharto Aceh governments, which have promoted 'the Islamic way to interpreting gender equality', as opposed to Western conceptions of gender equality that have been negatively associated with 'free for all action'.[95]

The attitudes of Indonesian national government officials about Aceh's Islamic legal system have been somewhat mixed since the tsunami, but generally speaking, political support for sharia has been high. This strong support has been shown by Jakarta's concession to Aceh to implement Islamic law in its entirety. Since 1998, there has been a growing trend among Indonesia's political leadership to view sharia as a form of compensation for the past suffering of the Acehnese people under the New Order. Islamic law has also been used as a political weapon by government and military leaders to discredit GAM's separatist cause in the eyes of the international community by portraying the rebels as Muslim 'fundamentalists' or 'terrorists'. There have been dissenting voices in Jakarta, but these still constitute the minority. In August 2006, for instance, more than 50 members of Indonesia's national parliament unsuccessfully petitioned President Susilo Bambang Yudhoyono to abolish Islamic law.[96] Disturbed by the spread of sharia to other provinces (some 30 regional governments have passed moral regulations since 2001 reflecting conservative Islamic values), they argued that Islamic law went against the pluralist spirit of the 1945 constitution. Most Indonesian political leaders, however, like many Acehnese government officials and ordinary civilians, have remained reluctant to criticize Aceh's sharia laws because they do not want to be labelled un-Islamic by conservative Islamist groups. This fear of being thought a 'bad Muslim' was perhaps seen most clearly shown in 2002 by Indonesia's then Speaker of the People's Consultative Assembly (MPR), Amien Rais, who strained Indonesian-Malaysian relations by describing Malaysia's practice of caning illegal Indonesian workers as 'inhumane' and 'insulting', while remaining conspicuously silent about Aceh's decision to publicly cane violators of Islamic law.[97] Such concerns about upsetting conservative Islamists have tended to suppress healthy public debate on what form Aceh's Islamic legal system should take, and to what end.

Implementation of sharia

On balance, the application of sharia in post-tsunami, post-conflict Aceh has contributed little towards helping Acehnese communities to regain a sense of control over their own lives and livelihoods. While Islamic law could potentially assist the Acehnese people in coming to terms with their legacy of violence and social trauma (for example, by application to serious crimes such as murder, rape and corruption), Aceh's sharia framework is still in its infancy and the religious bureaucracy has been reluctant to search for new ways to address the province's serious social and economic issues through Islamic law. The following observations, while limited, highlight the need for greater critical reflection on the role of Islamic law in the reconstruction process and its implications for the kind of society that will emerge as Aceh continues to rebuild itself.

Of particular concern to both Acehnese and outsiders involved in the reconstruction effort are legal ambiguities within Aceh's Islamic system. For instance, while the Law on Governing Aceh (LoGA) only stipulates that Muslims domiciled in Aceh must 'comply with and practise Syariat Islam', it states that 'all individuals residing or present in Aceh are obliged to respect the implementation of Syariat Islam'.[98] There is no elucidation on whether non-Acehnese Muslims are required to submit to Aceh's Islamic laws, or the level of 'respect' for sharia that is required of non-Muslims. The most confusing Islamic provision in the LoGA is Article 129 on Islamic criminal law (*jinayah*), which stipulates that:

> *(1) In* jinayah *cases where criminal acts are committed by two or more people that include non-Muslims, then the non-Muslim perpetrators may choose to voluntarily surrender to* jinayah *law, (2) Each non-Muslim who commits a criminal act not regulated by the Criminal Code or in the criminal stipulation set outside the Criminal Code will be subjected to* jinayah *law, (3) Acehnese citizens who commit criminal acts outside Aceh are subject to the Criminal Code.*

Not surprisingly, non-Muslims have expressed concerns about how this law will affect their rights to freedom of religion and expression. Article 129 does not clarify whether non-Muslim perpetrators may 'choose' to submit to civil law in *jinayah* cases, or whether non-Muslims will be punished for committing sharia crimes not included in Indonesia's Criminal Code (for example, the sale and consumption of food and beverages during Ramadhan, which in Aceh is punishable by up to six lashes, one year in jail or a maximum fine of Rp3 million (US$330)). Another concern about religious freedom pertains to *Qanun* no 11/2002, which includes a penalty of up to two years' imprisonment and a maximum 12 strokes of the cane for 'anyone who disseminates misguided understandings or ideologies'.[99]

Some of the ambiguities in Aceh's Islamic legal system point to a lack of experience on the part of the legislators. Many of the *ulama* who were involved in drafting the sharia *qanun* from 2002 to 2004 came from Islamic boarding schools and had no legal background. This inexperience is reflected in *Qanun* no 11/2002 (Chapter VIII, Article 21), which states that Muslims who fail to attend prayers for three consecutive Fridays without an acceptable reason are liable to punishment by up to three strokes of the cane or six months' imprisonment. While it is relatively easy to monitor mosque attendance in villages with only one mosque, and where most villagers live below the poverty line, it is far more difficult in urban areas, and the law does not account for travel for work, family visits or other legitimate reasons.

The most worrying legislation in terms of the zeal and discriminatory manner with which it has been enforced by the *Wilayatul Hisbah* has been in the field of criminal law (*jinayah*). Significantly, although Aceh's sharia courts are authorized to settle cases in the fields of civil law (*mu'amalah*), family law (*ahwal al syakhsiyah*) and criminal law, the only area that has expanded under the new system has been *jinayah*. Civil and family law cases have continued to be determined in the same manner as religious courts elsewhere in Indonesia, which are subject to the 'Compilation of Islamic Law' (*Kompilasi Hukum Islam*, KHI), which was introduced via Presidential Decree in 1991 to achieve greater national consistency in religious court rulings. According to one Islamic law expert:

> *From what I have observed at the Mahkamah Syari'at [sharia court] in Banda Aceh during visits in 2006–2007, the overwhelming bulk of its caseload remains in the field of family law, within which divorce cases still comprise the majority. Divorce, inheritance, and the signif-icantly rarer cases of* waqf *[charitable endowments] in contemporary Aceh generally appear to still be decided according to the 1991* Kompilasi Hukum Islam, *rather than any more recent, specifically Acehnese Islamic law. In this sense most of what happens in Aceh's Mahkamah Syari'at is not terribly different from established practice in the Islamic religious courts (*Pengadilan Agama*) elsewhere in Indonesia.*[100]

Despite the fact that most cases handled by Aceh's sharia courts have dealt with divorces, *jinayah* cases have generated the most publicity, especially the moral offences of *khalwat*, or close proximity between men and women, gambling (*maisir*), and the sale and consumption of alcohol (*khamar*) and other illegal substances. *Khalwat* is defined in *Qanun* no 14/2003 as 'the act of being alone by two or more people who are not married or in a relationship sanctioned by Islam (*muhrim*), which could lead to immoral sexual acts or the opportunity to commit adultery.' It carries a maximum sentence of nine public lashes, a Rp10 million rupiah fine (US$1,100), or up to six months' imprisonment.[101] The decision by the drafters of the *khalwat qanun* not to impose a separate punishment for adultery (*zina*) appears to have been based on the assumption that the *khalwat* penalties were a sufficient deterrent for would-be adulterers. The maximum penalty for gambling is 12 strokes of the cane or a minimum fine of Rp15 million (US$1,640) and a maximum fine of Rp35 million (US$3,800).[102] Consuming alcohol/illegal substances carries a fixed sentence of 40 lashes, up to Rp75 million (US$8,200) in fines, or a maximum one year jail term.[103] Because no *qanun* have yet been passed to deal with serious criminal offences such as murder, theft and rape, all of the criminal cases that have been tried by Aceh's sharia courts since the tsunami have been in these three areas of *khalwat*, gambling and the sale or consumption of alcohol/narcotics. According to Aceh's sharia agency, of the 107 Islamic criminal convictions in 2005, 79 were for gambling, 20 were for drinking/substance abuse, and eight were *khalwat* offenders. In 2006, 44 of the 85 *jinayah* court convictions were gambling cases, 20 were for drinking alcohol and 21 were *khalwat* cases.[104]

Although the sharia courts have dealt with more than twice as many gambling cases as *khalwat* offences since the tsunami, the media, feminist and human rights NGOs and Indonesian and foreign academics have portrayed Islamic law enforcement in Aceh as primarily focusing on monitoring and preventing *khalwat*.[105] There are several reasons for this. First, *khalwat* cases are more attractive to the mass media than gambling offences. Second, while Acehnese feminists (who, unlike gamblers, have established accessible NGOs) have been marginalized in Aceh, their opinions have been valued by many Western observers who themselves oppose Islamic law. Third, the great majority of *khalwat* cases never go to court. Fourth, the *Wilayatul Hisbah* has gained notoriety for its handling of several high-profile *khalwat* cases through its raids on segregated beauty salons, hotels and public humiliation of women who do not wear 'Islamic' dress. Fifth, the WH has itself expressed considerable interest in searching for *khalwat* offenders. The WH district secretary for Banda Aceh, has described his unit's civic duties as largely focusing on 'socializing' Islamic law, counselling unmarried couples and women to wear Islamic dress, and ensuring respect for the ban on gambling and alcohol:

> *We often go near the beach in the afternoon or late at night. Most of the time, we only give guidance and ask the couples to go home. It's only in cases of severe or repeated breaches that we make a report.*[106]

In fact, the WH's authority is limited to conducting identity checks, and they are required to obtain police assistance before undertaking investigations and making arrests. Despite this, there have been numerous reports of their involvement in more intrusive forms of behaviour. Even Aceh's WH chief admitted that 'If we see a woman date her boyfriend, we take her away from him.'[107] This problem of the WH encroaching on police authority was illustrated in February 2006, when the WH detained three women NGO activists who were participating in a UNDP workshop for not wearing headscarves while they were talking in their hotel corridor at about 11.30pm, and forced them to sign statements admitting their guilt.[108] Foreigners, too, have been illegally targeted. In one notorious incident in September 2006, the United Nations was forced to lodge a complaint with the Indonesian government after the WH raided the World Food Programme's Banda Aceh compound in search of development workers behaving in un-Islamic ways.[109]

Such incidents have made the WH widely unpopular, and have earned it a reputation for aggressiveness and poor professionalism. There is a common perception in Aceh that women and poor people have been the principal targets of WH raids. This view that Islamic justice has been dispensed unevenly, and largely restricted to those who can financially afford it, has been reinforced by the penalty system for *jinayah* offences. Many of the men caught gambling have only raised stakes of a few dollars, and are unable to pay the minimum fine of Rp15 million (US$1,640). In one typical case in August 2005, five young men who were arrested for playing dominos had only Rp30,000 (US$3.30) between them.[110] People who are able to pay fines for gambling, *khalwat*, and alcohol consumption are not subjected to the public humiliation and physical distress of being caned. This selective application of Islamic justice has created resentment among the civilian population and reinforced the general perception that sharia has been reduced to a political elite commodity. Reflecting this sentiment, one Banda Aceh resident asked: 'Why is the caning sentence only targeting the gamblers, drinkers and those who have committed adultery? It should apply also to the graft convicts.'[111] From a different perspective, one 'lashing executioner' (*algojo hukuman cambuk*) contended that 'The law is equal for everybody. It's just that the people who have been caught are poor people.'[112] Those responsible for monitoring and enforcing Islamic law have also been fond of emphasizing that corporal punishment in Aceh is the most humane in the world, because a doctor must oversee public canings, which must stop if the person being caned is unable to bear the pain; and, unlike parts of the Middle East and Africa, Aceh does not amputate the hands of thieves[113] or stone adulterers to death.

An interesting paradox in Acehnese perceptions about sharia is that while many people have viewed the current enforcement of Islamic law as unfair and discriminatory, corporal punishment has been very popular. Public canings have attracted enthusiastic audiences and have generally been characterized by a carnival quality. They have also been frequently televised for mass consumption in other parts of Indonesia and also in neighbouring Malaysia, where stricter interpretations of sharia in provinces such as Kelantan, Negeri Sembilan and Kedah have been viewed by conservative Acehnese Muslims as a model for Aceh. The obvious explanation for this popular support is that such public spectacles are a form of free entertainment. Another possible reason is that the belief that the Acehnese people caused the tsunami through their collective sins remains alive and well in Aceh. In June 2006, for instance, hundreds of Islamic boarding school students descended on a beach resort near Lhokseumawe and ordered people out of the sea on the grounds that their 'wicked deeds' might invite another tsunami.[114] While such vigilantism has caused considerable concern among moderate Muslims and non-Muslims, the lingering question asked by many Acehnese about whether they were ultimately responsible for the tsunami continues to be answered in sermons by *ulama* arguing that the Acehnese people could become better Muslims by strict adherence to sharia.

Still, there remains a pronounced gap between in-principle support for Islamic law, and public resentment over its practical application. Contrary to the claim by Aceh's sharia agency chief that Islamic law will allow the Acehnese people to work with greater peace of mind,[115] sharia has been one of the most socially divisive issues in the reconstruction effort. The dominant emphasis by Aceh's religious authorities on punishments for moral offences has generated anger and mistrust among the civilian population. There have also been tensions between Aceh's recently elected GAM governor, Irwandi Yusuf, who has opposed the imposition of Islamic law, and the religious bureaucracy, which has been intent on increasing its own power and jurisdiction through its continued expansion. GAM's opposition to sharia in turn has implications for the capacity of Aceh's new executive to constructively engage with both Jakarta officials and Aceh's religious administration in resolving current and future problems arising from the implementation of sharia. The vigilantism of the WH and other opportunistic Islamist groups has also impeded efforts by foreign aid agencies to build more coordinated relationships with their Acehnese partners.

Aceh's Islamic legal system is likely to continue to make a negligible contribution towards the large-scale reconstruction effort, unless the current focus on public morality as an end in itself is supplanted by a stronger emphasis on social welfare and justice as means to the greater goal of empowering local communities to recover from the conflict and tsunami.

The easy option, given the expansionary tendencies and ambitions of Aceh's Islamic administration, would be to further the existing trend towards emphasizing Acehnese morality. This trend is likely to continue for the foreseeable future, given the currently high levels of support for Aceh's sharia laws in Jakarta and among conservative Islamist groups, as well as the policy of 'neutrality' adopted by large sections of the international development community, and the uncritical acceptance of Islamic law by many Acehnese people.

The hard option would be to critically consider what Islamic law has actually achieved in terms of helping the Acehnese people to rebuild their lives and communities. Harder still, would be to rethink how sharia could be interpreted and applied in Aceh to create a fairer and more equal society. As a starting point, regulatory mechanisms would need to be introduced to make Aceh's religious bureaucracy more accountable for its interpretation and enforcement of Islamic law. Punitive action would also need to be taken against opportunistic Islamist groups who take the law into their own hands. Finally, a rights-based approach is necessary if Islamic law is to play any constructive role in the rebuilding of Aceh. Though the new sharia system could potentially offer an alternative legal order in post-tsunami, post-conflict Aceh, considerable obstacles remain to ensuring that this new form of rule *by* law can also ensure meaningful rule *of* law in this long-troubled region. What is required in Aceh's sharia justice system, especially in the field of criminal law, is a stronger focus on defending and protecting the Acehnese people against the threat and physical act of violence, and less emphasis on punishments for minor moral infringements.

References

Ahmed, E. (July 2005) 'A dangerous mix: religion and development aid', *Challenging Fundamentalisms*, www.whrnet.org/fundamentalisms/docs/issue-aid_religion0507.html
Consultative Group on Indonesia (CGI)/Bappenas (19–20 January 2005) *Indonesia: Notes on Reconstruction. The December 26, 2004 Natural Disaster,* http://siteresources.worldbank.org/INTINDONESIA/Resources/Publication/280016–1106130 305439/reconstruction_notes.pdf, 211pp
de Jong, K., Prosser, S. and Ford, N. (28 June 2005) 'Addressing Psychosocial Needs in the Aftermath of the Tsunami. MSF shares its observations from its programme in Aceh, Indonesia', http://medicine.plosjournals.org/perlserv/request=indexhtml?request=get-document&doi=10.1371/journal.pmed.0020179
Dexter, P. (July 2004) *Historical Analysis of Population Reactions to Stimuli – A Case Study of Aceh,* Edinburgh, South Australia, Australian Government Department of Defence, Defence Science and Technology Organisation, Land Operations Division, Systems Sciences Laboratory, 45pp

Felten-Biermann, C. (2006) 'Gender and Natural Disaster: Sexualised Violence and the Tsunami', *Development*, vol 49, no 3, pp82–86

Forrester, G. (April 2005) *Staying the Course: AusAID's Governance Performance in Indonesia*, Sydney: The Lowy Institute for International Policy, 50pp

Inge, V. (July 2006). Working Paper: 'Women, Gender and Work in Nanggroe Aceh Darussalam Province', www.ilo.org/public/english/region/asro/jakarta/download/ genderinaceh.pdf, 15pp

Interchurch for Development Cooperation (ICCO) (2007) *Lasting Peace in Aceh? Strengthening civil society as an active mediator for peace*, Brussels, Europe External Policy Advisors, EEPA

Internal Displacement Monitoring Centre (19 July 2006) *Indonesia: Support Needed for Return and Re-Integration of Acehnese Following Peace Agreement. A profile of the internal displacement situation*, Geneva, Internal Displacement Monitoring Centre, 305pp

International Crisis Group (31 July 2006) *Islamic Law and Criminal Justice in Aceh*, Asia Report no 117, Jakarta/Brussels, International Crisis Group

Kell, T. (1995) *The Roots of Acehnese Rebellion, 1989–1992*, Ithaca, NY, Cornell Modern Indonesia Project

Mashni, A., Reid, S., Sasmitawidjaja, V., Sundhagul, D. and Wright, T. (27 August 2005) *Multi-Agency Evaluation of Tsunami Response: Thailand and Indonesia*, CARE International and World Vision International, 76pp

Miller, M. (2004a) 'From reform to repression: the post-New Order's shifting security policies in Aceh', *Review of Indonesian and Malaysian Affairs*, vol 38, no 4, pp129–162

Miller, M. (2004b) 'The Nanggroe Aceh Darussalam Law: A Serious Response to Acehnese Separatism?', *Asian Ethnicity*, vol 5, no 3, pp333–352

Miller, M. (2006) 'What's Special About Special Autonomy in Aceh?' in Anthony Reid, ed. *Verandah of Violence. The Background to the Aceh Problem*, Singapore/Seattle, Singapore University Press in association with University of Washington Press, pp292–314

Miller, M. (2008). *Rebellion and Reform in Indonesia. Jakarta's Security and Autonomy Policies in Aceh*, London, Routledge

Miller, M. and Feener, R. (2009) 'Emergency and Islamic law in Aceh', in Ramraj, Victor. V. and Thiruvengadam, Arun K., eds *Emergency Powers in Asia. Exploring the Limits of Legality*, Cambridge, Cambridge University Press

Reid, A. (2006) 'Introduction' in Anthony Reid, ed *Verandah of Violence. The Historical Background of the Aceh Problem*, Singapore/Seattle, Singapore University Press in association with University of Washington Press, pp1–21

Said, M. (1999) 'Psikologi Politik Masyarakat' in Tulus Widjanarko and Asep S. Sambodja, eds *Aceh Merdeka dalam Perdebatan*, Jakarta, PT. Cita Putra Bangsa, pp73–79

Schulze, K. (29 June 2007) *Mission Not So Impossible: The AMM and the Transition from Conflict to Peace in Aceh, 2005–2006*, Singapore, S. Rajaratnam School of International Studies, 64pp

Seibel, H. with the collaboration of Wahyu Dwi Agung (June 2006) *Islamic Microfinance in Indonesia*, Cologne, Development Research Centre, University of Cologne, 72pp

Tiro H. (1984) *The Price of Freedom: the unfinished diary of Tengku Hasan di Tiro*, London, National Liberation Front of Aceh Sumatra

United Nations Development Programme (UNDP)/Indonesian National Development Planning Agency (Bappenas) (2006) 'Access to Justice in Aceh. Making the Transition to Sustainable Peace and Development in Aceh', www.undp.or.id/pubs/docs/Access%20to%20Justice.pdf, 182pp

Zoraster, R. (Jan–Feb 2006) 'Barriers to Disaster Coordination: Health Sector Coordination in Banda Aceh Following the South Asia Tsunami', *Prehospital and Disaster Medicine*, vol 21, no 1, pp13–18

Interviews

Abdullah, Prof. Dr Abdul Gani (Director General of Legislation), 22 November 2001, Jakarta

Abubakar, Alyasa (NAD sharia Agency Director), 25 July 2006, Banda Aceh

Ahba, Zulfitri (Village leader), 1 August 2006, Lampuuk, Aceh Besar

Feener, Michael (Associate Professor, Asia Research Institute, National University of Singapore, 28 September 2007, Singapore

Sudarsono, Dr Ir. (former Director General of Regional Autonomy/ Director of Education and Training Office, Home Affairs Department), 21 November 2001, Jakarta

Yusuf, Irwandi (former GAM representative/current Governor of Aceh), 6 August 2006, Banda Aceh

Indonesian Government Legislation

Tunggal, Hadi Setia (compiler). (1999). *Undang-Undang Nomor: 44 Tahun 1999 tentang Penyelenggaraan Keistimewaan Propinsi Daerah Istimewa Aceh*, Jakarta, Harvarindo

Undang Undang Nomor 11/2006 tentang Pemerintahan Aceh

Qanun no 10/ 2002 tentang Peradilan Syariat Islam

Qanun no 11/ 2002 Tentang Pelaksanaan Syariat Islam Bidang Aqidah, Ibadah dan Syi'ar Islam

Qanun no 12/ 2003 tentang Minuman Khamar dan Sejenisnya

Qanun no 13/ 2003 tentang Maisir (Perjudian)

Qanun no 14/ 2003 tentang Khalwat (Mesum)

Qanun no 7/2004 tentang Pengelolaan Zakat

Notes

1   In 2004, 97.5 per cent of Aceh's population was registered as Muslim, 1.8 per cent as Catholic and 0.7 per cent as Hindu or Buddhist. Patricia Dexter (July 2004). *Historical Analysis of Population Reactions to Stimuli – A Case Study of Aceh* (Edinburgh, South Australia: Australian Government Department of Defence,

Defence Science and Technology Organisation, Land Operations Division, Systems Sciences Laboratory), p9.

2   Anthony Reid (2006) 'Introduction' in Anthony Reid, ed *Verandah of Violence. The Historical Background of the Aceh Problem*, Singapore/Seattle, Singapore University Press in association with University of Washington Press, p10.

3   M. Mas'ud Said (1999) 'Psikologi Politik Masyarakat' in Tulus Widjanarko and Asep S. Sambodja, eds *Aceh Merdeka dalam Perdebatan*, Jakarta, PT. Cita Putra Bangsa), p75.

4   The Darul Islam rebellion started in West Java under the leadership of S. M. Kartosuwirjo, who pronounced an 'Islamic State of Indonesia' in West Java on 7 August 1949. Michelle A. Miller. (2004). 'From reform to repression: the post-New Order's shifting security policies in Aceh', *Review of Indonesian and Malaysian Affairs*, vol 38, no 4, p133.

5   The complete 'Declaration of Independence of Acheh Sumatra' can be found in Tengku Hasan di Tiro (1984) *The Price of Freedom: the unfinished diary of Tengku Hasan di Tiro*, London, National Liberation Front of Aceh Sumatra, pp15–17.

6   (11 December 2000). Amni Marzuki (GAM negotiator) in 'Interview: Islamic Law to Soothe Aceh', *Reuters*.

7   Tunggal, Hadi Setia (compiler). (1999). *Undang-Undang Nomor: 44 Tahun 1999 tentang Penyelenggaraan Keistimewaan Propinsi Daerah Istimewa Aceh* (Jakarta: Harvarindo), Chapter III, Article 3(d) and 5(1), (2).

8   Michelle Ann Miller (2008) *Rebellion and Reform in Indonesia. Jakarta's Security and Autonomy Policies in Aceh*, London, Routledge, p52.

9   Michelle Ann Miller (2006) 'What's Special About Special Autonomy in Aceh?' in Anthony Reid, ed *Verandah of Violence. The Background to the Aceh Problem*, Singapore/Seattle, Singapore University Press in association with University of Washington Press, p298.

10 During DOM, the Indonesian military sent teams of MUI *ulama* to the worst conflict areas to hold prayer meetings, make door-to-door visits and distribute propaganda material. In July 1990, Aceh's former MUI Chairman, Ali Hasjimy, announced that the MUI was ready to 'spearhead' the Indonesian government's efforts to crush GAM. Tim Kell (1995) *The Roots of Acehnese Rebellion, 1989–1992*, Ithaca, NY, Cornell Modern Indonesia Project, pp77–82.

11 (11 August 1999). 'Rakyat Lebih Mendengar Mahasiswa dan LSM Ketimbang Para Pejabat dan Ulama', *Kontras*.

12 Teungku Syamaun Risyad (HUDA Representative) in (18 November 1999). 'Referendum Sudah Final', *Serambi Indonesia*.

13 According to Indonesian sources, approximately 350 people were killed in Aceh in 1999, 841 were killed in 2000 (including 676 civilians, 124 Indonesian security forces personnel and forty-one GAM rebels), 1028 civilians were reportedly killed in 2001 (as well as 315 GAM rebels and 134 Indonesian security forces personnel); there were at least 1228 civilian fatalities in 2002, and between May, 2003 and July 2004, when Aceh was under emergency rule, the TNI claimed to have killed 5871 'GAM rebels'. (29 December 1999). 'Evaluasi Akhir Tahun LBH Banda Aceh: Peluru, Darah Dan Air Mata Masih Warnai Aceh', *Waspada*; (9 December 2000). 'Perbarui Mekanisme Penyelesaian Konflik Aceh', *Kompas*; (5 March 2002). 'Report on Human Rights in Indonesia 2001 (11)', *Laksamana.net*; (29 November

2002). '1,228 Warga Aceh Tewas Selama 2002 Akibat Konflik', *Media Indonesia*; (22 July 2004). 'Aceh death toll mounts', *Laksamana.net.*

14 For a detailed description of Law No.18/2001 and its implementation, see M. A. Miller (2004) 'The Nanggroe Aceh Darussalam Law: A Serious Response to Acehnese Separatism?', *Journal of Asian Ethnicity*, vol 5, no 3, pp333–351.

15 M. A. Miller (2008) *Rebellion and Reform in Indonesia. Jakarta's Security and Autonomy Policies in Aceh*, London, Routledge, pp91, 131.

16 *Qanun No. 10/2002 tentang Peradilan Syariat Islam; Qanun No.11/2002 Tentang Pelaksanaan Syariat Islam Bidang Aqidah, Ibadah dan Syi'ar Islam; Qanun No. 12/ 2003 tentang Minuman Khamar dan Sejenisnya; Qanun No. 13/2003 tentang Maisir (Perjudian); Qanun No. 14/2003 tentang khalwat; Qanun No. 9/2003 tentang Hubungan Tata Kerja Majelis Permusyawaratan Ulama dengan Eksekutif, Legislatif dan Instansi Lainya pada Ketentuan Umum; Qanun No.7/2004 tentang Pengelolaan Zakat.*

17 *Undang Undang Nomor 11/2006 tentang Pemerintahan Aceh*, XVII (125, 126).

18 (21–22 November 2001). Interviews with Dr Ir. Sudarsono (Director General of Regional Autonomy) and Prof. Dr Abdul Gani Abdullah (Director General of Legislation), Jakarta.

19 International Crisis Group (ICG). (31 July 2006). *Islamic Law and Criminal Justice in Aceh*, Asia Report No. 117 (Jakarta/Brussels: International Crisis Group), p11.

20 The functions and duties of the *Wilayatul Hisbah* are outlined in *Qanun* No.11/ 2002, Article 14, *Qanun* No.12/2003, Article 17, Qanun No.13/2003, Article 15, and *Qanun* No.14/2003, Article 14.

21 (24 August 2007). 'WH Tangani 770 Kasus', *Serambi Indonesia.*

22 ICG. (2006). *Islamic Law and Criminal Justice in Aceh*, p14.

23 M. A. Miller (2008) *Rebellion and Reform in Indonesia. Jakarta's Security and Autonomy Policies in Aceh*, London, Routledge, pp175–176.

24 Michelle A. Miller and R. Michael Feener (2009) 'Emergency and Islamic law in Aceh' in Ramraj, Victor. V. and Thiruvengadam, Arun K., eds. *Emergency Powers in Asia. Exploring the Limits of Legality*, Cambridge, Cambridge University Press.

25 (6 August 2006). Interview with Irwandi Yusuf, Banda Aceh.

26 It is important to make a distinction between NGOs that are underpinned by Christian principles but are predominately humanitarian agencies (such as World Vision) and those NGOs that undertake humanitarian activities to support their primary focus of evangelization (such as WorldHelp).

27 Ayman Mashni, Sheila Reid, Virza Sasmitawidjaja, Danai Sundhagul and Tim Wright. (27 August 2005). *Multi-Agency Evaluation of Tsunami Response: Thailand 28.*

28 Kaz de Jong, Sue Prosser and Nathan Ford. (28 June 2005). *Addressing Psychosocial Needs in the Aftermath of the Tsunami. MSF shares its observations from its programme in Aceh, Indonesia*, http://medicine.plosjournals.org/perlserv/request= index-html?request=get-document&doi=10.1371/journal.pmed. 0020179.

29 United Nations Development Programme (UNDP)/Indonesian National Development Planning Agency (Bappenas) (2006) 'Access to Justice in Aceh. Making the Transition to Sustainable Peace and Development in Aceh', www.undp.or.id/pubs/docs/Access%20to%20Justice.pdf, p66; citing (March 2006) *Aceh: Peace After the Waters? Aceh: Challenges of Reconstruction and Peace One Year Later*, Global Exchange, p6.

30 (8 January 2005) 'Preacher: Failed Muslims Brought Disaster', *WorldNetDaily*.

31 Nick Meo (22 December 2005) 'Tsunami was God's revenge for your wicked ways, women told', *timesonline.uk*.

32 Claudia Felten-Biermann (2006) 'Gender and Natural Disaster: Sexualised Violence and the Tsunami', *Development*, vol 49, no3, p85, fn1.

33 Internal Displacement Monitoring Centre (19 July 2006) *Indonesia: Support Needed for Return and Re-Integration of Acehnese Following Peace Agreement. A profile of the internal displacement situation*, Geneva, Internal Displacement Monitoring Centre, p.142; citing (March 2006) *Global Exchange*, pp6–7.

34 The great majority of proselytizing NGOs worldwide are Christian missionaries. Of these, approximately one in every two missionaries is US-based and one in three is evangelical. Eman Ahmed (July 2005) 'A dangerous mix: religion and development aid,' *Challenging Fundamentalisms*, www.whrnet.org/fundamentalisms/docs/issue-aid_religion0507.html, citing David Van Biema (22 June 2003) 'Missionaries Under Cover', *Time Magazine*.

35 (14 January 2005) 'Pemerintah Indonesia Bantah Berikan Izin ke World Help', *TempoInteraktif*.

36 Ahmed (2005) 'A dangerous mix'.

37 (15 January 2005) 'Soal Adopsi 300 Anak Aceh, PGI Bentuk Tim Investigasi', *Jawapos*; Adian Husaini (18 January 2005) 'Misi Kristen untuk Anak-anak Aceh', *Republika*; Stevanus Subagijo (19 January 2005) 'Anak Aceh, WorldHelp, dan Isu Pemurtadan', *Pikiran Rakyat*.

38 Rev Vernon Brewer (WorldHelp President) in Alan Cooperman. (14 January 2005) 'Tsunami Orphans Won't Be Sent To Christian Home', *The Washington Post*.

39 Myles Fish (International Aid President) in (7 May 2005) 'IA: Indonesia Invites Christian Aid Group to Stay', *Indonesia Relief News*.

40 (12 January 2005) 'Tsunami aid workers suspected of trying to convert Muslims', *Associated Press*.

41 Since the mid-1980s, IFEES has emerged as the only internationally recognized NGO to view environmental protection and sustainability within a sharia frame-work. Fazlun Khalid (September 2006) 'Islamic law and the environment', *EcoIslam*, no2, p3.

42 WWF-Indonesia (8 February 2006) 'Perlindungan lingkungan hidup bagian penting dari ajaran Islam', *Press Release*.

43 In 2006, the CGI forum collectively pledged US$5.4 billion in fresh loans to Indonesia. In January 2007, however, President Susilo Bambang Yudhoyono announced that the CGI was no longer needed because Indonesia paid off the last of its IMF loans from the 1997–98 economic crisis in 2006. (25 January 2006). 'Presiden Putuskan Membubarkan CGI', www.rri-online.com.

44 Consultative Group on Indonesia (CGI) and Bappenas (19–20 January 2005) *Indonesia: Notes on Reconstruction. The December 26, 2004 Natural Disaster*, http://siteresources.worldbank.org/INTINDONESIA/Resources/Publication/280016–1106130305439/reconstruction_notes.pdf, p56.

45 *Ibid*, p57.

46 *Ibid*.

47 (23 February 2006) 'Acehnese accuse religious police of 'arrogance' and thuggery', *The Jakarta Post*.

48   Aceh Monitoring Mission website, www.aceh-mm.org/, accessed, 27 August 2007.
49   Kirsten Schulze (29 June 2007) *Mission Not So Impossible: The AMM and the Transition from Conflict to Peace in Aceh, 2005–2006*, Singapore, S. Rajaratnam School of International Studies, p39.
50   *Ibid.*
51   Bill Guerin (29 June 2005) 'Flogging for Islamic Law', *Asia Times Online*.
52   Barbara Slavin and Kathy Kiely (6 January 2005) 'Could U.S. aid to survivors alter anti-Americanism among Muslims?', *USA Today*.
53   Ed McWilliams (former political counsel, U.S. Embassy, Jakarta) in Diana Farsetta (2005). 'USAID in Indonesia: Expecting Waves of Gratitude', *PR Watch.org Newsletter*, vol 12, no 4.
54   For more detailed analysis of AusAID's Islamic education programmes in Indonesia, see Geoff Forrester (April 2005) *Staying the Course: AusAID's Governance Performance in Indonesia*, Sydney, The Lowy Institute for International Policy, p13 or Kingham, R. (2007) 'Basic Education in Indoenesia', in M. Clarke and S. Feeny (eds) *Education for the End of Poverty*, New York, Nova Publishing.
55   (8 February 2005) 'Saudi Charity's Aid to Indonesia Worries West', *Indonesia-Relief.org*.
56   Simon Henderson (Gulf Affairs researcher, The Washington Institute for Near East Policy) in (8 February 2005) 'Saudi Charity's Aid to Indonesia Worries West', *Indonesia-Relief.org*.
57   David E. Kaplan, Monica Ekman and Aamir Latif (15 December 2003). 'The Saudi Connection: How billions in oil money spawned a global terror network', *US News and World Report*.
58   Zachary Azuba (28 January 2005) 'Out of the Woodwork: Islamist Militants in Aceh', *The Jamestown Foundation News*.
59   Ridwan Max Sijabat (24 September 2007) 'BRR sharia comment slammed', *The Jakarta Post*.
60   Interview with UNDP staff, 23 August 2007.
61   Richard M. Zoraster (January–February 2006) 'Barriers to Disaster Coordination: Health Sector Coordination in Banda Aceh Following the South Asia Tsunami', *Prehospital and Disaster Medicine*, vol 21 no 1, p16.
62   *Ibid.*
63   Shaela Rahman (24 April 2006) 'Aceh Diary: hazards and risks', http://psdblog. worldbank.org/psdblog/2006/04/aceh_diary_secu.html.
64   Shaela Rahman (4 May 2006) 'Aceh Diary: On the Weekend, work or ... ?', http://psdblog.worldbank.org/psdblog/2006/05/aceh_diary_on_t.html#more;   see also David Lawrence (29 November 2006) 'Aceh Diary: a visit to Nias Island', http://psdblog.worldbank.org/psdblog/2006/11/aceh_diary_a_vi.html.
65   (17 January 2006) 'Gerilya Misi di Serambi Makkah', *Redaksi*; Trisno S Sutanto (20 January 2005) 'Aceh dan Politisasi Isu Agama', *Suara Pembaruan*; (7 March 2005) 'Siapa Bilang tidak Ada Kegiatan Kristensiasi di Aceh?', *Fakta*.
66   (12 January 2005) 'Relawan FPI Tidur di Kuburan', *TempoInteraktif*.
67   Philip Conford (29 January 2005) 'Fighters for God on a Holy Mission', *The Age*.
68   Mathew Moore (6 January 2005) 'Radical Groups Arrive in Force', *The Age*.
69   *Ibid.*

70 Zachary Abuza (28 January 2005) 'Out of the woodwork: Islamist Militants in Aceh', *The Jamestown Foundation*.
71 Jundi (Laskar Mujahidin member) in (7 January 2005) 'Radical Islamic Group Aiding Relief Cause', *Japan Today*.
72 Abuza, 'Out of the woodwork'.
73 (10 January 2005) 'Relawan Majelis Mujahidin Diusir dari Aceh', *TempoInteraktif*.
74 (5 January 2005) 'Yang Penting Kuburkan Mayat', *TempoInteraktif*.
75 Interview, Lampuuk, 1 August 2006.
76 (14 January 2005) 'MMI Siap Tampung 10,000 Anak Aceh', *TempoInteraktif*.
77 Hasri Husan (FPI member) in (21 January 2005) 'Tsunami aid workers suspected of trying to convert Muslims', *Associated Press*.
78 The Government of the State of Acheh (PNA), Ministry of Information (9 January 2005) 'Regarding the Islamic Defenders Front and the Indonesia Mujahidin Council in Acheh', *Press Release*.
79 *Ibid*.
80 (12 December 2006) 'Irwandi-Nazar Memimpin. Hasil Perhitungan Sementara LSI, JIP dan Jurdil Aceh', *Rakyataceh.com*.
81 Irwandi Yusuf in (12 December 2006) 'Aceh 'will not have Islamic law', *Bangkok Post*.
82 Ridwan Max Sijabat and Nani Farida (17 December 2006) 'Amputation bill riles Acehnese', *The Jakarta Post*.
83 (16 February 2002) 'GAM Tolak Konflik SARA di Aceh', *Kompas*.
84 Interchurch for Development Cooperation (ICCO) (2007) *Lasting Peace in Aceh? Strengthening civil society as an active mediator for peace*, Brussels, Europe External Policy Advisors, EEPA, p9.
85 *Ibid*.
86 Aguswandi (26 January 2006) 'Why Islamic conservatism is up in Acch?', *The Jakarta Post*.
87 Alyasa Abubakar in (6 October 2006) 'Unease in Indonesia's Aceh as morality police get tough', *AFP*.
88 (25 July 2006) Interview with Alyasa Abubakar, Banda Aceh.
89 ICG (2006) *Islamic Law and Criminal Justice in Aceh*, p9.
90 Jane Perlez (3 August 2006) 'In religious Aceh, Islamic law is taking hold', *International Herald Tribune*.
91 Mardiyah Chamin (16 April 2006) 'The Trouble with Syariah', *Indonesia Matters*.
92 (26 October 1999) 'Aceh policewomen to wear veils', *The Jakarta Post*.
93 Suraiya Kamaruzzaman in (April 2000) 'Defending women's rights in Aceh', *Tapol Bulletin*, no 157.
94 Inge Vianen (July 2006). *Working Paper: Women, Gender and Work in Nanggroe Aceh Darussalam Province*, www.ilo.org/public/english/region/asro/jakarta/download/genderinaceh.pdf, p5.
95 *Ibid*, pp.5–6; citing Raihan Putry Ali Muhammad (2001) *Gender Dalam Perspektif Islam*, Banda Aceh, Biro Pemberdayaan Perempuan Setda Provinsi NAD.
96 Michael Renner (17 August 2006) 'Conservatives pushing religious law in Aceh, *Worldwatch Institute*.
97 (28 August 2002) 'Mahathir, 'Kami Tidak Berniat Membalas', Warga Malaysia Terjamin?', *Pikiran Rakyat*.

98   LoGA, Chapter XVII(126).

99   Qanun No11/2002, Chapter VIII, Article 20(1).

100 (28 September 2007). Interview with Michael Feener, National University of Singapore.

101 Qanun No 14/2003 tentang Khalwat (Mesum), Chapter VII(22–24).

102 Qanun No 13/2003 tentang Maisir (Perjudian), Chapter VII(23).

103 Qanun No 12/2003 tentang Minuman Khamar dan Sejenisnya, Chapter VII(26).

104 (8 June 2007) 'Pelaku Ulangi Khalwat Dengan Wanita Berbeda', *Serambi Indonesia*.

105 (12 June 2007) 'Khalwat Dominasi Pelanggaran di Banda Aceh', *Serambi Indonesia*.

106 Mehdi Chebil (22 August 2007) 'Photoessay: Aceh's Shariah law', *The Diplomat*.

107 (6 October 2006) 'Unease in Indonesia's Aceh as morality police get tough', *AFP*.

108 ICG (2006) *Islamic Law and Criminal Justice in Aceh*, p9.

109 Shawn Donnan (6 October 2006) 'Aceh enforces Sharia law with lash of cane', *Financial Times*.

110 (24 August 2005) 'Diduga Main Judi, 5 Pemuda Ditangkap', *Serambi Indonesia*.

111 Nani Farida (23 June 2005) 'Public canings to start in Aceh for gamblers', *The Jakarta Post*.

112 Musdaruddin in Shawn Donnan (6 October 2006) 'Aceh enforces Sharia law with lash of cane', *Financial Times*.

113 In December 2006, a bill on amputating the hands of thieves was rejected by Aceh's new governor, Irwandi Yusuf.

114 Michael Renner (17 August 2006) 'Conservatives pushing religious law in Aceh', *Worldwatch Institute*.

115 Alyasa Abubakar in (6 October 2006) 'Unease in Indonesia's Aceh as morality police get tough', *AFP*.

3

Political Reconstruction in Aceh

Damien Kingsbury

Introduction

The political environment of Aceh has undergone profound change in the period since the tsunami of December 2004. Given the normative qualities associated with such alteration, Aceh's political change could be understood as a political reconstruction. This is especially so when compared with the province's previous political under-development. Aceh's recent history had been one of Jakarta-appointed governors operating in a corrupt system and working with the military in effect as an administration of occupation within a conflict environment, with all the abrogation of civil and political rights that implies.

The removal of Aceh's last Jakarta-appointed administrator in July 2004 and the more conciliatory rule of his temporary successor marked an important shift in Aceh's political life. However, the signing of a peace agreement in 2005, known as the Memorandum of Understanding (MoU), ended the province's 29-year-old separatist conflict, significantly reduced the military and police presence and disarmed the Free Aceh Movement (*Gerakan Aceh Merdeka* – GAM), which reorganized as a civil political party, Partai Aceh (Aceh Party). The outgoing temporary governor ensured that the provincial administration employed or re-employed staff identified with the previously illegal GAM, thus 'Acehnizing' the civil administration. Parallel to this, Aceh civil society groups and NGOs re-emerged as active and vocal political participants, while new political groupings operated in what was widely embraced as a largely free political environment. Perhaps most importantly, these changes allowed for the creation of local political parties, and the elections of a new governor and district officials, all of which marked a further and more profound development in Aceh's political reconstruction. This chapter assesses Aceh's political paradigm shift following the signing of the MoU, itself in significant part an outcome of the impact of the 2004 tsunami.

The term 'political reconstruction', as it is often used, implies that a political environment has been reconstructed or restored to its previous state. In Aceh, the previous political environment was not restored or rebuilt, but overturned and replaced by a normatively better political environment. In this chapter, then, 'reconstruction' refers to a regeneration and renewal of Aceh's political landscape. Aceh's political landscape prior to the 2004 tsunami was marked by a long history of warfare, along with an associated failure on the part of the state to actively promote the welfare of its local citizens. In this respect, Aceh existed at a low level of political development (on 'political development', see Kingsbury, 2007a), meaning that it had a low or functionally non-existent level of political participation and representation in which there had not previously been free and fair elections, that civil and political rights were limited or entirely abrogated, and that state institutions were often dysfunctional, malignant and sometimes predatory (see Evans, 1995). Political reconstruction thus implies political development, where the political environment was redeveloped to better reflect both the aspirations of the people of Aceh, as well as to correspond more closely with normative political values around representation, participation, accountancy and transparency.

The particular relevance of political reconstruction within the context of wider post-tsunami reconstruction is three-fold. The MoU signed between GAM and the government of Indonesia, which ended the long-running separatist war, was reached within the context of the post-tsunami environment in Aceh and was, if not entirely an outcome of it, then at least in part a consequence of the impact of the tsunami. Secondly, the peace agreement allowed material post-tsunami relief and reconstruction to proceed unhindered. The third element of post-tsunami relevance was that the MoU established many of the normative criteria of political development. In this sense, the tsunami metaphorically wiped away much of the pre-existing political infrastructure in Aceh, and allowed the construction of a new political framework.

Aceh to 1976

Aceh's political history, depending on criteria, dates to (or before) the 9th century CE (Stein, 1907: p34), being an internationally recognized state from the 16th century. Until the Dutch invasion of 1873, Aceh was a Sultanate comprising regions ruled by local lords (*uleebalang*) under what has been described as a federated system in which there were, if somewhat overstated, checks and balances on the exercise of political power (see Kingsbury, 2007b). The Dutch invasion was fiercely resisted, with Aceh only succumbing in 1903, with some continuing resistance until 1912. More limited resistance to the Dutch continued until the Japanese invasion of 1942, with Aceh contributing to the war of independence from the Dutch after World War II. Some historians disagree as to the Acehnese political intentions, but there continue to be claims that Aceh contributed to the war for independence in order to regain its own independence, or a high level of self-rule within a loose federated structure (see Nessen, 2006).

Independence in 1949 allowed Aceh a relatively high degree of self-rule, but Indonesia reconstituted its provinces and subsumed Aceh into North Sumatra, confirming that with its shift to being a unitary state in 1950. Unable to resolve this political loss, Aceh joined the Darul Islam rebellion against the central government in 1953, declaring the Federated State of Aceh (Negara Bahagian Acheh – NBA), later joining the PRRI-Permesta rebellion as a means of securing this claim.[1] Aceh's rebellion against Jakarta ended in 1963, with the promise of 'special administrative status', although beyond relative autonomy in religious, educational and cultural matters, this turned out to have little practical meaning. A change of government in Jakarta in 1966 was supported in the predominantly anti-communist Aceh, but the central and authoritarian tendencies of the New Order government under Suharto quickly alienated many Acehnese, especially following the discovery in 1972 of large gas deposits off the coast of Aceh and the loss to outsiders of jobs, land and revenue that many Acehnese believed to rightly belong to them.

Responding to a growing, or renewed, sense of alienation, and drawing strongly on many Acehnese' sense of distinction from other Indonesians, on 4 December 1976, Teungku [Lord] Hasan di Tiro founding the Aceh-Sumatra National Liberation Front, which came to be better known as GAM, and declared Aceh's independence from Indonesia. As a former participant in the Darul Islam rebellion, and claiming descent from Aceh's last leader against the Dutch, Teungku Cik di Tiro, di Tiro drew on a long political pedigree and tapped into a strong sense of Acehnese history.

The separatist conflict period

Following di Tiro's declaration of Aceh's independence, the Indonesian government responded with the mass arrests of GAM members. GAM members have claimed that it was initially almost exclusively political in its orientation, and that its armed rebellion did not begin until after the initial mass arrests.[2] Following the 1976 crackdown, GAM activists went underground, beginning the first phase of the rebellion, and from 1986 around 500 cadres went to Libya for military training (ending in 1990), forming the core of the movement in the late 1980s and leading to increasing attacks against police and military installations. In what has been identified as the second stage of the conflict, in response, in 1989 the Indonesian military launched what was called the Military Operations Area (Daerah Operasi Militar – DOM) operation, in which around 15,000 externally based troops were moved into the province. This counter-insurgency operation struck at GAM's military capacity, and a year later, with many field commanders killed or captured, the government claimed that GAM had been 'crushed'. In the period from 1989 until 1998, it has been variously estimated that between 10,000 and 26,000 people were killed.[3] There is little doubt that the DOM period was one of great disruption and hardship in Aceh, with thousands of homes burned, and by mid-1999, between 150,000 and 200,000 people being turned into internal and external refugees (HRW, 2000a), suspected GAM supporters summarily executed and their bodies often left in public (see AI, 2001; HRW, 2000), mass killings and the wide-spread use of rape (Kamaruzzaman, 2003) as a tool of intimidation and retribution. At least 10 mass graves were found from this time, containing the bodies of between 1000 and 1500 people (Martinkus, 2004: p11). The DOM strengthened resentment against rule from Jakarta and continued to fuel, rather than resolve, separatist sentiments.

The DOM campaign had a significant impact in Aceh, but failed to defeat GAM, which continued its sporadic attacks on police and the army from 1990. Following the fall of President Suharto in 1998 and the beginning of Indonesia's democratization, there were brief reversals of Indonesia's official militaristic policy on Aceh, such as the withdrawal of Kopassus (special forces) troops in 1998 and the formal lifting of military operations. Reversing this situation, in January 1999, the Indonesian military, the TNI (Tentara Nasional Indonesia) under the technical auspices of Polri, launched Operasi Wibawa (Operation Authority), which was notable for its massacres of civilians (see Tapol, 2000a; 2000b). In response to these continuing attacks, during the general elections in June 1999 the GAM effectively closed down polling operations in the areas it controlled, including the regencies of North Aceh and Pidie, and continued its attacks against Indonesian soldiers, police and government officials.

There was a brief and passing proposal by President Abdurrahman Wahid in early 2000 about the option of Aceh having a referendum on independence, which was immediately reinterpreted by a TNI spokesman, but which recognized a distinct political identity as existing in Aceh. But the TNI was reined in again with a signing of a 'humanitarian ceasefire' on 12 May 2000, and again for three months from June 2000. It was around this time that Aceh's 'civil society' movement reached the peak of its influence, generally reflecting calls for a referendum. The civil society movement peaked with the march of several hundred thousand (some claim up to a million) people in Banda Aceh on 8 November 1999, and a similarly large rally in November the following year. If there was ever any doubt about how Acehnese people generally felt, a rally by around one in four of the population – most from outside the capital of Banda Aceh – was stunning confirmation of a desire for the opportunity to determine their own political status.

On 19 January 2001, a seven-month old ceasefire was extended for another month, following all-party talks in Switzerland. With the introduction of Indonesia's 'regional autonomy' legislation (RI 18/2001), Aceh was made a 'special administrative region', renamed Nanggroe Aceh Darusslam ('Peaceful State of Aceh'), which in theory gave it greater provincial autonomy than that granted to sub-provincial regions. In January 2002 the government announced the introduction of special autonomy status, including the implementation of Islamic shariah law and greater revenue-sharing of its natural resources, as stipulated in the 2001 legislative special autonomy provisions. However, in practical terms, as the original special autonomy legislation draft was so watered down by the Indonesian legislature (DPR) before being passed, that status was widely seen to be much longer on rhetorical purpose and shorter on implementation. Rather than resolving the conflict, the imposition of 'special autonomy' appeared to exacerbate it. By early 2001, GAM was estimated to control around 60 per cent of the territory of Aceh, and in those areas it controlled had assumed responsibility for government services such as education, health care and infrastructure. In 2001, the TNI again increased troop numbers in Aceh to more than 30,000, and established or increased local militias (GAM, 2005a; TNI, 2004; RMLA, 2004; Acehkita, 2004), while leading generals overwhelmingly rejected President Wahid's peace efforts and again pushed for a full-scale military 'resolution' to the insurgency. Hopes for a negotiated settlement were again dashed when, in January 2002, GAM's commander since 1989, Abdullah Syafei, was killed in an ambush of his jungle home, and Kodam Iskandar Muda (Iskandar Muda Regional Military Command) was established specifically for Aceh.

However, following a failed encirclement campaign against a GAM contingent, in December 2002, and under increasing international pressure, GAM and the government of Indonesia negotiated a 'Cessation of Hostilities Agreement' (CoHA). While the CoHA held some hope of movement towards peace, the TNI could only envisage a military solution. Both the TNI increasingly tested the limits of the CoHA (Aspinall and Crouch, 2003), with the TNI and GAM engineering an end to the ceasefire at the final CoHA meeting in Tokyo on 19 May 2003 by escalating claims already agreed to by GAM to a point where, eventually, GAM was required to functionally surrender. Martial law was declared the following day, until May 2004 (a state of emergency being declared thereafter). The belated sacking of the Acehnese governor, Abdullah Puteh, in July 2004 was a small step towards redressing local grievances. It has been widely estimated that in the years following the ending of the DOM, some 1000 or more people were killed in Aceh each year, with double that figure in the year following the launching of a major military campaign from May 2003 (AI, 2004).

GAM's democratization

Apart from the impact of the tsunami, there were two issues critical to the political reconstruction of Aceh, the first being the increasing if at times uneven democratization of Indonesia after the fall of Suharto in 1998. This democratization eventually allowed agreement for the implementation of democratic processes in Aceh, including local elections and the creation of local political parties. The second issue was GAM's own democratization, initially announced at Stavanger, Norway, in 2002, but not meaningfully given effect until the post-tsunami peace talks in Helsinki. During these talks, the Indonesian government initially offered GAM political authority if it would give up its struggle for independence. While prepared to consider alternatives to complete independence, on the basis of creating a better environment for post-tsunami reconstruction as well as achieving in political terms many of its aims, GAM rejected this offer as an inadequate response to the political problems of representation or participation in Aceh. Reluctantly, GAM 'prime minister' Malik Mahmud and 'foreign minister' Zaini Abdullah were persuaded to go down a more substantive democratic path, hoping that GAM could win a democratic contest. However, others of the GAM negotiating team thought that it would be pointless if GAM took power in as corrupt and authoritarian a manner as its predecessors, and believed that short of independence, substantive democratization held the best hope for Aceh's future. Engaging in an open political contest then became GAM's official policy (e.g. see GAM, 2005b) and within months led to the organizational democratization of GAM.

The importance of GAM making the transition from a military organization to a civil political party cannot be overstated within the context of Aceh's political reconstruction. If GAM had not made the transition, Aceh would have remained at war and its political environment would have been essentially unaltered. Hence the success of GAM's transition to civil politics was critical to the larger political process. The first test of GAM's democratic participation was to be the *Pilkada* (Pemilihan Kepala Daerah dan Wakil Kepala – election of Regional Head and Deputy Head, including district and sub-district elections), held on 11 December 2006. This election was the first real test of GAM's popularity and, more importantly, its commitment to democratic processes, especially if it had fared poorly.

Since the signing of the MoU in Helsinki on 15 August 2005, there had been much discussion within GAM about who could lead it in an electoral contest, with several names being discussed, including representatives who had attended the 'civil society' meeting that had been run in parallel to the Helsinki peace talks. In October 2005, GAM had established its formal non-military structure, including the Majelis Nasional (National Council), replacing a previous Malaysia-based Majelis, and the Aceh Transition Authority (Komite Peralihan Aceh – KPA), which was primarily responsible for the demobilization and reintegration of former GAM fighters. These were supposed to be the two principal organizations that GAM would employ for such political decision-making.

However, in early 2006, at the invitation of Malik Mahmud and Zaini Abdullah, Acehnese academic and member of the United Development Party (PPP), Humam Hamid, and Zaini's brother, Hasbi Abdullah, traveled to Stockholm to seek GAM's endorsement of their candidacy for the positions of governor and deputy governor of Aceh. Malik conferred the pair as GAM's preferred candidates, which sent a wave if dismay through the organization. Humam was not a GAM member and Hasbi, despite having served time in prison as a GAM member, was not viewed as a central GAM figure. Malik's decision was, therefore, widely seen within GAM as a mistake and at worst a bid to retain control of GAM from Stockholm, which contradicted the organization's democratic premise. Malik's tactical errors during the Helsinki peace talks were widely seen to have included, despite having ample warning of the need to do so, failing to hand over timely information on the number of GAM combatants to be demobilized. This meant that the TNI was able to also withhold its remaining troop numbers until such time as the matter could not be debated, thus leading to a much larger number of TNI to remain in Aceh than originally discussed. This failure angered many GAM members, including field commanders as well as negotiating team members. Following from what was perceived to be Malik's lack of input to the Helsinki peace process some GAM members openly doubted his ability to lead the organization in other than a figurehead capacity.

Another of Malik's errors, which led to serious disagreement between GAM negotiators, was his private agreement to meet Indonesian negotiators outside the negotiations framework. This would have allowed the Indonesian government to claim that it was no longer holding discussions within an internationally brokered context but had 'internalized' the discussion. This action was in direct contravention of existing GAM policy and was openly rejected by the negotiating team. In response to this rejection,

Malik and Zaini threatened to resign their positions, and although persuaded not to while the negotiations were still in process, they refused to attend a GAM media conference that evening.[4] This event marked the clearest division within the negotiating team and later came to represent the division within GAM between authoritarian and collective decision-making. The characterization that the later division within GAM was between its 'old guard' and 'young turks', or even a Stockholm/Aceh division (e.g. ICG, 2006b) was incorrect; it was more accurately a division between an authoritarian and unaccountable form of leadership, and a more participatory and democratic approach to decision-making.

With the Majelis and KPA established, but Malik continuing to try to rule the organization from above, the formalization of GAM's transformation to a civil political party did not take place until a meeting of senior GAM leaders in Stockholm over 5–8 April 2006. At this time, Malik was still in Stockholm, refusing to return to Aceh. Malik had told GAM members that he intended to take out Swedish citizenship and to retire in Sweden. More directly, he was not convinced that returning to Aceh would be safe. However, he wanted to continue to organize GAM in Aceh from Stockholm, and to retain effective control over the organization. In order to put in place his plans for GAM, Malik persuaded the Swedish NGO, the Olof Palme International Centre, which had funded the GAM-Aceh civil society meetings, to fund a meeting of senior GAM leaders, to come to Stockholm in April 2006. However, while there was a faction of the group that attended that was loyal to Malik, most attendees were dismayed and upset by Malik's nomination of Humam and Hasbi, and were by this stage close to open rebellion. The four-day meeting was notable for a number of outcomes. The main outcomes were an agreement on the structure of GAM as a democratic political party, in which representatives, formally located within the Majelis, effectively constituting GAM's central committee, would select candidates for election, at the district and sub-district level on the recommendation of local party branches. The party structure itself was to be based upon the KPA. The party structure would, therefore, follow GAM's previous organizational structure. On the afternoon of 6 April, the meeting voted to confirm that the relationship between the Majelis and the organization's then leadership (principally Malik and Zaini, but formally also including the ageing and infirm Hasan di Tiro), was to be one of respect for founders of the movement, who would thereafter only occupy symbolic positions in relation to the party. They were, it was decided, not to have any further authority in the new party structure. To confirm this, the meeting agreed that party members must be Acehnese residents, which excluded the leadership which continued to reside in Stockholm.[5]

The last day of the meeting was presided over by GAM's ageing founder, Hasan di Tiro, which added formality to the occasion. Malik also agreed to return to Aceh and make a public statement about the formation of the party along the above lines, and its system of selecting candidates, which in effect meant handing over authority to GAM's Aceh-based leadership as represented by the Majelis. The decisions of the April Stockholm meeting were to be put to the Majelis for approval, even though a number of senior Majelis figures were present at the meeting.

Internal splits

As agreed at the Stockholm meeting, Malik and Zaini returned to Aceh on 19 April, and were widely feted at a number of ceremonies around the province. While Malik made speeches at these events, he did not announce details of the then recent Stockholm agreement on democratization of the party which, so far as most participants at the Stockholm meeting had been concerned, was his primary purpose in returning to Aceh. In particular, as the signatory to the MoU, Malik continued in his role as leader of GAM, despite having agreed in Stockholm to step down from an active leadership position. Those who had been at the Stockholm meeting were dismayed, as were local GAM members who had been privy to details of the agreement.

Serious cracks were beginning to show within the senior ranks of GAM. The divisions within the negotiating team during the Helsinki peace talks over competence and inclusive decision-making had begun to widen, and there was now a sense of a fundamental division between the authoritarian (top-down authority) and democratic (bottom-up decision-making) wings of the organization. The factions representating these positions faced each other when the Majelis met in Banda Aceh in May, being chaired by former GAM 'finance minister' and, until jailed in 2003, CoHA negotiatior, Muhammad Usman Lampoh Awe. Former GAM military[6] commander Muzakkir Manaf was elected as head of security, demonstrating the military structure's subordination to GAM's political structure, while 'defence minister' and former arms buyer Zakairah Saman was elected head of the political wing.[7]

At this meeting, the Majelis voted to elect former jailed GAM negotiator Teugnku Nashiruddin bin Ahmed and Muhammad Nazar (from SIRA, who had joined the political wing of the Majelis) as its candidates for the positions of governor and deputy governor of Aceh. Nashiruddin was seen as a compromise candidate between the now clear factions in GAM, while Nazar was seen to represent civil society groups. Despite the agreement at the April Stockholm meeting, the decision of the Majelis was thwarted. The

Majelis voted in favour of Nashiruddin and Nazar over Hasbi and Humam, proposed by Lampoh Awe, 39 to 34 for the governorship and 31 to 24 for the deputy governorship. However, despite being given a clear majority, following discussions with Zakaria, Nashiruddin withdrew his candidature. Having persuaded Nashiruddin not to stand for governor, Zakaria then attempted to have the candidate for vice-governor, Muhammad Nazar, withdraw his candidacy. However, Nazar had been chairman of the pro-referendum NGO, the Aceh Referendum Information Centre (Sentral Informasi Referendum Aceh – SIRA) and was not influenced by Zakaria or Malik's position within GAM. These actions cast into serious doubt GAM's capacity for democratic reform, and opened the split within the organization that had, until this time, been carefully papered over.

With Nashiruddin's withdrawal, Malik announced that second-placed Hasbi should be GAM's candidate for governor, and Hasbi chose Humam as his running mate. A number of Majelis members protested at this and called for another vote. Malik refused and instead said that, as the Indonesian government had not yet passed MoU-linked legislation allowing the registration of a formal political party, GAM would not contest the elections as such. Under the provisions of the Law on the Governing of Aceh (LoGA) that did apply, GAM candidates who wished to stand, in effect as independents, would require the signatures of 3 per cent of the 2.6 million registered voters.

With no formal endorsement from GAM, Humam was endorsed by the PPP as its candidate for governor, with Hasbi as his running mate. By June it had become clear that most GAM members were disenchanted with Malik's interference with Nashiruddin's candidature and his support for Humam and Hasbi, and were again casting around for more representative GAM candidates. Nazar had decided to remain in the contest, possibly as candidate for governor, based on support from his organization SIRA, and was looking for a running partner. Muhammad Nur Djuli nominated himself, but failed to receive support from the KPA.

A 'kitchen cabinet' GAM-SIRA meeting was held in Kuala Lumpur in August to consider a response to the proposed LoGA, which was regarded as having failed to fulfil the complete requirements of the MoU. This meeting was notable for the absence of pro-Malik faction supporters, who had no involvement in the formulation of the MoU and were disconnected from its translation into law. During a break in this meeting, Irwandi Yusuf was persuaded to stand for the position of governor, with Nazar as his deputy. Irwandi had come third in the Majelis' vote for gubernatorial candidacy, but remained popular among GAM commanders, as well as having developed his political capacity as GAM's representative to the decommissioning of its weapons and the welfare of GAM members following the signing of the

MoU. Formerly a veterinary science lecturer at the Syah Kuala University in Banda Aceh, Irwandi had previously been a propagandist for GAM and was instrumental in GAM establishing an intelligence wing in 2000. He was arrested at the home of US journalist William Nessen in Jakarta in 2003, escaping from prison in Banda Aceh when it was destroyed by the 2004 tsunami. Irwandi was spirited out of Indonesia and thence to Stockholm and Helsinki for the peace talks, where he played a back room role. Once Irwandi and Nazar had agreed to run, they then appealed directly to the KPA, as the organizational base of GAM's mass membership.

In response to this growing rebellion against his authority, Malik influenced Muzakkir to publicly endorse Humam and Hasbi's candidature. At a meeting of GAM commanders called by Malik on 22 August 2006, Muzakkir publicly endorsed Humam and Hasbi as GAM candidates. To clarify his political allegiance, on 6 November Muzakkir Manaf issued a further statement, in concert with district KPA leaders, in which he said that GAM withdrew its support for Hasbi and Humam. He said that as head of the KPA, along with regional KPA leaders, he would take a neutral stand in the coming election for the period of 2007–2011. Muzakkir added that the 'KPA respects highly the esteem values of democracy in line with the MoU Helsinki' and that 'We fully accept and support any candidates that are rightfully and democratically elected by the Acehnese people in this coming election' (Manaf et al, 2006). By withdrawing his support for Humam and Hasbi, this statement was widely interpreted as Muzakkir stating his support, and that of most KPA leaders, for Irwandi and Nazar. Importantly, however, a small number of GAM commanders from East Aceh, and in particular from the Abdullah family's base at Pidie, chose to support Hasbi and Humam, which meant there would indeed be a contest between candidates supported by the different factions of GAM.

On 11 November, a statement was released claimed to be on behalf of the Majelis, saying that support for Hasbi and Humam was final. However, several Majelis members said they had no knowledge of the statement having been prepared, indicating that it had not been endorsed by the Majelis as such. On 22 November 2006, less than three weeks before the elections, a convoy containing Humam and Hasbi was attacked by protesters at Matang Glumpang Dua in Birueun District. Humam was punched and banners were burned, although there were no serious injuries from this incident (ANFREL, 2006: p3). The attack was widely attributed to supporters of Irwandi and Nazar, and while there were claims of provocation, Irwandi promised that such attacks would not be repeated.

The Manaf-KPA 6 November statement was made public on 27 November, delineating the split within GAM. In this environment, in which

GAM was in effect pitted against itself, on 11 December 2006 the elections were held. There were in all eight pairs of candidates for the positions of governor and vice-governor, five from larger Jakarta-based parties including Golkar,[8] PPP, PBB,[9] PDI-P,[10] PAN[11] and PBR[12] (which shared a joint ticket) and PKS,[13] as well as three pairs of independents. Many observers predicted that GAM would fare poorly in the elections, being split and having little money or organizational capacity compared to the established parties (see ICG, 2006a; Aspinall, 2006), a view that was supported by public opinion polls[14] (IFES, 2006). In that some observers believed that GAM-backed candidates could succeed, they tended to favour the Humam-Hasbi team backed by GAM's Swedish leadership.

In the end, the two leading pairs of candidates for the gubernatorial elections both represented GAM, with Irwandi and Nazar winning 38.3 per cent of the just over two million votes cast[15] (the lower number of actual voters reflecting, in large part, difficulties many had in registering for the elections), comfortably exceeding the 25 per cent required sufficient to avoid going to a run-off ballot (the assumption being that in a run-off election the remaining votes would at least double). Humam and Hasbi received about 17 per cent of the vote. Had there been a run-off election, the contest would have been, in effect, between factions within GAM, with Jakarta-supported party candidates, as well as other independents, being deleted from the competition. The situation at the district level was similar, with GAM winning 15 of the 19 district elections, including in areas not thought to be GAM strongholds. The results were a major political endorsement of GAM and constituted an equally significant rejection of Jakarta-based political parties. There was also considerable discussion about the failure to accurately predict the outcomes of the elections but, as noted by journalist William Nessen, there was doubt about the reach of surveys beyond major urban areas, or the willingness of Acehnese to speak honestly to surveyors (pers. comm. 15, 16.12.2006). A massive demonstration in Banda Aceh in favour of the MoU on 15 August 2006 was probably a more accurate indicator at that time of popular sentiment than any public opinion polling could hope to be.

In that some observers were critical of the outcome, it was a salient lesson that President Yudhoyono and Vice-President Jusuk Kalla had only received 33.58 per cent of the vote in the first presidential round in 2004. This made Irwandi and Nazar's 38.3 per cent look relatively emphatic. Translated into a run-off vote, based on the first vote, Irwandi and Nzar would have received a landslide 77 per cent of the vote or, interestingly, very close to the same vote that delivered independence to East Timor in 1999. The result in favour of Irwandi and Nazar over Humam and Hasbi also meant that, should there have been a run-off election, even though Humam and Hasbi were formally endorsed by PPP, the election would have more accurately been between factions within GAM.

Not surprisingly, the result of the *pilkada* sent reverberations throughout the rest of Indonesia, in particular Jakarta, where it was both welcomed as a demonstration of democracy at work and, by some nationalist chauvinists, as a portent of a continuing Acehnese desire for independence. The factionalism within GAM and the way in which the Majelis had been subverted spelled its functional death, with Malik suspending its operation in 2007. This left Irwandi as governor as the principle official representative of GAM, and Irwandi was careful to assure Jakarta that GAM no longer desired independence but sought only to serve the people of Aceh. In that Irwandi represented the majority of the KPA, and the KPA had always been regarded by GAM members as the foundation of the party, it did legitimately appear as though the aspiration for independence had been laid to rest.

While the KPA was the basis for the new party, there was considerable dismay, again, at the announcement of the formation of the party by Muzakkir Manaf at Malik's behest, on 7 July 2007. In particular, there was concern, particularly in Jakarta, that the new party's name continued to be 'GAM', but without spelling out what it stood for,[16] and using the red, black and white crescent and star flag that GAM had fought under. A common view within GAM was that the flag should become the flag for Aceh, and not that of one political party among many contesting elections in Aceh. The furore over the party name and the flag, however, abated as GAM waited somewhat patiently for its party registration to be approved by the central government.

Following the *pilkada* and the strong victory for GAM's pro-democracy faction, the split within GAM began to reduce, with GAM members again coalescing around the KPA. However, this coalescing also reflected a changing of the political order of the organization, as explicitly planned in the April 2006 Stockholm meeting. Malik continued to act as GAM's public head and tried to expel former GAM military spokesman and second in command, Sofyan Dawood, who had been a strong supporter of Irwandi and public critic of Malik's. But following from the announcement of the party name and use of the former flag, Malik's judgement was again called into doubt. Sub-provincial run-off elections held in March 2007, in Aceh Barat and Aceh Barat Daya, and in August 2007 in the former militia stronghold of Aceh Tengah, again produced substantial GAM victories and confirmed GAM's popular standing. In August 2008, GAM formally re-registered itself as Partai Aceh, while its members moved to heal the divisions within it. SIRA also reorganized itself as a political party, retaining its acronym under the name of Suara Independen Rakyat Aceh (Independent

Voice of the People of Aceh), while other smaller parties also organized, including the Partai Rakyat Aceh (Aceh People's Party).

With access to the benefits of office at both the provincial and sub-provincial levels, and benefitting from the good performance in office of Governor Yusuf[17], Partai Aceh consolidated ahead of the 9 May 2009 provincial legislative elections. In particular, in office, Governor Yusuf reorganized and restructured much of the local government apparatus to make it more[18] efficient, transparent and accountable, as well as implementing a ban on logging, citing Aceh's rainforest heritage value, moved to improve education, notably through the granting of international scholarships, promoted more accessible health care and moved to rein in the widely unpopular *wilayatul hizbah* ('sharia police'). Governor Yusuf has said that he wants Aceh to set an example to the rest of Indonesia by becoming its most progressive province. Governor Irwandi, and others, also want to see a more complete implementation of the 2005 Helsinki Peace Agreement, which in effect means more autonomy for Aceh. Countering this relatively strong performance have been attempts to engineer the secession of parts of the province based on local ethnic identity (notably among the Gayo and Alas peoples of Aceh's highlands), as well as continued provocations by members of the TNI, the continued operation of some illegal military businesses (and some extortion by former GAM members). Similarly, while central leadership has been strong, some former GAM members elected as sub-provincial representatives have not performed as competently in office as was hoped.

The capacity of Partai Aceh to deliver on its only generally articulated programme set against many Acehnese' high expectations could have reduced its political appeal in Aceh. But with most provincial legislators already having recognized which way the political wind was blowing, Partai Aceh appeared to have secured itself a political future.

Set against Aceh's violent past, the period between the 2005 peace agreement and the May 2009 legislative elections was largely peaceful. Over this time, there have been several violent incidents, mostly involving criminal activity, which is not uncommon in post-conflict environments in which the full social and economic reintegration of former combatants has been inadequately addressed. However, in the weeks leading up to the May 2009 elections, there were a number of more overtly political violent incidents, with at least four people having been killed in more than 13 attacks against Aceh Party members and buildings. Despite its slow if general reform, in particular since 2005, the prevailing view was that elements of the Indonesian military (TNI) were behind the attacks against Partai Aceh offices and officials. Senior TNI officers in Aceh had expressed concern that a strong win for the Aceh Party would again fan the flames of separatism, and some military figures admitted ordering the tearing down of Aceh Party flags and banners. Aceh Party leaders, however, continued to assert that separatism remained firmly off their agenda.

Despite such ham-fisted efforts to limits its activites, Partai Aceh appeared to remain popular, with estimates of its vote ahead of the provincial elections ranging between 40 and 70 per cent. A 40 per cent win would have meant a legislative coalition with the second most popular party, SIRA, which should receive between 15 and 20 per cent of the vote. SIRA's younger, more urban support base has long been close to the Aceh Party's older, more rural supporters, each taking a different approach to their earlier approaches to achieving independence. The third most likely popular party, PRA, was also close to both the Aceh Party and SIRA, and could also join a coalition legislature. Based on the policies they had announced, each of these parties were broadly social-democratic and reformist in outlook. While there were other, smaller, locally based parties and national parties contesting the provincial elections, it was unlikely they would have any capacity to form a majority coalition. That is, Aceh could look forward to a medium-term political future in which former proponents of independence had captured both of the local executive and the local legislature, delivering to them the type of political control that some former combatants had said was the original aim of the separatist movement, in its first iteration, in the 1950s.

Regardless of the precise ordering of the vote, what was most important about the elections, and GAM's internal conflicts and reorganization, was that after never previously having had free and fair elections, a genuine democratic process appeared to be consolidating in Aceh. Like the continuation of the peace following the signing of the MoU, this outcome was beyond the most positive expectations of virtually all observers, and was an overwhelming confirmation that the creation of a genuine democratic space could sustain peace. In this respect, the political and, consequently, social landscape of Aceh has been and continues to be, fundamentally reconstructed.

Conclusion

This chapter has traced the development of the recent peace process in Aceh and the factors that contributed to its success, most importantly the way in which it was underscored by a genuine commitment to democratic processes. The significance of the peace for the future of Aceh cannot be overestimated. Without peace, reconstruction cannot go beyond a series of hollow technical interventions. What is noticeable about the evaluations of Aceh's reconstruction processes is the extent to which they ignore the contribution of the peace process in developing a holistic form of reconstruction that takes seriously the need for political, as well as social, physical and economic security, and the way in which moves towards good governance underpin other forms of development.

References

Acehkita (2004) *The Formation of Peoples' Resistance Action*, Acehkita Network, 30 July 2004

AI (2004) *Indonesia: Human rights sacrificed to security in NAD (Aceh)*, Amnesty International, News Service no 120, 11 May 2004

ANFREL (2006) *ANFREL First Week Observation Mission Report: Aceh Election: December 11, 2006*, Asian Network for Free Elections, Bangkok

Aspinall, E. (2006) *Aceh: Elections and the Possibility of Peace*, Austral Policy Forum 06–37A 18 December 2006 http://nautilus.rmit.edu.au/forum-reports/0637a-aspinall.html (accessed 27 August 2007)

Aspinall, E. and Crouch, H. (2003) *The Aceh Peace Process: Why It Failed*, Washington, East-West Center. Policy Studies 1

Evans, P. (1995) *Embedded Autonomy*, Princeton University Press

GAM (2005a) *Data Orang Sipil (Cuwak, Milisi) Yang Dipersenjatai Oleh Tni/Polri Di Acheh*, Free Acheh Movement intelligence assessment

GAM (2005b) GAM Statement On Political Parties for Acheh, Aceh-Sumatra National Liberation Front, Stockholm, 14 July 2005

HRW 2000a 'Indonesia: Civilians Targeted in Aceh', Press Backgroundeer, Human Rights Watch, May 2000

ICG (2006a) 'Aceh's Local Elections: The Role of Former Guerrillas' (media release), Jakarta/Brussels, International Crisis Group

ICG (2006b) *Aceh's Local Elections: The Role of the Free Aceh Movement*, International Crisis Group, Jakarta/Brussels, 29 November 2006

IFES (2006) *Opinions and Information on the Pilkada Aceh Elections 2006: Key Findings from an IFES Survey*, Washington DC, International Foundation for Election Systems

Kamaruzzaman, S. (2000) 'Defending Women's Rights in Aceh', *Tapol Bulletin*, no 157, April

Kingsbury, D. (2007a) *Political Development*, London and New York, Routledge

Kingsbury, D. (2007b) 'Islam, Democratisation and the Free Aceh Movement', *Journal of Contemporary Asia*, vol 36, no 4, May

Manaf, M. (2006) Public statement by Muzakkir Manaf and 18 Heads of KPAs, Banda Aceh, 27 November 2006

Martinkus, J. (2004) *Indonesia's Secret War in Aceh*, Random House, Sydney

Nesen, W. (2006) 'Sentiments Made Visible: The Rise and Reason of Aceh's National Liberation Movement', in Reid, A. *Verandah of Violence: The Background to the Aceh Problem*, Singapore, NUS Press

RMLA (2004) 'The Formation of People Resistance Action Front in the Territory of NAD Province', Regional Martial Law Authority, The Province of Aceh, Intelligence Taskforce Unit, March

Stein, M. (1907) *Ancient Khotan,* vol 1

Tapol (2000a) *Bantaqiah trial: an examination of the indictment by TAPOL,* TAPOL Report, 25 April 2000

Tapol (2000b) *A Reign of Terror: Human Rights Violations in Aceh 1998 – 2000,* Tapol, March 2000

TNI (2004) *Pembentukan Aksi Perlawanan Rakyat Di Wilayah Provinsi Nad,* Penguasa Daurat Militer Daerah, Satuan Tugas Intelijen, Kodam Islankar Muda, TNI, March 2004

Notes

1   While DII was not a separatist rebellion, many Acehnese, including the ASNLF, claim that Aceh's participation in it was for the purposes of securing either independence or a high degree of local autonomy, which is borne out by the declaration of the NBA in 1955. The main part of this period of rebellion ended in 1957, although with some hold-outs lasting until 1959 and others until 1963 with the ending of Darul Islam.

2   Based on discussions with senior GAM members, Stockholm and Helsinki, 2005.

3   The lower death toll was based on bodies identified, the higher death toll as claimed by GAM.

4   The media conference was addressed by GAM spokesman Bakhtiar Abdullah, negotiators Muhammad Nur Djuli and Nurdin Abdul Rahman, and Irwandi Yusuf and the author in the capacity of adviser.

5   These details were taken from a report for the Olof Palme International Centre written by the author, who chaired the meeting.

6   Formally known as Aceh National Army (Tentera Nasional Aceh – TNA), but more commonly known as GAM Forces (Angkatan GAM – AGAM).

7   Zakaria had returned to Aceh in 2005 to act as, in effect, Malik's political commissar to the military commanders.

8   The party of former President Suharto and of Vice-President Jusuf Kalla.

9   The Islamist Partai Bulan Bintag (Moon Star Party).

10 Partai Demokrasi Indonesia-Perjuangan (Indonesian Democratic Party-Struggle), which under President Megawati Sukarnoputri had authorized martial law in May 2003.

11 The Partai Amanat Nasional (National Mandate Party), based on the modernist Islamic organization Muhammadiyah with a strong nationalist, was anti-GAM.

12 The Islamist Partai Bintang Reformasi (Reform Star Party).

13 The Islamist Partai Keadilan Sejahtera (Prosperous Justice Party) had helped Susilo Bambang Yudhoyono achieve the presidency in 2004. Yudhoyono had given agreement to the local party provision in the MoU, allowing the peace agreement to go ahead.

14 However, about 40 per cent of respondents replied that their intention was 'secret' or that they did not yet know.

15 Interestingly, if extrapolated into a final or run-off figure, this would have produced a final result very similar to the 78.5 per cent that produced East Timor independence in 1999.

16   There had been earlier discussion about the party being called GAM, but standing for *Gerakan Aceh Maju*, or Advance Aceh Organization.
17   The quality of Yusuf's performance in office came in spite of serious health issues, not least of which was a debilitating stroke in August 2008.
18   Notably in personal conversation with the author, Banda Aceh, November 2007, Melbourne, March 2009.

4

Reconstruction through Participatory Practice?

Sue Kenny

Introduction

One of the most significant changes in the aid and development industry over the past two decades has been the growing commitment to a people-centred, participatory approach to development projects and programmes (Chambers, 1983; Bhatnagar and Williams, 1992; Eade and Williams, 1995; Long, 2001; Nederveen Pieterse, 2001: p75; Bennett and Roche, 2002; Groves and Hinton, 2004: p4). This shift has accompanied the idea that development is more than just externally driven and managed technical and economic interventions (Robb, 2004), but involves respecting, listening to and working with local people (Hinton and Groves, 2004; Fukuda-Parr et al, 2002). By the end of the 20th century this new development paradigm, which was concerned with establishing methods for participatory development and promised the empowerment of local people, was beginning to permeate the programmes of large international institutions, non-government organizations (NGOs) and donor governments alike (Godinot et al, 2006; World Bank, 1996).

The participatory, empowering approach to development is premised on the view that the people who are affected by a problem or issue should participate in the development process. In its strongest form it means that people are empowered to own the development process. Local participation in, and ownership of development programmes is deemed essential for effective processes and outcomes, because local people can grasp the local context in which change is being promoted; they understand best 'what will work' and 'what will not work' and they clearly have to 'wear' the decisions they make. The people-centred, participatory approach is linked to two key discourses which have begun to shape development policies in recent years. These are the discourse of civil society and the discourse of human rights.

Since the early 1990s there has been increasing global interest in civil society as the site which offers the best leverage for sustainable development

(Edwards and Gaventa, 2001). In its most common usage today, civil society is identified as a sphere in which people come together freely and independently to discuss issues and to work collectively to influence and shape society (Cohen and Arato, 1995; UNDP, 1997; Van Rooy, 1998; Howell and Pearce, 2001). The sphere of civil society can be contrasted with the sphere of the state, which is organized around political power, and the sphere of the market, which is organized around the quest for profit. In the development context, state-driven change has often been marked by corruption and incompetence and works to (further) disempower the populace. People tend to be suspicious of, and alienated from the top-down methods of government officials. Similarly, the quest for market success in development programmes has usually benefitted elites more than ordinary people, and has often damaged a whole country, such as in the failed 'structural adjustment' programmes of the 1990s. What is particularly interesting about the centring of civil society in development discourse is how it draws attention to the idea of people as active agents in their society, rather than passive recipients of aid. Importantly, people will only become active citizens when they believe in the efficacy of human action. Moreover, as Edwards and Gaventa (2001: p2) point out, people come together in the arena of civil society 'because they care enough about something to take collective action'.

People-centred policies are linked to human rights principles (Eade and Williams, 1995: pp9–10). The ascendancy of human rights discourse has reinforced commitment to the empowerment of ordinary people. For example, the rights-based approach means that aid agencies are accountable as much to 'beneficiaries' as to donors (Eyben and Ferguson, 2004). The human rights agenda draws attention to what Chandler (2002: p2) identifies as the 'normative project of human progress'. It prioritizes the value of human dignity over other drivers of development, such as narrow self-interested politics, the quest for economic growth and opportunistic policies of national governments.

Forms of participation

To appreciate the role of participatory approaches it is important to understand that the idea of participation does not rest on one unitary approach to development. Indeed, a number of commentators have pointed out that there are different forms and levels of participation and different reasons for developing participatory programmes (Arnstein, 1969; Eade and Williams, 1995; Pretty, 1995; Smith, 1998; Cooke and Kothari, 2001; Cornwall, 2008). Most of these ways of differentiating types of participation do so

within a clear normative framework based on a commitment to empowerment of local people. This normative framework is adopted in this chapter.
The work of Arnstein (1969: p216), in particular, has been influential in
setting out 'a ladder of participation' which ranged from non-participation
(therapy and manipulation) to tokenism (including informing, and consultation) to citizen power (including partnership and citizen control). For the
purpose of this chapter analysis is constructed upon a continuum beginning
with participation as *manipulation,* where agendas are set externally and
consultation is entirely tokenistic; to *consultation,* where agendas and plans
are set externally, but allow for comment on proposals which can actually
modify planning; to *partnership* between funding bodies and governments,
where for example, people might take the initiative in developing a programme; and finally to self-mobilization and *ownership* of the whole process
by those who are affected. As Pretty (1995) and Cornwall (2008) point out,
self-mobilization may or may not involve challenging existing distributions
of wealth and power.

In the first two points on the continuum, external experts or authorities
maintain control. Recipients and potential recipients of aid are informed of
actions. In these models it is outside professionals, such as donor governments and United Nations agencies, who set agendas, identify needs
and propose interventions and strategies. That is, participation involves
responding to plans and strategies designed externally. These models tend
to be informed by the idea of deficit, which focuses on 'what is missing' in
communities. They can be used as a legitimating device and can offer an
expedient way of achieving goals. As Gunewardena and Schuller (2008:
p34) point out, such types of humanitarian intervention promote Western
forms of behaviour, management, organization and accountability. They
impose 're-designed terms of engagement' and they define 'successful outcomes' in Western terms of reference. Indeed they provide a 'conveyor belt
for Western rationality'. These models of participation are predicated on
asymmetrical power relations, which are based on a clear distinction
between the external 'expert' and the beneficiaries of aid.

At the other end of the continuum, control is either shared or squarely in
the hands of the recipients of aid and support. The third model is organized
around equal power sharing and a commitment to mutual learning on the
part of all participants in the development process. The final model of participation is premised on the principles of community development.
Community development involves the ownership of agendas, strategies and
action by those who are affected. It aims to construct cooperative and active
communities which can identify their own needs and assets, define
problems, strengthen capacities, ensure resource availability, develop and
enact strategies and facilitate mutual aid (Campfrens, 1997; Kenny, 2006).

Importantly, community development rests on the view that 'At all levels of society, down to the very lowest, participation must be enhanced ...' (Campfrens, 1997). While community development does involve external interventions, Campfrens argues that as much as possible and feasible, activities should rely on the capacity and initiatives of the community members themselves, in order to foster confidence and increase competency within the community. That is, community development prioritizes self-mobilization over external interventions. Community development thus eschews the asymmetrical power relations which have been so embedded in the development industry.

Disaster in Aceh

It was in the context of continuing interest in these types of commitments to participatory approaches that humanitarian and development organizations were greeted with the news that in the morning of 26 December 2004, a massive earthquake off the coast of northern Sumatra, followed by a devastating tsunami, had hit the coast of Aceh (Nanggroe Aceh Darussalam). The humanitarian response to the wreckage left by what has come to be known as the Indian Ocean tsunami was unparalleled. Materials, funds and aid workers poured into the tsunami-affected regions, which included Sri Lanka, India and Thailand as well as northern Sumatra. What was particularly significant in the aid effort was the sheer number of non-government institutions and agencies involved and the apparent 'luxury' of sufficient funds to cover both the immediate humanitarian relief and the longer-term reconstruction process. What would be the effect of the unparalled international support on the participation of local people in the reconstruction effort? Could a people-centred, participatory approach be applied here? This chapter considers these questions. Taking the emergency relief, and the recovery, rehabilitation and reconstruction (often referred to simply as the reconstruction effort; this chapter follows this approach) of the province of Aceh as a case study, it identifies ways in which people-centred, participatory approaches can be manifested in post-disaster situations.[1]

What is evident in all the discussions and reports of the reconstruction effort is the immensity and complexity of the tasks involved. Importantly, there is not one perspective on what has been done or should have been done. There are many perspectives. This chapter cannot do justice to the myriad of views. What it aims to do is to draw out a range of experiences and views of the people-centred approaches applied in the reconstruction effort.[2]

Participatory approaches and the reconstruction of Aceh

As indicated above, mapping the changing activities of the players in the post-tsunami reconstruction process is a complex task. Different players, different locations and different points of time affected the many experiences and perspectives of how the response unfolded. The players in the reconstruction were the local Acehnese survivors, Acehnese NGOs (mainly consisting of those that were established in the aftermath of the tsunami), the Acehnese diaspora who were elsewhere at the time of the tsunami and rushed to Aceh immediately after the tsunami; Indonesians from outside Aceh, including Indonesian government officials, religious leaders and NGOs who also hurried to the province immediately following the tsunami; and international players, including foreign government representatives and NGOs, both large and small. For the purposes of this chapter a key distinction is made between the recipients of aid, also known as local Acehnese survivors, who were the subjects of reconstruction, and the other players in the reconstruction, referred to as external agencies, Acehnese diaspora, and international and Indonesian organizations.

One approach to understanding the activities of the different players at different points of time involves the identification of phases, constructed around the idea of an emergency phase in which emergency relief dominated the interventions, and a rehabilitation and reconstruction phase. For the purpose of analysis this chapter adopts this approach but with several caveats. First it is important to note that using this distinction does not mean that it is necessary to accept that each phase has clearly differentiated activities and needs. As Buchanan-Smith and Fabri (2005: p5) point out, different needs and types of response might coexist simultaneously. Second, if development is constructed holistically, then an emergency situation is just one aspect of the whole picture of development that calls for on-going infrastructure development rather than a knee-jerk response to a rupture.

What types of participatory practices were evident in the reconstruction of post-tsunami Aceh? An overview of the relief and reconstruction effort, particularly over the first year, reveals that there was a wide variation in commitment to participatory practices, of any kind. Some external agencies articulated an official discourse of participation. Other external agencies were not convinced that any participatory practice was appropriate, partly because of the urgency imperative and partly because a participatory approach was not formally within the agencies' modus operandi. Extensive local participation by local Acehnese survivors was certainly not part of the practice of most Indonesian aid professionals. In the following section we consider perceptions of how far participatory activities were evident in the two phases of relief and reconstruction.

The relief phase

Relief work in the aftermath of the earthquake and tsunami involved activities for the immediate protection of people's lives, including the provision of water, food, medical supplies and shelter. It was in the first few days that the need for this support was most acute. There was a range of narratives regarding the types of participation that occurred immediately after the tsunami. In summary, these were: first, the view that the local Acehnese survivors were incapacitated by the devastation; second, the view that participation of local people really only involved tokenistic consultation by aid agencies; third, that the local Acehnese survivors themselves, assisted by international workers and the returning Acehnese diaspora, were active participants, working alongside the disparate emergency workers from elsewhere; and finally and more expansively, the view that many local Acehnese survivors were fully self-mobilized and thus actually drove the relief effort themselves. Given the interviews in a NGO capacity-building study undertaken by this author (see note 2), it would seem that there is evidence to support aspects of all these narratives.

In the first narrative, survivors were passive observers of the devastation. Participatory practices were negligible. Several international aid workers holding this particular viewpoint drew on comments by local Acehnese that the tsunami was God's punishment for lax adherence to Muslim discipline, and argued that passivity was a symptom of Acehnese fatalism. Ironically, several other respondents commented on the important role of the surviving Indonesian military personnel, or TNI, who did much to direct the early relief effort, by controlling the incoming aid, the camps for displaced persons and travel of the first emergency aid workers when they arrived. These emergency efforts, it was remarked, were essential to the prevention of the spread of disease, through, for example, the setting up of water purification bases. The second narrative was that while the rhetoric of participation was invoked, at most there was only desultory consultation with survivors. Indeed, given the need for urgent action and the immense pressures which occur in any relief effort, it was expedient to minimize participation to limited and at times only tokenistic communication. The third narrative was that during this week it was mainly the returning Acehnese diaspora that participated in relief projects and they provided local leadership by working in partnership with the external Indonesian and international aid workers. Finally there was the view that it was mainly the local Acehnese themselves, and particularly students, local NGOs and religious and village leaders, who directed the relief effort and also formed the bulk of the relief workers, especially in more remote areas. In this narrative it was this first week post-tsunami that afforded the greatest opportunity for an asset-based approach to participation, in so far as the survivors were able to draw on their considerable skills to organize aid. This latter narrative is consistent with asset-based community development, in so far as the local Acehnese identified their needs and developed interventions as they saw them. Wherever possible, families and villages organized accommodation and sustenance among themselves (Cosgrave, 2007). Local information centres, or *poskos*, were set up to provide information and centres for tracing relatives. Indeed, there has been much favourable comment from our interviewees on the role of the active Acehnese during the relief phase. The importance of a quick response was emphasized: 'Just doing it', as one Acehnese respondent commented. In this narrative, what dominated the relief period was self capacity-building (see Kenny, 2007). However, in general, according to our Acehnese respondents, the majority of Indonesian government and international agencies were not enthusiastic about local participation in the relief phase.

The reconstruction phase

The reconstruction phase was under way by the end of March 2005. In a reconstruction phase, the effort shifts from emergency relief to the rebuilding of the material and organizational infrastructure and regenerating people's livelihoods. There have been two discourses framing thinking about reconstruction. The first is the discourse of rehabilitation and recovery, where the emphasis is on restoration, or as our interviewees put it, 'going back to normal'. This is the discourse favoured by survivors. However, after such a disaster, the idea of 'going back to normal' is relative to what can be salvaged. The second discourse involves 'building back better'. This discourse has been favoured by government officials and international agencies.

Reluctance to involve local survivors on the part of external agencies continued into the reconstruction phase. Many agencies failed to even consult local leaders, which led to misplaced aid and over-ambitious programmes. For example, our respondents remarked on the large number of new houses that were designed in a way that was completely inappropriate to local needs. These respondents tended to differentiate between 'good' and 'bad' international agencies on the basis of the appropriateness and quality of their housing reconstruction. It is now clear that one of the main reasons for so much failure in housing reconstruction was that, with noticeable exceptions, small and large international agencies tended to control the process of needs identification. In some cases external aid agencies were seen to be in competition with one another to claim 'their' territory for housing redevelopment. They did not understand the local culture, production processes and protocols. This led to a range of misunderstandings and miscalculations, including unrealistic time-lines, failure to access or receive equipment and supplies, and delivery of poor quality materials (Christoplos, 2006; Masyrafah and Mckeon, 2008). This was exacerbated by the pressures on international aid agencies to demonstrate to donors in their home country that they were actually 'doing something'. In most cases, non-Acehnese staff in the agencies would prioritize needs, and draw up the projects as they saw them, specifying location, timescale and assessment processes. Only after completing this stage of the project would they consult (often on the basis of a workshop) with local people.

The experiences of such 'consultation', according to one Acehnese respondent, fed into the 'natural' Acehnese suspicion of large external and formal organizations. This suspicion in turn fed into criticism of some of the early attempts at participatory practice, which were clear illustrations of the deficit approach to local development that many agencies had brought with them when they first arrived in Aceh. Surprisingly, our respondents also commented unfavourably on participation which appeared to be asset-based, because it involved people spending a considerable amount of time articulating their needs and viewpoints, only to have their views ignored in the implementation of plans. While the dominant form of participation was of the consultative kind we can find examples of attempts to introduce both partnership and community development forms of participation. The following provides a case study of how one local Acehnese NGO was able to introduce both these forms.

Case study: The Development Forum

The Development Forum (TDF)[3] is a local Acehnese organization which was established almost immediately after the tsunami, when a number of Acehnese, including survivors of the events of 26 December 2004, and those living elsewhere in Indonesia, teamed up to form their own indigenous organization. The driving principle of the organization is that 'it is the people themselves who are best placed to identify their needs in order to improve their lives'. Their first task was to find out what the Acehnese survivors themselves prioritized as *their* needs. Members of the Development Forum argued that if their work was to be taken seriously it must be based on the priorities of people themselves. The overwhelming response was that they needed to 'get back to normal'. It was clear that they did not want to sit idly by, watching foreign workers 'rescue them'. The Development Forum respondents pointed out that while the Acehnese might have lost their homes, physical resources and loved ones, they still had many assets, including knowledge, skills and networks. They wanted to reclaim their livelihoods and their future. Members of TDF argued that if the reconstruction was to be effective, respect for the integrity of local people and acknowledgement of their resources should be at the centre of activities. As well as listening to and respecting survivors, one of the most important aspects to building trust for TDF was to 'actually do something immediately, however small', rather than 'just talk about what they could do'. They pointed out that working collaboratively to ensure the participation of local people was an essential step to recovery. TDF created what they called the 'brain and stomach approach', whereby the brain required education and knowledge, and the stomach required re-establishing livelihoods.

Within the 'brain and stomach' framework, two priorities stood out. First, for families with surviving school-age children, getting students back to school was a priority. For example, in the capital, Banda Aceh, where a large number of schools had been decimated and teachers killed, tent schools were set up in the foothills of the city. Many people offered to take on teaching roles to ensure that classes continued. One of TDF's first efforts was to work with local and other Indonesians to bring in teaching materials from all over Indonesia to support the teachers. From this small effort, TDF, working in partnership with both external agencies and local communities, moved to gain grants to establish a school in an area that had been badly affected by the tsunami. The school was up and running in 2006. This educational work has been complemented by a partnership arrangement with schools outside Indonesia, organized around scholarships for Acehnese young people.

Second, the other key priority for the Acehnese survivors was to be able to participate in society as active members, by reinstating their livelihoods. To do this they required an income. Mostly they wanted to return to their previous occupations. For many Acehnese this meant restoring their business. Using an asset-based approach, TDF began to work with those who had previously operated small businesses, beginning with discussions of what economic activities the survivors had practised before the tsunami. They calculated together what was needed to re-establish businesses. For some families, rebuilding a business meant having a replacement motorcycle taxi. For others it meant a set of saucepans to re-establish a way-side stall, or seeds and fertilizers to re-establish a farm. TDF set up a system of revolving small loans whereby they would purchase the materials needed on the basis of an agreement that recipients would repay the debt, either as an interest free loan or at a low interest rate, so that funds could be provided to another small business. In February 2009 TDF had made over 900 such loans, with few defaults on repayments. One of the reasons for the success of the revolving loans programme has been the employment of 'organic' leaders to both motivate and facilitate. These motivators/facilitators have been drawn from the villages, and most importantly, they are trusted by the villagers. They have not necessarily been village leaders, formal or otherwise. They are selected for their skills, experience and understanding of village needs. Facilitators attend programmes to deepen their knowledge of small business practices. They participate in workshops run by TDF, where general issues and strategies are discussed. After reviewing their activities at the end of 2008, TDF decided to restructure around three functions: the continual generation of income to ensure financial independence and long-term sustainability for the organization; continuation and development of micro credit revolving funds; and educational, social and advocacy functions. In 2009 the first stage of a community centre, which could provide a base for all the activities of TDF, had been completed.

There are a number of ways of explaining the success of organizations such as the Development Forum. First, as TDF staff point out, right from the beginning they had networks and understanding of the local traditions and cultures, so that they were able to develop trust among local people quickly and easily. For example, understanding the primary importance of verbal communication in local cultures meant that paperwork and formal requirements have been kept to a minimum. Second, TDF is committed to sharing understandings and the participation of all parties in their reconstruction efforts. From the perspective of TDF workers, the key to successful reconstruction is the collaborative way in which needs are identified and fulfilled. Third, a corollary of this approach is the importance of taking an asset-based approach to development. Fourth, a critical factor in TDF activities has been the principle of maximizing independence from funders, including international aid agencies and government. TDF has refused offers of external funds unless they served the real needs of local people. Funding agreements with external agents have been constructed as real partnerships, rather than the traditional donor, contractor, recipient categorization, based on asymmetrical power relations. In contrast to other local organizations which opportunistically accepted any funds, this strategic approach has assisted in ensuring the sustainability of TDF. Fifth, TDF is committed to a mutual learning environment, where all parties participate and learn as equals, including international agencies, TDF staff and participants in programmes. In this way there is a continual programme of capacity-building, for international agencies, their own staff and the Acehnese they are working with. Finally, there is continual follow-up and informal evaluation of programmes and projects, with the aim of developing solutions within a partnership framework, especially when people who are re-establishing their livelihoods run into difficulty.

Notwithstanding the success of TDF, and its strong asset based practices, its commitment to the community development principle that participation involves ownership of processes, strategies and decisions by those affected, even TDF does not offer a full participatory model. For example, while the recipients of revolving loans choose and propose their small business start-up endeavour, they do not participate directly in the decision as to whether they will be supported or not. Often they have little involvement in calculations regarding the repayment schedule, or the rate of interest when it is applied or the evaluation of their business outcomes. Why is this? There are a number of reasons. First, there is still the pressure for speedy outcomes. Participation involving full ownership of all processes slows down the process of 'getting families back on their feet economically'. Second, many of the recipients, particularly women, are reluctant to get involved in the decision-making. It is enough of a challenge for them to restart their small businesses.

There have been other issues facing TDF as well. These have included the issues of when to apply for and accept grants from Western agencies (involving calculation of how receipt of international funds might compromise their activities, especially in the eyes of some local Acehnese); and whether to expand the scope of their activities (at what point does growth in the scale of their activities undermine their ability to maintain community development participatory principles). These challenges, of course, are not unique to NGOs in Aceh. They are part of the common refrain about the dilemmas of asset based community development work internationally. However, when located in the volatile environment that is post-tsunami Aceh they have been particularly significant.

What this brief overview of the work of the Development Forum indicates is that, notwithstanding the growing commitment internationally to a people-centred, participatory approach to development and aid, the establishment of asset based participatory practice, has been far from easy in post-tsunami Aceh, even where an organization is based on a commitment to such principles. The difficulty of establishing participatory processes must be understood in the context of the profound challenges and constraints of the whole reconstruction process, to which we now turn.

Factors affecting participatory programmes and practices

Size and complexity of the reconstruction effort

The first type of challenge concerns the sheer size of the reconstruction effort, in terms of both funds and the extent of devastation. The complexity and enormity of the tasks required for rebuilding Aceh have been dominant themes setting the context for the many evaluations of both relief and recovery projects (see for example, Relief Web, 2006; Cosgrave, 2007; Masyrafah and Mckeon, 2008). While exact numbers vary, the estimates are that between 130,000 and 150,000 people died and over 700,000 people lost their livelihoods (AidWatch, 2006; Masyrafah and Mckeon, 2008). The cost of the damage has been estimated at US$4.45 billion (Masyrafah and Mckeon, 2008).

Rebuilding lives, physically, socially and emotionally, was always going to be very challenging. The geographic topography of much of the Acehnese coastline changed and whole communities were destroyed. Before homes could be rebuilt, land titles, equity, materials, unit costs, and quality issues had to be sorted out (Masyrafah and McKeon, 2008). The power of the earthquake and tsunami meant that not only was much of the material infrastructure demolished, but so too was the organizational and civil society infrastructure. The enormity of the tasks and the issue of 'where to start' affected local Acehnese wanting to participate in the relief and reconstruction, just as it did Indonesian and international agencies. As noted above, a normal response in post-disaster situations is a reluctance on the part of international agencies to involve local people. Aid agencies feel that they do not have the time for the 'luxury' of participation or consultation. Moreover, in addition to the disruption caused by the earthquake and tsunami, Acehnese life had already been destabilized through 30 years of violence and instability, centred around the struggle for independence for Aceh and the activities of the Indonesian military. By 2004, decades of military repression and overall human rights abuses had severely bruised Acehnese assessment of opportunities for self-determination. Such an environment of profound insecurity had meant that while the networks of bonding (in-group) social capital had been strengthened, bridging social capital (between groups) had been severely eroded.[4] If they were going to work together and with outsiders on reconstruction, the Acehnese had to trust each other and to work across old boundaries, which they did to a large extent, but it did take time. We discuss the impact of this climate of distrust further below. The unparalled funds available did mean that more could be achieved than in other reconstruction programmes, but it also encouraged opportunistic behaviour, whereby some local people were involved in tokenistic consultation and received funds which were then redirected for personal gain rather than community projects.

Tensions in contemporary delivery of aid

A second type of challenge constraining participatory practices is embedded in the tensions arising from the differing imperatives and assumptions of contemporary development and aid. Perhaps most important is the tension in the aid industry between what Edwards and Gaventa (2001) identify as development imperatives (accountability to recipients) and institutional imperatives (accountability to donors). For example, given the imperative of accountability to their donors in foreign countries, aid agencies tended to favour efficiency and compliance with set timelines over the flexibility usually required for participation involving partnership and community development processes. Contemporary aid tends to be controlled by time constraints, regulations and accountability protocols, rather than long-term commitment to the recipient communities with whom development practitioners are working (Hewitt, 2006).

Several respondents in international agencies commented on the new pressures emanating from the risk-averse context, or what Beck (1999) identifies as 'risk society'. For example, by having to confront the 'threatening sphere of bad possibilities' characterizing the new 'risk-oriented' society, workers are reluctant to 'risk' handing over power and responsibility for programmes to local people. In this context, compliance with international regulations and protocols, technical efficiency and cost-effectiveness within a neo-liberal framework are prioritized over the empowerment of the recipients of aid. Hewitt (2006) notes how one international NGO focused so much on conforming to the formal (risk-averse) international standards regarding humanitarian response, that it had no capacity to respond to the needs of local people. These priorities and pressures did not make for an environment suitable for nurturing strong forms of participation, particularly those based on the community development principle of local ownership.

It is in the context of the tensions between accountability to recipients and accountability to the donors funding their activities that international aid agencies and NGOs received such a bad press over the slowness and inappropriateness of much of their reconstruction work. Ironically, international NGOs were criticized for being both 'too slow' (not having sufficient 'outputs') and 'too fast' (producing the wrong outputs, without due consideration to consultation). As Hewitt (2006) points out, an imbalance in favour of development imperatives may result in the demise of the NGO through donor withdrawal. Too great a focus on donors' institutional imperatives can mean that the NGO loses its reason for existence. Of course, from a community development perspective it is not a matter of the pace of reconstruction, but whether the reconstruction efforts are owned by local communities, and how well they are calibrated with the needs of these communities.

Working through participatory methods while at the same time taking all local contextual factors into account generally takes more time than top-down methods. The argument for 'taking time' rests on the view that there is 'buy-in' in regard to the process, and thus the outcomes tend to be more secure and sustainable. Yet involvement must be more than tokenistic or consultative. In the case of the international NGOs involved in post-tsunami Aceh it was clear that while there was a desire to do more than tokenistic consultation, and the intent was usually to establish programmes which were responsive to real needs, the process of needs assessment was laboured. Survivors often felt 'over-consulted' and 'over-assessed', particularly when they were subjected to assessments by multiple NGOs (Hewitt, 2006; Cosgrave, 2007). Moreover, the intense level of assessment was rarely matched by the level of practical support or by further involvement by survivors, such as a right to veto actions. Indeed, even the most community development conscious programmes still managed to get weighed down by pressure for fast 'outputs' and the technocratic reporting processes. This sort of pressure, of course, was one of the reasons why the Development Forum has been so careful in considering whether to accept Western aid money. Given the imperative of expedient and effective projects in Western terms of reference, it was often easier for international agencies to consult with local leaders at the *kabupaten* (sub-provincial) level, in formal settings and meetings, rather than spending time working more informally at the village (*kecamatan*) level. Thus ordinary villagers, and especially women, were often by-passed in any participatory processes and certainly rarely participated as equal partners. Even local NGOs and other local bodies such as community committees, with whom international NGOs 'consulted' with relatively easily, can be unrepresentative, with 'women, the poor, the landless and other marginalized groups being side-lined in decision-making processes' (AidWatch, 2006: p13). Nonetheless many of the respondents in the Indonesian NGO capacity-building study pointed out that many spaces for women to operate in, including through jobs, have been opened up in the process of the reconstruction.

Contemporary delivery of aid also involves high turnover of international staff, often in the interest of ensuring that aid workers do not suffer excessively from stress and 'burn-out'. This high turnover has several consequences. First, it fractures the often close relationships between local people and aid workers, which is necessary in both partnership and community development based participation, and in so doing undercuts the trust which is the basis to such participation. Second it affects the continuity of programmes and alienates local people who perceive aid workers to be deserting them. Third, it fuels the cynical attitude that holds that when new staff arrive and programmes are reoriented, the newcomers need to 'make their mark' and thus change the programme again (see Bennet and Roche, 2002). Finally, all of these factors affect the preparedness of local people to give their time and energy to participating in the reconstruction processes. The Indonesian NGO capacity-building study revealed that these concerns about the constant turnover of international workers were very much present in post-tsunami Aceh.

Power factors affecting participation

A third category of constraint upon participatory approaches has arisen from the particular configurations of power relations affecting the reconstruction of Aceh. Respecting local customs, which as discussed above, is a central tenet of participatory community development, also means working with existing structures and power relations, including those based on inequalities, and dealing with the internecine conflicts that are experienced in most communities. In Aceh these internecine struggles dig deeply into community cohesion, based as they are on the often violent conflict around the movement for independence over many decades (see Chapter 3 in this book). As indicated above, negotiating different interests in the community for the purpose of coming up with collective decisions in the face of often lingering suspicion and distrust of outsiders has been a tall order. The background tensions between the independence movement (GAM) and the Indonesian military (TNI), and the power struggles between the military, police and the government, presented a difficult backdrop to the reconstruction effort (McCulloch, 2005). Initially few international organizations grasped the ways in which the background political tensions in Aceh affected the aid and reconstruction tasks and the complexities arising out of the tense historical and political context. Before the tsunami struck, much of the system of governance had been dysfunctional. There was a contested land rights system and a weak civilian bureaucracy, both of which had been under effective control by the military. A number of villagers who had been caught between the fighting had already been displaced and resettled in camps (Easton, 2005). At the same time, however, the years of conflict had also had the effect of fortifying the resilience of the Acehnese people. Many of our respondents commented on this resilience, and the way in which it was built on a long history of struggle and a strong sense of pride in Acehnese culture. But interestingly, Acehnese fortitude and commitment to self-determination did not necessarily convert into preparedness to get involved in post-tsunami decision-making, or ownership of reconstruction projects. The experiences of conflict were often translated into a general scepticism regarding the value of democratic participation in civil society.

While the effects of the earthquake and tsunami and the following reconstruction have cooled down many of the tensions associated with the historical struggles for independence, they have created yet other tensions. For example, perceived differences among local 'winners' and 'losers' from the rebuilding process have ignited community tensions. AidWatch (2006: pp19–20) documented a host of social tensions brought to the surface through the reconstruction activities. For example, where reconstruction (involving both passive receipt of support and active involvement) has focused on the more disadvantaged people, such as those directly affected in coastal settlements, this has fuelled new tensions between coastal settlements and other regions of Aceh. Inland regions not directly touched by the tsunami have nonetheless suffered significantly from the economic impact of the disaster (after decades of economic stagnation in the context of the civil conflict). Aid groups consulting with and favouring 'obvious' victims in barracks and camps overlooked survivors 'bunking in' with relatives, who often continued to live in very difficult conditions. These rifts have not made for a situation conducive to egalitarian participation or joint ownership of reconstruction projects.

Antagonism over 'who to liaise with and listen to' has also arisen between international and local NGOs. Some local NGOs expressed anger over the ready acceptance of government policies and plans by international agencies, especially the government Blue Print for rebuilding Banda Aceh which was produced early on in the reconstruction effort, without listening to the views of local communities. Given the community development rhetoric of participation and accountability to those affected, the view of these Acehnese respondents was that uncritical support for the Indonesian government on the part of international agencies was opportunistic.

There was yet another sensitivity in dealing with the Indonesian government that was noted by international NGOs. This concerns issues of human rights. Human rights are central to community development. When the earthquake and tsunami hit, there had been a long history of human rights abuses in Aceh arising from the deep conflict of the independence struggles. In their quest to enter Indonesia and to be able to remain to provide assistance for the duration of the reconstruction, international agencies were sensitive to any perception that they were being outspoken about human rights issues and that they could be caught up in the local struggles. While several international respondents commented that they were too busy delivering aid to get involved in human rights, others commented on their concerns about human rights abuses and the corruption of aid by the military and government officials. They referred to reports of the military siphoning off food, abusing young women and bullying families to move into camps. A particular concern was in regard to the organization of the barracks as emergency accommodation. For example, one Acehnese woman identified the way in which people were herded into barracks (when they wanted to remain in tents on their own land) as a human rights issue. Another woman referred to the exclusion of women from camp management as constituting an abuse of human rights.

Responding to information on human rights abuse is a difficult area for aid workers. Taking an overtly political line or becoming over-involved in local issues concerning human rights can rebound unfavourably on recipients of aid when an international agency works in partnership with local people in bringing up human rights issues. It can also result in aid agencies being expelled, or at least seriously curtailed in their activities (Chandler, 2002). Yet failing to respond to human rights issues can also undermine the legitimacy of community development methods in the eyes of local people, by compromising the integrity of aid and development workers.

Many of our respondents remarked on the contrast between the poorly paid local NGO workers and the exceedingly well-paid international workers, who have taken over some of the best accommodation, contributed to increases in the cost of living and have been able to fly out for luxurious 'R and R' leave. Several of the key NGO leaders expressed anger over their exclusion from the management of many of the international programmes. They commented unfavourably on the nationality prerequisites and the many layers of bureaucracy that froze them out of participation in the tendering process. Such exclusion clearly undermines the possibility of 'true' local participation, they argued. Some international agencies explained this exclusion on the basis of responsibility to the donor nations, lack of capacity among the Acehnese, lack of accountability procedures in Acehnese NGOs and its corollary, the potential for corruption. Westerners cited examples of projects that failed because of incompetent management and corrupt managers and officials. In reflecting on this rationale, one Acehnese respondent stated that while there are cases of corruption and incompetence, this does not excuse the failure of international agencies to ensure full participation of local people and to work collaboratively with local leaders and NGOs.

The final power factor affecting participation concerns the assumed value of participation. Some local people, understanding the asymmetrical power relations that are inherent in the whole concept of aid and development, are not convinced that they can influence development through their involvement in the planning or application of development projects. Others just do not want to be involved in a project for their own reasons. As Cooke and Kothari (2001) argue, participation can be a tyranny. It can be forced on people; it can mean giving away secrets to external authorities; and as indicated above, it can be manipulative and involve co-option.

Cultural factors

A fourth factor affecting participation concerns the role of culture. There are three key issues here, all of which require sensitivity. The first issue is culturalism. Development workers are increasingly required to be competent in cross-cultural practice. However, cross-cultural practice carries within it another set of tensions around the issue of culturalism, that is, the privileging of traditional knowledge over 'imported' or foreign knowledge. This view is sometimes translated into the assumption that respect for local communities should also mean acceptance of the integrity of all customs, including those that are oppressive within a human rights framework (Ife, 2001; Kenny, 2006). Pupavic (2006) has criticized the culturalism inherent in international development orthodoxies, including locally-grounded community development approaches, which reify traditional production systems while ignoring or discounting the importance of industrial production as a basis for economic advancement. He comments on what he calls the 'anti-modernization' development philosophies that champion local cultures, individual and community needs and the rural economy, while failing to address the capacity of the developing state, which without a developed economy and infrastructure, can hardly become a progressive re-distributive state that guarantees its citizens' welfare (Pupavic, 2006: p261).

The culturalist position fails to understand that all cultures are both diverse and continually changing. There is no 'pure' culture that is unassailable. Indeed women in patriarchal societies, when given the opportunity, will challenge their subordination in their practical activities. Culturalism is an important issue in participatory community development and must be handled sensitively. The resolution to a naïve culturalism does not lie in the rejection of participation or ownership of processes and projects by local people. It lies in education and understanding, for example through the introduction of human rights agendas, without the denial of respect for different views.

The second cultural issue concerns the deeply religious culture of Aceh. Some Acehnese respondents criticized what they saw as the failure of international agencies and NGOs to understand the Islamic nature of

Acehnese culture. Several members of Islamic organizations expressed concern about the lack of acknowledgement and formal participation in the reconstruction process on the part of religious leaders. They commented on how the importance of Islam was ignored in the government scheme for reconstruction when it was drawn up. Given the influence of religious leaders and the important role of local *dayah* or *pesantren* (Islamic boarding schools) in housing and educating the children left as orphans, our respondents were surprised that there was so little liaison between international workers and Islamic leaders. One explanation of this omission is the 'Othering' of the aid recipient, in which the recipient of aid is constructed as someone who is not 'like us', who can be a threat to 'our way of doing things' or requires skills and education to make him or her 'like us'. This 'Othering' which continues to frame many of the methodologies of aid and development, also helps explain the reluctance of Western agencies to implement participation through consultative, partnership or community development methods.

The final cultural issue to be discussed here involves the authoritarian and fatalistic elements of Acehnese culture. As indicated above, the community development approach is based on the views that the aim of development is effective self-determination and people must be the active agents of their own destinies. Even today, this social ontology often rubs up against authoritarian and fatalistic views resulting from the 30 years' experiences of repressive government control and deep religiosity of the Acehnese people. A corollary of experiences of authoritarianism and fatalistic attitudes is the way in which people recovering from disasters either fashion themselves as victims or are constructed by others as victims. In post-tsunami Aceh, the Indonesian and international media constructed their reporting within the narrative of victim-hood. Relief and reconstruction organized around the idea of victim-hood can open the way to competition between 'victims' regarding who is the most deserving, or what one respondent identified as 'victim entrepreneurs'. Indeed, even where there was commitment to consultation, partnership and asset-based community development, some communities actually wanted to rely almost entirely on outside facilitators to undertake the planning, decide the directions and oversee projects.

Engaging the state

The fifth factor affecting participation concerns the state. Notwithstanding all the current emphasis on civil society and the role of NGOs in aid and development, Nederveen Pieterse (2001: p24) reminds us that practices of aid and development require an understanding that the state is still a major 'conductor and conduit' of development. The perceptions and attitudes of the Indonesian authorities to both local and international NGOs has been very important to them. This is because international agencies want to avoid the 'neo-colonial' label which the governments of developing states might readily apply to their activities. There continues to be a fear that participation can involve social action and that collective activity might be seen to be a form of political agitation by the authorities, as it was over the past few decades. In addition, partnerships between local and international NGOs and application of community development methods can be seen to compromise national sovereignty. Indeed an issue that was particularly sensitive at the beginning of 2005 was constructed around Indonesian national sovereignty. Given the history of separatist conflict within the province, the Indonesian government and the TNI (Indonesian military) were wary of contact between international agencies and the independence movement and possible interference by foreigners in existing administrative arrangements, which were constructed pre-tsunami and where the TNI had the 'upper hand'. At the beginning of the relief and reconstruction process the geographical reach of the international agencies was restricted (Easton, February 2005) and several times the Indonesian government threatened that it would demand that they depart from the region altogether. While this did not occur (although one UN agency did leave, reportedly after some informal pressure) it made many of the international agencies uncomfortable about their grass roots interventions and encouragement of participatory community development. At the same time, according to our Acehnese respondents, local NGOs and villagers, having experienced decades of conflict, were at times suspicious of strangers and afraid of possible punitive consequences resulting from their liaison with foreign groups, NGOs and agencies outside their own families or villages. Participatory community development built on principles of trust and mutuality is quite difficult to organize in such circumstances.

Marketization of aid

The final constraint we need to consider concerns the new contextual factors that are now affecting all aid and development programmes. An important change influencing the delivery of aid and development programmes, which is often overlooked in analysis of the difficulties of the Aceh reconstruction effort, is the growing marketization of aid. There are two elements of marketization. First, the enormity of the funds available encouraged instrumentally directed involvement in the aid effort, such as by establishing small local NGOs. This sometimes meant that local people used the rhetoric of participation opportunistically, to access funds. Second, the aid and development industry has increasingly involved profit companies as well non-profit organizations and state institutions. In the context of the dominance of neo-liberal policies which support market driven economics, non-profit aid organizations are often in competition with for-profit companies for contracts. Western corporations now see aid programmes as an opportunity for their own development. Both the for-profit and the non-profit sectors have cashed in on the lucrative contracts to manage and deliver expert reconstruction in Aceh. Klein (2005, 2007) argues that countries that have been 'smashed to rubble, whether by so-called Acts of God or by Acts of Bush' offer new terrain for capitalist enterprise. We are witnessing the rise of what she identifies as disaster capitalism. From this perspective, aid has become another mechanism for developing global markets for large corporations. Commenting on the sources of funding of non-profit organizations, Foroohar, writing in the *Civil Society Observer* (January–February 2005), argues that 80 per cent of the aid pie goes to the largest well-branded non-profit organizations, who receive most of their money from governments. The marketization of aid ensures that agencies focus on their competitive edge and branding strategies. From this perspective, participation is no more than an instrument to obtain consent for activities undertaken by international agencies or corporations. Community development is only relevant in so far as it contributes to the competitive position of such organizations.

Conclusion

We now return to the questions posed at the beginning of this chapter and draw the evidence together. Have people-centred, participatory approaches to development been applied in the reconstruction of Aceh? If so, how have they been manifested? Our investigation has indicated that the international and Indonesian aid agencies arrived in Aceh with a view of the capacities of the Acehnese that focused on their deficits, yet in the early relief phase many Acehnese survivors not only participated in the relief effort, but also organized activities. As the relief phase moved into recovery and the social, political and physical rebuilding of Aceh, most of the players in the reconstruction effort were aware of the value of local participation. While this participation tended to be of the consultative kind, and sometimes involved manipulation, there have been examples of NGO activities that involved asset-based community development, such as the Development Forum.

The evidence overall indicates that even when aid programmes articulated commitments to participation, they found it difficult to implement these commitments. This is because of the many challenges facing them, but also because they failed to examine assumptions upon which they work. For example, the assumption of unequal power relations between donor, aid worker and aid recipient that are embedded in disaster relief and recovery are left unexamined. If we are to embrace a truly asset-based, people-centred and participatory approach to aid and development we need to understand our interconnectedness as human beings who operate in a globalized world, and to approach aid and development through the principle of mutuality. We need to structure participation as a process and practice that involves developing the capacities of all players in the development field, which in the case of Aceh, includes a wide range of participants, including those in the Indonesian and foreign governments and agencies, those involved with international and Indonesian NGOs, as well as those local Acehnese and NGOs.

What this analysis suggests, then, is that the adoption of the discourse of participation does indicate the growing hegemony of the new aid paradigm based on people-centred, participatory approaches to aid and development, but there remain many constraints and challenges, and often the activities undertaken in the name of participation belie the rhetoric. These constraints and inconsistencies should be understood.

Lessons

This final section of the paper sets out some reflections on what we can learn from the experiences of participation in post-tsunami Aceh. These are:

1. The importance of understanding the different forms of participation and how they might be manifested differently in different contexts.
2. The importance of articulating and communicating the approaches taken to participation by your agency.
3. While it is imperative to develop participatory approaches to post-disaster reconstruction it is also important to avoid using participatory processes tokenistically, opportunistically or as a form of manipulation.
4. Beginning with an asset-based approach.
5. As far as possible, ensuring that the planning, needs identification, strategies and activities are owned by survivors. For example, prioritizing the fulfilment of the needs of survivors as they see them.
6. The importance of operating on the principle of mutuality. For example, understanding that all parties learn from the experiences.
7. The importance of understanding and validating the role of local people in the reconstruction process, especially at the very beginning of the relief phase, when the temptation is to exclude them.

8. Ensuring that the processes, limits, reasons for involvement, expectations of time, effort and resources, constraints and expected outcomes are articulated from the perspective of each stakeholder. This is essential for smooth coordination.
9. Being wary of making promises that might not be kept.
10. The importance of understanding that local people have different ways of participating and degrees of interest in participation and that some people just do not want to be involved at all.

References

AidWatch (2006) 'National Audit Slams $1 Billion Government Tsunami Aid Program', AidWatch Media Release, 28 July 2006, available at www.aidwatch.org.au (retrieved 3 August 2006)

Arnstein, S. (1969) 'A Ladder of Citizen Participation', *Journal of the American Institute of Planners*, vol 35, no 4, July 1969, pp216–224

Beck, U. (1999) *World Risk Society*, Cambridge, Polity Press

Bennett, F. and Roche, C. (2002) 'Developing Indicators. The scope for participatory approaches' in *New Economy*, vol, 7, Issue 1, pp24-28

Bhatnagar, B. and Williams, A. (1992) *A Participatory Development and the World Bank: Potential Directions for Change*. vol 183, Washington, World Bank Discussion Papers

Buchanan-Smith, M. and Fabri, P. (2005) *Linking Relief and Rehabilitation and Development – A review of the Debate*, London Tsunami Evaluation Coalition

Campfrens, H. (ed) (1997) *Community Development Around the World*, Toronto, University of Toronto Press

Chambers, R. (1983) *Rural Development: Putting the First Last*, London, Longman

Chandler, D. (2002) *From Kosova to Kabul & Beyond, Human Rights and International Intervention*, London, Pluto Press

Christoplos, I. (2006) *Links between Relief, Rehabilitation and Development in the Tsunami Response*, Tsunami Evaluation Coalition

Cohen, J. and Arato, A. (1995) *Civil Society and Political Theory*, Cambridge, MA, MIT Press

Cooke, B. and Kothari, U. (eds) (2001) *Participation: The New Tyranny?*, London, Zed Books

Cornwall, A. (2008) 'Unpacking "Participation": models, meanings and practices', *Community Development Journal*, vol 43, no 3, July pp269–283

Cosgrave, J. (2007) *Synthesis Report: Expanded Summary. Joint Evaluation of the international response to the Indian Ocean tsunami*, London, Tsunami Evaluation Coalition

Eade, D. and Williams, S. (1995) *The Oxfam Handbook of Development and Relief*, Oxfam

Easton, M. (February, 2005) 'Civil Society and Human Rights in Aceh after the Tsunami', Members Briefing, Human Rights First, New York and Washington

Edwards, M. and Gaventa, J. (eds) (2001) *Global Citizen Action*, London, Earthscan

Eyben, R. and Ferguson, C. (2004) 'How can Donors Become More Accountable to Poor People?' in Groves, L. and Hinton, R. (eds) (2004) *Inclusive aid changing power and relationships in international development*, London, Earthscan. pp163-180

Foroohar, R. (January 2005) 'Wary of Aid', *Civil Society Observer*, viewed 13 May, 2005, www.un-ngls.org/cso/so6/wary.htm

Fukuda-Parr, Lopes, C. and Malik, K. eds (2002) *Capacity for Development. New Solutions for Old Problems*, New York, Earthscan and UNDP

Godinot, X. and Wodon, Q. (eds) (2006) *Participatory approaches to attacking extreme poverty: case studies led by the International Movement ATD Fourth World*, Washington, World Bank Publications

Groves, L. and Hinton, R. (eds) (2004) *Inclusive aid changing power and relationships in international development*, London, Earthscan

Gunewardena, N. and Schuller, M. (2008) *Capitalizing On Catastrophe: Neoliberal Strategies in Disaster Reconstruction*, Lanham, USA, Altamira Press

Hewitt, A. (2006) Being Risky and Trustworthy: Dilemmas Facing a non-government development agency, in *Community Development and Global Risk Society Conference Proceedings*, Centre for Citizenship and Human Rights, Deakin University, Melbourne, pp124–133

Hinton, R. and Groves, L. (2004) 'The Complexity of Inclusive Aid' in Groves, L. and Hinton, R. (eds) *Inclusive aid changing power and relationships in international development*, London, Earthscan, pp3–20

Howell, J. and Pearce, J. (2001) *Civil Society and Development. A Critical Exploration*, London, Lynne Reinner Publishers

Ife, J. (2001) *Human Rights and Social Work: Towards Rights-Based Practice*, Cambridge, Cambridge University Press

Kenny, S. (2006) *Developing Communities for the Future*, Melbourne, Thomas Nelson ITP

Kenny, S. (2007) 'Reconstruction in Aceh: Building whose capacity?', *Community Development Journal, An International Forum*, vol 42, no 2, pp206–221

Klein, N. (2005) 'The Rise of Disaster Capitalism', *The Nation*, viewed 23 May 2005 www.the nation.com?doc.mhtml?i=20050502&s=klein.htm

Klein, N. (2007) *The Shock Doctrine: The Rise of Disaster Capitalism*, London, Penguin

Long, C. (2001) *Participation of the Poor in Development Initiatives*, London, Earthscan

Masyrafah, H. and Mckeon, J. (2008) *Post-tsunami Aid Effectiveness in Aceh. Proliferation and Coordination Reconstruction*, Wolfensohn Center for Development Working Paper 6, Wolfensohn Centre for Development at Brookings

McCulloch, L. (2005) *Aceh: Then and Now*, Minority Rights Group International

Nederveen Pieterse, J. (2001) *Development Theory Deconstructions/Reconstructions*, London, Sage

Oxfam (2005) 'Oxfam: Aceh Weekly Tsunami Response Programme', *Weekly Update*, 8 April 2005

Pretty, J. (1995) 'Participatory learning for sustainable agriculture', *World Development*, vol 2, no 8, pp1247–1263

Pupavic, V. (2006) 'The Politics of Emergency and the Demise of the Developing State: Problems for Humanitarian Advocacy', *Development in Practice*, vol 16, nos 3 & 4, June, pp255–269

Putnam, R. D. (2000*)* *Bowling Alone. The Collapse and Revival of American Community,* New York, Simon & Schuster

Relief Web (2006) *Indonesia: About half million Aceh tsunami victims still live in refugee camps* www.reliefweb.int/rwarchive/rwb.nsf/db900sid/VBOL-6MWEHX?Open Document&Click=

Robb, C. (2004) 'Changing Power Relations in the History of Aid', in Groves, L. and Hinton, R. (eds) (2004*)* *Inclusive aid changing power and relationships in international development,* London, Earthscan, pp21–41

Smith, B. C. (1998) 'Participation without empowerment: Subterfuge or development' *Community Development Journal,* vol 33, no 3, pp197–204

United Nations Development Programme (UNDP) (1997) *Capacity Development, Technical Advisory Paper 2,* Management Development and Governance Division, New York, UNDP

Van Rooy, A. (1998) *Civil Society and the Aid Industry,* London, Earthscan

World Bank (1996) *The World Bank participation sourcebook,* World Bank Social Policy and Resettlement Division, World Bank. Environmentally Sustainable Development, Washington

Notes

1   The analysis draws on different sources. These include reports coming out of Western aid and development agencies, official Indonesian figures and reports and interviews with a number of people involved in the reconstruction (hereafter identified as interviewees or respondents), including local Acehnese, government officials, and participants in Acehnese NGOs, Indonesian NGOs and international NGOs and agencies, who were interviewed over the period from February 2005 until February 2009.

2   The first-hand research described in this chapter has been part of a six-year project, funded by Deakin University and the Australian Research Council, which began in 2003 and undertaken with co-researchers, Dr Ismet Fanany and Professor Greg Barton. The project, which in this chapter is referred to as the 'Indonesian NGO capacity-building study', set out to study the perceptions of capacity-building among members of moderate Islamic non-government organizations (NGOs) in Indonesia and to track the ways in which NGOs have interpreted and responded to change. During the process of research, the northern coastal region of Sumatra was devastated by an earthquake and subsequent tsunami. After the tsunami a new area of focus was added to the study. This was capacity-building and NGOs in Aceh. Discussion in this chapter draws on interviews with 96 respondents in the period from February 2005 until February 2009. Respondents included individuals who were involved in international agencies and NGOs, Indonesian agencies and NGOs, Acehnese NGOs, local village and religious leaders, activists and political commentators. Without the generous giving of time by the respondents, this report would not have been possible.

3   The terms on which research funding was received meant that pseudonyms must be used, so this is not the real name of the NGO.

4   Social capital refers to the features of social organization, such as trust, reciprocity, norms and networks, that facilitate coordination and cooperation for mutual benefit and increase a society's productive potential (Putnam, 2000). Bridging social capital occurs when networks develop between groups, when social relations and ties are established between groups of people, while bonding social capital strengthens the bonds within a group (Putman, 2000: 22).

Section Two

Case Studies

5

Towards a Model of Constructive Interaction between Aid Donors and Recipients in a Disaster Context: The Case of Lampuuk

Ismet Fanany

Introduction

The 2004 tsunami that struck the Indonesian province of Aceh was covered heavily by the world media, and today remains an example of the damage nature can inflict on human settlements. The devastation left behind in the wake of the tsunami was particularly severe in Lampuuk, a settlement like many others in Aceh. While the initial devastating impact of the tsunami on Lampuuk did not differ much from the fate suffered by many of its neighbours, as well as other villages across the region, the settlement's recovery and the process by which it was rebuilt in the aftermath of the disaster has distinguished it as an example of a successful reconstruction, based to a large extent on an effective aid donor–recipient relationship.

The settlement of Lampuuk is located about 20km southwest of Banda Aceh, with a population of around 6000. Prior to the tsunami, the settlement did not merit special attention and did not stand out from thousands of others in Aceh. After the tsunami, however, all that remained of Lampuuk was the local mosque and about 1000 of its original inhabitants. The site quickly became a photo opportunity for high-profile visitors to the disaster zone, with former US presidents Bill Clinton and George Bush touring the site on 20 February 2005. Half a million US dollars was quickly allocated to the settlement by the Clinton-Bush Tsunami Fund. In response, its two main streets were renamed for the two presidents.

Following the initial interest in the settlement, the residents of Lampuuk were still left with the challenge of rebuilding houses and infrastructure destroyed by the flood waters. Not surprisingly, the local organization that was quickly formed to coordinate the rebuilding effort received a number of offers of aid. Oxfam, for example, undertook to repair water systems to the settlement. Several aid donors were prepared to assist with housing. One of these, and the agency whose offer was eventually accepted, was the Turkish Red Crescent.

This chapter describes the process by which the residents of Lampuuk negotiated with the Turkish Red Crescent and which led eventually to the rebuilding of houses for the surviving inhabitants of the settlement. It is a somewhat unusual story in that the recipients of this aid were heavily involved in the process and were very satisfied with the results. Irrespective of any other achievement, this outcome is an important one and suggests that the experience of Lampuuk might serve as a model for cooperation between aid donors and recipients and, as such, may provide valuable insight for future endeavours.

The role of aid

Recent years have seen increased interest in understanding the factors that cause aid programmes to succeed or fail. This has been manifested in a shift from stand-alone projects to partnerships and mutual accountability on the part of donors and recipients (World Bank, 1998). The significance of institutions in the region in question receiving aid and the existence of good governance has been established (Svensson, 1999; Burnside and Dollar, 2000; 2004; and Dollar and Svensson, 2000). The method by which aid is disbursed has also been shown to be significant (Dollar, 2003; Cordella and Dell'Ariccia, 2002; 2003).

It should be recalled that the role and function of development aid has changed over time. Our current conception of aid and aid organizations is quite different from the prevailing concepts of the 1950s, when the current system took form. At that time, lack of development, meaning development in recipient nations that was behind the standard of the west, was seen to result from a lack of capital. Aid, during this period, generally took the form of investment projects intended to result in capital transfer. Growth-oriented programmes and anti-poverty efforts that followed were often unsuccessful, however, and, by the 1980s, the focus had changed to conditional programmes aimed at forcing a change in policy and practice in recipient nations. More recently, it has become clear that lack of appropriate institutions has been an impediment to development in many recipient countries (Paul, 2006). It is for this reason, that programmes based on process conditions and political monitoring are features of many aid efforts (Adam and O'Connell, 1999; Thorbecke, 2000).

At the present time, non-governmental organizations (NGOs) are active in the disbursement of aid. While NGOs raise only a small amount of funds themselves, they are increasingly important as channels for the distribution and implementation of aid and are often seen as possessing desirable characteristics felt to be lacking in governments and official organizations in the developing world. In addition to more traditional concerns, NGOs have become involved in a range of causes, including issues like gender equality and environmentalism that have had a place in Western society for some time but are new to many of the societies which receive aid (Burnell and Morrissey, 2004). This is certainly the case in Indonesia, where a plethora of NGOs have appeared, mirroring social concerns in the West that frequently have little relevance to the majority of the public.

Needless to say, NGOs are not new, but their role in the implementation of aid has changed greatly over the last two decades. These organizations have long functioned in the provision of educational and health services in many developing countries (Edwards and Hulme, 1996). Now, however, NGOs are seen by many aid donors as more effective and less costly agents of funds disbursement, a pattern that began in the 1990s at the end of the Cold War (Meyer, 1992; Vivian, 1994). A driving force in the trend toward NGO involvement in the aid process is the view that democratic governance (in the Western model) is necessary for economic development. NGOs are often taken to be central to the process of democratization and integral to the functioning of a civil society (World Bank, 1994; Edwards and Hulme, 1996).

In Indonesia, there are some 8000 NGOs (ADB, 1999). While international aid bodies have been largely convinced as to the usefulness of NGOs in the development process, a certain amount of scepticism regarding their activities is observable in Indonesia. Indonesian scholars and researchers who are familiar with the working of their society, which is known for high levels of endemic corruption, have noted the complexity of Indonesian society, the need for foreign aid organizations to work through Indonesian NGOs, but also the propensity for these same NGOs to misuse the funds they receive (see, for example, Lounela, 2001; Situngkir, 2003; Situngkir and Siagian, 2004). This difference in perception of NGOs on the part of Indonesians and foreign donors is interesting and takes on great significance in the context of post-tsunami reconstruction as it is virtually impossible for foreign organizations of any kind to operate without an Indonesian partner organization brokering the funds available (USAID, 2004).

The experience of Lampuuk

The experience of the people of Lampuuk immediately following the Indian Ocean tsunami centred on their relationship with the Turkish Red Crescent. Lampuuk, as described above, has been held up as an example of successful reconstruction and has served as the face of the tsunami's aftermath. The area is classified as a *kemukiman*, a settlement, that is part of the *kecamatan* of Lhuk Nga in the *kabupaten* of Aceh Besar. Under the current administrative system, *kabupaten* (sometimes translated as 'regency') is roughly equivalent to a county, and is the level at which Regional Autonomy was conferred beginning in 2001. *Kabupaten* are typically divided into a number of *kecamatan*, similar to townships, with the exact division dependent on the size of the *kabupaten*. In many parts of Indonesia, these divisions roughly correspond to traditional administrative units that preceded the modern state and may also follow language and/or ethnic lines. The settlement of Lampuuk is located on the western, or Indian Ocean, side of the province and is composed of five villages, or *meunasah*. These are Meunasah Balee, Meunasah Lambaro, Meunasah Blang, Meunasah Cut, and Meunasah Mesjid. The Turkish Red Crescent built houses in all five villages and also renovated the Lampuuk mosque.

The people of Lampuuk are not certain how many people were in the settlement when the tsunami struck the area. Their estimates range from 5000 to 6000 and reflect the fact that daily activities in the area tend to be fluid, meaning that significant numbers of people may be in one location one day and in another the next, depending on the nature of work to be done that day, or other activities that might be taking place. Immediately following the tsunami, however, residents are reasonably sure of the survivors, who numbered about 400. The population gradually increased in the months and years following the disaster, as former residents of Lampuuk who had been living elsewhere chose to return home. In 2007, the population had reached 1050 people who were occupying 701 new houses.

Because it is located close to the beach, Lampuuk was almost completely destroyed by the tsunami. Only the hill region north of the settlement escaped devastation, because of its elevation. The mosque was spared, however, and became one of the more photographed emblems of the disaster. Once the water receded, many survivors left the settlement to stay in temporary shelters that had begun to appear in other locations. That same day, however, as soon as it was safe, 28 residents returned to Lampuuk. It was these individuals who became the main actors in the reconstruction of the settlement.

This group of 28 was composed of 20 men and eight women, ranging in age from nine to 60. These residents returned to their villages immediately to try to find out what had happened to their family and friends. The bodies of some of the dead were eventually found; others remain missing. The initial 28 returnees built temporary huts using materials they happened to find and decided among themselves that they would do whatever they could to locate the missing and rebuild the village.

The group worked to exhaustion every day and discussed future plans every night. Without realizing it, they made themselves into an operational team that would be central to the eventual reconstruction of the settlement and in the administration of aid in their local environment. There can be no doubt that this response had important psychological benefits for the survivors, and emerged as a spontaneous attempt to normalize an extremely disturbing situation.

Aid arrived in Lampuuk almost immediately and increased by the day. In the first week following the tsunami, the people of Lampuuk were given trucks, tools, building materials and money to build temporary housing. Within a month, the population of the settlement had increased to 100. The remaining survivors stayed in the barracks that had been quickly set up by various aid organizations until permanent housing was available in their villages. The 100 or so residents who returned to the settlement in those early days took an active role in the reconstruction of Lampuuk, under the leadership of the original 28.

The residents of Lampuuk soon realized they would not have to rely on their own devices to rebuild their villages. They heard about the massive relief effort and began to be visited by representatives of the many aid organizations of all kinds that were setting up in Aceh following the tsunami. Some residents felt they should discuss their needs individually with those willing to provide aid, but the group of 28 believed the residents would achieve better results if they negotiated as a group. Their argument was that reconstruction of the settlement would require not just houses but also infrastructure. Roads, water systems, and electrical installations had all been destroyed. Taking the advice of the USAID representative, the group formed the Lampuuk Recovery Center (LRC) some two months after the disaster. The USAID representative explained that they would be better off having a formal organization that would represent them in discussions with aid providers as it would serve as a conduit for the wishes of the survivors as a group, and would allow them to rebuild the whole community together.

Most of the members of the LRC were drawn from the group of 28, but its chairman was a resident who had been visiting Medan, North Sumatra, when the tsunami struck. It should be noted that many people in Aceh are reluctant to have their names used in any public context, because they fear political repercussions relating to the conflict between the central government and the Free Aceh Movement (GAM) from the mid-1970s to

2005. The Aceh conflict persisted into the first stages of the reconstruction, and several Lampuuk residents were killed during this period. Among the first decisions of the LRC was to clear debris from the settlement before attention could be given to rebuilding roads and houses. This, the members felt, would be appropriate for them to do themselves before any aid organizations became involved. It would also assist them in assessing their own needs and determining the best way in which to meet these needs. Members of the LRC felt this would be an opportunity to redesign the settlement, perhaps in a more efficient manner.

Their idea was to build roads such that blocks were created where houses would be built. Prior to the tsunami, the villages had evolved organically, with individuals positioning their houses however they liked on their own land, and roads coming into being wherever people had habitually walked. The new plan, they felt, would require that every resident give up 10 per cent of their land to be used for roadways. Before the tsunami, houses were scattered across the countryside, many with no proper access to main roads. It was this sort of situation that the LRC wanted to avoid through systematic rebuilding.

The LRC faced strong opposition from many of Lampuuk's residents, however. Many did not want to sacrifice land for roads. Interestingly, many of the objectors were former residents of the settlement who had been living elsewhere but who had returned to Lampuuk because their relatives had been killed. They retained strong ties to land that had been in their family for generations, and were unwilling to give it up for the LRC's concept of civic good. Another group that opposed the plan of the LRC was Lampuuk's surviving female residents, who, more than men, believed the value of the land was more important than civic good and that they would be betraying the memory of the dead by giving up land. The LRC used a number of methods to persuade protesters. One of the most effective came from their realization that aid was being offered without any demand for payment and that the many foreign organizations were under no obligation to help them in any way. This being the case, they argued, it was only fitting that residents give something to the reconstruction effort as well. If strangers were willing to help all the residents of the settlement, then the residents themselves should also do something to help their fellow citizens. In this case, that would be to give up land for municipal use. Nonetheless, the LRC also had to resort to threats. They determined that no houses would be built in areas without roads. This was backed up by exemplary action with members of the LRC building dirt roads on their own land and on land owned by the community leaders who supported their ideas. This eventually brought most of the residents around to the view of the LRC.

Nine months after the tsunami, the residents of Lampuuk met with the Turkish Red Crescent for the first time. This meeting was more an accident of fate than an intentional plan. It happened that a woman, who came from Lampuuk, was head of the Banda Aceh City Planning Office at the time. She had official contact with the Turkish Red Crescent as part of her job. At this point, the residents of Lampuuk had already dealt with a number of aid organizations. PT Exindo, an Indonesian technology and consulting firm, had given them Caterpillar earth-moving machinery to clear land and build roads. Mercy Corps, a US-based wide-ranging aid organization, provided tools, trucks for carrying timber and other supplies. They also set up a business start-up programme in the area to allow people to develop new sources of income.

One experience that made an impression on the residents of Lampuuk concerned Habitat for Humanity, a non-profit ecumenical Christian organization that works through local affiliates around the world. Habitat offered Lampuuk prefabricated houses that could be ready for occupation much sooner than traditionally-built homes. The LRC decided to reject this offer, because they felt permanent structures would be more desirable. Their refusal caused some friction within the Lampuuk community because some residents thought it was inappropriate and ungrateful to refuse an offer of houses, when many of them badly needed shelter. The fact that Habitat's houses could be ready in a couple of months was an additional benefit. Members of the LRC, perhaps wary following the tsunami, feared that the prefab units Habitat was offering would not be able to withstand the strong winds that the region experienced annually. This did turn out to be the case, when some houses built by Habitat elsewhere in Lhuk Nga suffered severe damage during the windy season. Residents who had been against the refusal did come to thank the LRC for its stance at a later date, but the initial decision to reject Habitat's offer caused a great deal of bad feeling and embarrassment on the part of residents who had been tempted by the possibility of having a new house as soon as possible.

The LRC's first meeting with the Turkish Red Crescent did not impress members or the residents of Lampuuk. While they liked what they heard from the organization, the LRC was not convinced that it was seriously interested in reconstructing their villages. They visited the organization's offices dozens of times, each time being reassured that their houses would be built but never getting an exact date for the construction to begin. Three months later, there was still no indication that construction was about to commence. At a meeting with the LRC, the residents expressed concern that they might have to pay the Turkish Red Crescent to begin work on their houses, a state of affairs that is familiar to all Indonesians. They began to seriously consider the possibility they had made a mistake trying to work with this organization as, one year after the disaster, no construction had taken place, and they were not even sure the Turkish Red Crescent would do any building in the end.

Finally, early in 2006, an Indonesian consulting firm hired by the Turkish Red Crescent began building a sample house. Now sure they would get their houses, the LRC agreed that the Turkish Red Crescent would have 701 houses built and would also renovate the mosque. When the sample house was finished, the Turkish Red Crescent called for tenders. The job was won by another large construction company based in Jakarta, who would build the houses at a cost of Rp88 million each. It was rumoured at this time that this contractor had subcontracted the construction to several smaller companies, an action that was not covered by their agreement with the Turkish Red Crescent. The residents heard that the subcontractors would be building for Rp66 million per house. Therefore, the contractor was said to be earning Rp22 million per building without doing any work and was free to tender for other business.

Many of the residents of Lampuuk felt cheated and decided to take action. The *Mukim*, the head of the settlement, requested that the LRC take the matter up with the Turkish Red Crescent. When it was confirmed that the contractor had, in fact, subcontracted out the project without its agreement, the organization cancelled the contract. It permitted the contractor to complete the 200 houses that had been started by that time, but did not allow the subcontractors to work on the remaining 501 structures that were to be built. Contracts for these remaining homes were given to other firms. It is interesting to note that these actions were not unusual in the context of the Indonesian construction industry. However, since the end of the Suharto government in 1997, the era of *Reformasi* (Reform) in Indonesia has brought a much greater sensitivity to corruption on the part of the public and, with it, a greater intolerance to activities that would have been routinely accepted a decade ago.

This incident highlights a significant aspect of the participation of the people of Lampuuk in the reconstruction of their villages, that of control. They had gained perspective as well as confidence from their experience with Habitat for Humanity, which gave them the nerve to challenge the contractor's behaviour. They took a chance that the Turkish Red Crescent would take the company's actions seriously, but feel that they succeeded in maintaining the value of their houses in line with what that organization originally offered.

Despite the slow pace at which construction progressed, the residents of Lampuuk were very satisfied with the Turkish Red Crescent's management of the building. The organization allowed, and even encouraged, them to directly present any concerns they had, and continued to invite this kind of input even after the contractors were at work. The residents were also free to influence the design of their houses, as long as they stayed within the budgetary limits that had been set, even if their preferences did not correspond to the organization's recommendations. For example, the Turkish Red Crescent originally suggested that houses be built on stilts, due to the settlement's proximity to the beach and as a precaution in the case of future tsunamis. Lampuuk residents wanted 'modern' houses, a request to which the organization acceded. The residents were also able to choose building materials for their homes, again as long as their preferences were covered by the fund allocation. While the Turkish Red Crescent approved most of what they wanted, tiled floors were ruled out, because they would have brought the cost per unit to well over Rp 88 million.

Ensuring that the contractors built the houses to the specifications they had prescribed was another challenge faced by the Turkish Red Crescent and the LRC. In this as well, the residents were highly satisfied with the actions of the organization. It hired Lampuuk residents as field supervisors and required each contractor to put up a Rp 400 million bond before work began. If the job was not carried out in accordance with the contract, the firms faced significant financial loss. Having been alerted to the possibility of corruption by their previous experience, the residents were on the lookout for any possible repeat. It did happen that inferior concrete was used in some houses, and low quality wood was used for fittings, but the Turkish Red Crescent demanded that the contractors fix the problems at their own expense.

Two years after the tsunami, in April 2007, the Turkish Red Crescent handed over the keys to 701 new houses to the residents of Lampuuk. Those who had been living in temporary accommodation of various kinds were able to return to their villages. With the formation of the LRC and their unprecedented action to take responsibility for their own fate, the residents had shown an unusual unity and solidarity of cause. Despite sometimes serious disagreements, the residents waited until everyone could move into the new houses at the same time, even though some dwellings had been ready much earlier.

In June of 2007, when the last of the author's fieldwork in Lampuuk was conducted, the residents had been in their new homes for about two months. There was a palpable air of excitement and satisfaction in the settlement. Nonetheless, a number of problems had already emerged. Despite the supervisory role the Turkish Red Crescent had given them and their own vigilance, many roofs leaked, doors did not close fully, and paint was peeling. Technically, the contractors were still responsible however, and the Turkish Red Crescent had asked for a list of problems it could take up with them. Some of the residents were ashamed by the defects they found because the donor, the Turkish Red Crescent, was an international organi-zation that had come to Indonesia to help them, while the contractors were all local or national firms, whom they felt should have behaved better. Many were determined to report any problems they encountered, because experi-ence had shown them this was the only way to get such issues addressed. Some, however, did not bother to complete the checklists the Turkish Red Crescent had given them because they were exhausted by the whole process and just wanted to be rid of contractors trying to effect repairs.

Lessons learned in Lampuuk

There has been considerable work on evaluating the effectiveness of tsunami relief efforts in Aceh and elsewhere. These reports, agency brief-ings and scholarly papers agree on a number of points. These include the fact that coordination was perhaps the greatest challenge faced by all involved. The large number of organizations present in the disaster area and the unprecedented level of funds to be disbursed meant greater resources were available but also that logistics tended to be complicated, and lack of coordination was seen as hindering the aid effort in some cases. Pressure felt by NGOs to provide shelter to survivors and to spend money rapidly and in a visible manner has been widely cited. This led, in some cases, to housing being built in remote areas, a lack of infrastructure required to make dwellings habitable, and an oversupply of accommodation in some locations. Also, significant differences in housing quality led to tension and conflict between intended residents, as some organizations offered bigger or more modern dwellings. Additionally, it became apparent that disaster planning and preparedness efforts were almost entirely lacking in the regions affected by the tsunami. This, of course, falls within the sphere of responsibility of national and local governments, but has been taken up by the UN as a concern of the international community (see, for example, Canny, 2005; Schulze, 2005; CPBI, 2006; Takeda and Helms, 2006). Finally, it has been noted that the lessons of the Indian Ocean tsunami do not differ much from what was learned from other disasters in the past. The problem, some suggest, is that little has been done to act on these lessons (CPBI, 2006).

These comments and observations, while important, focus on the larger sphere of organizations and programmes and represent, for the most part, the views of agencies and their interpretations of the perceptions of the recipient public. There are other lessons to be learned, however, from the experience of individuals, who often know little about organizations and processes beyond their immediate environment but who frequently have very clear ideas about what happened to them and how they feel about it. This is the case with the residents of Lampuuk.

From the start, the people of Lampuuk were aware that aid was available, and were quick to take advantage of it. They were also cognisant of the fact that these organizations were under no obligation to help them and that they had some responsibility to help themselves. This response is somewhat different from the condition of gratitude discussed extensively by Korf (2005; 2006; 2007) and others. While the people of Lampuuk did express their gratitude for the assistance they received, they believed they had to 'give back' something to the donors in the form of work on their own behalf. They felt strongly that they had to show initiative in order to earn the confidence of potential donors.

After some initial hesitation, the residents, through the LRC, realized they had the ability to pick and choose among potential donors and that they were not bound to accept anything offered, if it was not what they wanted or felt they needed. Again, this is a manifestation of their willingness to take on part of the responsibility for their own fate but also a result of their growing confidence. Not surprisingly, their willingness to deal directly with aid organizations and express their views grew as reconstruction progressed. This is somewhat unusual in the Indonesian context, where individuals tend to avoid confrontation, especially with authority. Foreign organizations and individuals certainly fall into the category of authority, and Westerners who have worked in Indonesia often comment on the outwardly passive and accepting behaviour they encounter, only to find that the individuals they deal with rebel behind their backs and refuse to do what they agreed to.

Corruption is endemic in Indonesia, and it is not surprising that the residents of Lampuuk encountered it during the reconstruction of their villages. While it has always been part of business and official dealings in Indonesia, *Reformasi* has made it much more acceptable to report or complain about corrupt behaviour of individuals or companies. This is likely the reason the people of Lampuuk felt they could bring the actions of the house building contractor to the attention of the Turkish Red Crescent. In the experience of many Indonesians, it would have been more natural to simply accept that the company would skim funds intended for home construction, and they would end up with inferior dwellings. This is usual practice in Indonesia (PwC, 2005), and, in fact, the Asian Development Bank and the OECD held a major international meeting on corruption in the tsunami relief effort in Jakarta in 2005 as part of their Anti-Corruption Initiative for Asia and the Pacific.

Additionally, there can be no doubt that the high level of involvement in reconstruction experienced by the residents of Lampuuk helped them to deal with the devastation and loss caused by the tsunami. They had been helpless to prevent or escape the tsunami but felt that at least they could do something towards their recovery from it. This provided a kind of psychological diversion, especially in the early days following the disaster that helped them to recover emotionally and feel that they were making progress towards a normal life. This process was exhausting, as many residents report, and it is likely that true psychological healing will take many years. Nonetheless, they were able to weather the first months and years following the tsunami in a state of activity that provided an occupation and allowed time to distance them from the disaster.

A possible model of interaction between aid donors and recipients

There are three stages that follow any disaster, and the Indian Ocean tsunami was no exception. The role of aid donors will be different in each of these phases, whose nature must be considered carefully if the desired results are to be achieved. The first stage following any disaster is the period of emergency. During this time, issues of life and death are most pressing, and the main priority must be to locate and treat survivors. It is also necessary to locate the dead if possible, as this is usually of great importance to those who have survived. In the case of the tsunami, as noted, there were relatively few injured, many dead, and survivors tended to be comparatively well.

The second stage is reconstruction and rehabilitation. This includes the physical aspects of the environment, such as roads, buildings, infrastructure, and so forth, but also the activities of daily life. Survivors need a way to make a living, educational opportunities, forums for religious and cultural expression and also emotional sustenance. While it is fairly straightforward to determine what the physical needs of a community might be following a disaster, it is much more difficult, even for the survivors, to know how to replace the more intangible losses they have suffered.

The third stage involves evaluation and verification of the results of reconstruction and rehabilitation. Completed work may not meet the required standards. Reconstruction may be incomplete. It may, for a number of reasons, be impossible for survivors to return to something resembling normal life because certain of their needs were overlooked. Evaluation is difficult and may be omitted by donors. This may be the reason some contractors feel that misappropriation and the cutting of corners will not be noticed. When evaluation is carried out, it often focuses on easily enumerable aspects of rebuilding, such as number of houses, schools and clinics built, miles of roadway opened, and so forth. Emotional and lifestyle rehabilitation may be ignored because they are not straightforward to evaluate.

The model of interaction proposed here will focus on the second and third stage of reconstruction. What is required in the first stage of response following a disaster will depend on the nature of the event and often requires medical and emergency care. This is a highly specialized area of aid that is typically provided by organizations that focus on this area, such as the International Medical Corps and Doctors Without Borders, often in conjunction with the International Red Cross/International Red Crescent and other agencies.

An important element of Lampuuk's experience came into existence by chance. The formation of the LRC was a result of advice received by the community from outside, but the existence of this group allowed the resident, to interact more effectively with potential donors. The LRC was set up before the Turkish Red Crescent appeared on the scene and even before the residents knew that they would be receiving foreign aid. The formalization of the group took place when the original group of 28 survivors decided to take charge of the reconstruction effort themselves.

The LRC was instrumental in working with the Turkish Red Crescent to convey the views and wishes of the residents of Lampuuk. It also presented the settlement's refusal to Habitats for Humanity. Without the LRC to present an impersonal but united front, it is highly likely that some residents would have accepted Habitat's offer. The houses it offered would likely have proven inappropriate for Lampuuk, as they did in other locations in the region, but acceptance of the offer would have split the residents and might well have led to long-term problems and factionalism in the settlement. The LRC also offered residents a forum for community debate about what course of action should be taken at various points in the reconstruction effort. Individuals found it easier to set aside their own emotions and consider the issues logically in the context of a group than they might have otherwise. The setting-up and functioning of the LRC itself represented an attempt to return to normalcy as members took care to run the organization in the way such bodies normally had been before the tsunami. This, in turn, made it possible for them to interact effectively with aid providers and to present their views in a measured and unemotional manner.

This strongly suggests that recipient participation is a key factor in effective donor–recipient interaction, and this is the first lesson to be learned from the experience of Lampuuk. Aid will be much more effective if the intended recipients can be involved at every stage of its provision. This may present a problem in Indonesia, in particular, where it has been noted that aid is most often distributed using broker organizations. These brokers are often NGOs that jockey for relationships with international donor organizations. While it is possible to consider the LRC to be an NGO of sorts, it is notable in that it was formed entirely of Lampuuk residents who survived the tsunami and who had a vested interest in the reconstruction of the region. They did not stand to make a profit, as many Indonesian NGO staff do, nor was membership of the LRC their job. The direct involvement of the aid recipients in this manner ensures that the most pressing needs of the community are addressed and that its desires are at least known to the donor. These requirements and preferences may be obscured when a donor goes through a broker organization that may not be aware of or sensitive to the recipients' condition. Ideally, the donor would encourage the formation of a local organization representing residents of a disaster area and indicate that it will work through this organization in the disbursement of aid.

A second lesson from Lampuuk concerns the importance of eliminating any obstacles to participation in the aid process that may be faced by potential recipients. In practice, many of these hindrances may be emotional. This was the case in Lampuuk, where residents felt it was shameful, rude, or inappropriate for them to reject aid that was freely offered. Others felt that it was not right for them to ask for anything, even when they had clear preferences about the design of housing, the materials to be used and so forth. Ideally, recipients should feel that their input is important and any sort of comment will be accepted by the donor. Again, this is an issue where the participation of a broker organization may be detrimental, as in Indonesia, in any case, these brokers often have their own agenda beyond reconstruction of the disaster-affected area. Organizational structure and hierarchy may also become an impediment to reconstruction if recipients feel they do not have access to those in decision-making positions. The residents of Lampuuk, for example, stressed over and over again how significant it was that they were encouraged to take their concerns directly to the Turkish Red Crescent, even after contractors had begun to work.

A third lesson from the reconstruction of Lampuuk is that a method for recipient participation should be established before any aid is made available. In Lampuuk, this began with the group of 28 and continued with the formation and formalization of the LRC. Representing the whole community, the LRC eliminated a need for individuals to interact directly on their own behalf with the donor and allowed difficult decisions to be presented through an anonymous front representing everyone involved. This was very important because most Indonesians avoid confrontation and have great difficulty conveying bad news, especially to an authority figure. Additionally, if individuals had had to negotiate for themselves, the inevitable result would have been a range of quality and designs of houses, which likely would have led to conflict within the community. This sort of thing was observed elsewhere in Aceh, where a great deal of bad feeling was generated when some residents were perceived by others to have received superior dwellings. The appointment of Lampuuk residents as field supervisors also turned out to be an effective mechanism for participation, although the Turkish Red Crescent remained responsible for presenting any complaints or problems to the builders. In other words, the residents were given the authority to oversee construction but were not required to take on the difficult role of challenging the contractors. As the provider of funds for the project, the Turkish Red Cross acted as the ultimate supervisor of work, which was no doubt the most effective way this could have been managed in this case. The builders likely felt compelled to comply with instructions from the donor, where they might have ignored complaints from the residents. These contractors were large local and national firms who might have felt able to steamroll the residents, but would not attempt this with an international donor, especially as the Turkish Red Crescent had demanded they post a bond.

The experience of Lampuuk suggests a fourth lesson, that donors should participate in the disbursement of aid, even when work to be done is undertaken by contractors or other organizations. In Lampuuk, this was clearly important in the success of the rebuilding. As described, the Turkish Red Crescent was instrumental in dispute resolution and in management of the tender process. Donors naturally have an interest in seeing that the funds they provide are properly used, but, unlike recipients, are capable of exerting control over contractors and organizations they have hired to do work. Direct participation, even if a broker organization is used as well, also allows a donor to take financial responsibility for aid disbursed, which is itself a legal requirement as well as a moral obligation to those who have made charitable contributions to its cause.

The fifth lesson learned in Lampuuk is that the layers of administration required for aid disbursement should be as few as possible. In this case, there were three: the donor organization, the contractors who delivered required services, and the recipients. In some cases, it may be practical for the donor organization to deliver aid itself. If not, however, it is vital to minimize the number of middlemen and separate organizations that distance it from the recipients. Each additional layer may add cost, time, and confusion and might contribute to outcomes diverging significantly from what was intended. Further, each additional layer of administration makes it more difficult for the donor to control what is going on in the field. This would have been the case in Lampuuk if the housing contractor had been permitted to use a number of subcontractors who would have had no contact with the Turkish Red Crescent. From the point of view of recipients as well, fewer layers of administration are better. As the party with fewest resources, recipients benefit from closer contact with the donor and, as in

Lampuuk, may be more confident in expressing their concerns to the aid provider than to members of a local organization or to contractors.

The final lesson from Lampuuk is that the aid donor must take a continuing responsibility for reconstruction work for a reasonable period after that work is completed. In Lampuuk, defects were noted in the completed houses commissioned by the Turkish Red Crescent. That organization had contracted with builders to provide homes of specified quality that would pass inspection upon occupation. This certification would have to take place before the contractors' bond could be released, and the donor undertook to ensure the end quality of the dwellings. Without this assurance, even though some residents chose not to pursue it, recipients would have no means to call builders on their actions and get repairs made. This kind of accountability is unusual in Indonesia, even under normal circumstances. It provided a level of reassurance to residents that is usually absent, even when consumers pay for housing or other services. Nonetheless, aid donors often forgo precautions of this kind once they have discharged their basic responsibility, as there may be little inducement for them to remain involved once the emergency has passed.

The Indian Ocean tsunami was a disaster of unusual magnitude that led to extreme conditions under which reconstruction had to occur. The specific cultural conditions of Aceh and Indonesia contributed to the way in which reconstruction took place and in which aid was disbursed. Nonetheless, there are undoubtedly similarities between this situation and others that have been experienced, and will be experienced in the future, in other locations around the world. While there are aspects of each disaster that are unique, there are many lessons and issues in common. Due to the magnitude and extent of the Indian Ocean tsunami, many of these have now been discussed in the literature and will figure in the future planning of international agencies and governments alike. This profile of the experience of the Lampuuk settlement and its residents, it is hoped, will add to our understanding of the mechanisms of international aid and provide useful insight into the perceptions and views of the recipients themselves.

References

ActionAid (2006) *Tsunami Response: A Human Rights Assessment*, London, ActionAid

Adam, C. and O'Connell, S. (1999) 'Aid, Taxation, and Development in Sub-Saharan Africa', *Economics and Politics*, vol 11, no 3, pp225–253

Afrida, N. (2005) 'Acehnese Women lead the Way Home', IPS Asia-Pacific, www.ipsnewsasia.net/writingpeace/features/indonesia2.html

Asian Development Bank (1999) *A Study of NGOs in Asia*, Manila, ADB

Aspinall, E. (2005) 'Indonesia After the Tsunami', *Current History*, vol 104, no 680, pp105–109

Balderas, V. (2006) 'New Song on Volunteerism and Tsunami Released', World Vounteer Web, www.worldvolunteerweb.org/browse/volunteering-issues/volunteering-advocacy/doc/new-song-on-volunteerism.html

Barnett, C. (2005) 'Ways of Relating: Hospitality and the Acknowledgement of Otherness', *Progress in Human Geography*, vol 29, no 1, pp5–21

Blumenthal, S. (2005) 'The Neocons Have a Hand in Aceh, Too', *The Guardian*, 6 January

Burnell, P. and Morrissey, O. (2004) *Foreign Aid in the New Global Economy*, Cheltenham, UK and Northampton, MA, Edward Elgar Publishing

Burnside, C. and Dollar, D. (2000) 'Aid Policies, and Growth', *American Economic Review*, vol 90, no 4, pp847–868

Burnside, C. and Dollar, D. (2004) 'Aid, Policies, and Growth: Revisiting the Evidence', *Policy Research Working Paper No 3251*, World Bank, Washington, DC

Canny, B (2005) *A Review of NGO Coordination in Aceh Post Earthquake/Tsunami: A Report Sponsored by the International Council of Voluntary Agencies*, Geneva, ICVA

Clark, N. (2005) 'Disaster and Generosity', *Geographical Journal*, vol 171, pp284–386

Clinton Presidential Center (2005) 'Presidents Visit Tsunami-Affected Area', www.clintonpresidentialcenter.org/02005-nr-cf-ee-tsu-idn-fe-presidents-tour-tsunami-zone-indonesia.htm

Cosgrave, J. (2006) *Tsunami Evaluation Coalition: Initial Findings*, London, Tsunami Evaluation Coalition

Centre for Peace Building International (2006) Lessons of Recovery Assistance after the 2004 Tsunami: Summary Report from International Symposium, May 5, www.cpbintl.org/Documents/TsunamiSymposiumSummaryMay06CPBI-AU.pdf

Cordella, T. and Dell'Ariccia, G. (2002) 'Limits of Conditionality in Poverty Reduction Programs', *IMF Working Paper No 02/115*, Washington, DC, International Monetary Fund

Cordella, T. and Dell'Aricchia, G. (2003) 'Budget Support versus Project Aid', *IMF Working Paper 03/88*, Washington, DC, International Monetary Fund

The Diplomad (2005) 'The USA responds, and the UN?' http://diplomadic.blogspot.com/2005/01/usa-responds-and-un.html

Diprose, R. (2002) *Corporeal Generosity: on Giving with Nietzsche, Merleau-Ponty, and Levinas*, Albany, NY, SUNY Press

Dollar, D. (2003) 'Eyes Wide Open: On the Targeted Use of Foreign Aid', *Harvard International Review*, vol 25, no 1, pp48–53

Dollar, D. and Svensson, J. (2000) 'What Explains the Success or Failure of Structural Adjustment Programmes?' *Economic Journal*, vol 110, no 466, pp894–917

Edwards, M. and Hulme, D. (1996) 'Too Close for Comfort? The Impact of Official Aid on Nongovernmental Organizations,' *World Development*, vol 24, no 6, pp961–973

Eye on Aceh (2006) *People's Agenda? Post-Tsunami Aid in Aceh*, Eye on Aceh/Aid Watch, www.acheh-eye.org/data_files/english_format/ngo/ngo_eoa/ngo_eoa_2006_02_00.pdf

Goodman, P. S. (2005) 'Tsunami's Unpredictable Outcome: Few injuries', *Washington Post*, 3 February

Howitt, R. (2002) 'Scale and the Other: Levinas and Geography', *Geoforum*, vol 33, pp299–313

Korf, B. (2005) 'Sri Lanka: The Tsunami After the Tsunami', *International Development Planning Review*, vol 27, no 3, ppi-vii

Korf, B. (2006) 'Disaster, Generosity, and the Other', *Geographical Journal*, vol 172, pp245–247

Korf, B. (2007) 'Antinomies of Generosity: Moral Geographies and Post-Tsunami Aid in Southeast Asia', *Geoforum*, vol 38, pp366–378

Lipscombe, B. (2005) 'Aceh Village Still Split by Tsunami', BBC News, http://news.bbc.co.uk/2/hi/asia-pacific/4123678.stm

Lounela, A. (2001) 'Indonesia: Abundant Foreign "Democritisation" Money has Corrupted the NGO Movement', *KEPA Newsletter*, http://teksti.kepa.fi/international/english/information/newsletter/2030/?searchterm=None

Meyer, C. (1992) 'A Step Back as Donors Shift Institution Building from the Public to the "Private" Sector', *World Development*, vol 20, no 8, pp1115–1126

Muslim Aid (2005) 'Aceh Tsunami Survivors Still in Uncertainty', http://www.muslimaid.org/subpages.php?section=news&sub=currentaffairs&down=yes&id=168

Nanthikesan, S. (2005) 'Post Tsunami Posturing', *Lines Magazine*, vol 3, no 4, www.lines-magazine.org/Art_Feb05/Editorial_Nanthi.htm

Novib (2005) *The Tsunami's Impact on Women*, Oxfam International Briefing, The Hague, Novib

Paul, E. (2006) 'A Survey of the Theoretical Economic Literature on Foreign Aid,' *Asian-Pacific Economic Literature*, vol 20, no 1, pp1–17

Popke, E. J. (2003) 'Poststructuralist Ethics: Subjectivity, Responsibility and the Space of Community', *Progress in Human Geography*, vol 27, no 3, pp298–316

Post, U. (2006) 'Attention Deficit: Disasters and the Media', *Magazine for Development and Cooperation*, vol 46 no 1) www.inwent.org/E+Z/content/Archive-eng/index.html/

Pricewaterhouse Coopers (2005) *Economic Crime in the Construction Industry*, London, PWC

Schulze, K. (2005) *Between Conflict and Peace: Tsunami Aid and Reconstruction in Aceh*, London, London School of Economics

Situngkir, H. (2003) *Moneyscape: The Generic Agent-Based Model of Corruption*, Working Paper, Bandung, Bandung Fe Institute

Situngkir, H. and Siagian, R. (2004) *NGOs and Foreign Donations*, Working Paper, Bandung, Bandung Fe Institute

Svensson, J. (1999) 'Aid, Growth, and Democracy', *Economics and Politics*, vol 11, no 3, pp275–297

Takeda, M. B. and Helms, M. M. (2006) 'Bureaucracy Meet Catastrophe: Analysis of the Tsunami Disaster Relief Efforts and their Implications for Global Emergency Governance', *International Journal of Public Sector Management*, vol 19, no 2, pp204–217

Tarrant, B. (2005) 'Be It So Humble, Tsunami Survivors Long for Home', Reuters, 3 November

Telford, J. et al (2006) *Joint Evaluation of the International Response to the Indian Ocean Tsunami: Synthesis Report*, London, Tsunami Evaluation Coalition

Thorbecke, E. (2000) 'The Evolution of the Development Doctrine and the Role of Foreign Aid', in Tarp, F. and Hjertholm, P., eds *Foreign Aid and Development –*

Lessons Learnt and Directions for the Future, London and New York, Routledge, pp17–47

Till, F. (2005) 'Tsunami – Delivering Aid Stymies UN,' *The National Business Review*, 4 January

US Geological Survey (2005) *Tsunamis and Earthquakes: Gallery of Northwestern Sumatra*, http://walrus.wr.usgs.gov/tsunami/sumatra05/Lampuuk.html

USAID (2004) *USAID Strategic Plan for Indonesia 2004–2008: Strengthening a Moderate, Stable, and Productive Indonesia*, Washington, DC, USAID

Vivian, J. (1994) 'NGOs and Sustainable Development in Zimbabwe: No Magic Bullets,' *Development and Change*, vol 25, pp181–209

World Bank (1994) *Governance: The World Bank's Experience*, Washington, DC, World Bank

World Bank (1998) *Assessing Aid: What Works, What Doesn't, and Why?* Policy Research Report, New York, Oxford University Press

Young, I. M. (1997) *Intersecting Voices*, Princeton, NJ, Princeton University Press

Village Government in Aceh, Three Years after the Tsunami*

Craig Thorburn

Introduction

The Memorandum of Understanding signed between the government of Indonesia and the Free Aceh Movement (*Gerakan Aceh Merdeka* – GAM) in August 2005 was, if not entirely an outcome of, at least in part due to the impact of the Boxing Day 2004 tsunami. The MoU and subsequent Law on the Governing of Aceh[1] ended 29 years of separatist conflict and what was in effect an administration of occupation, with all the abrogation of civil and political rights this implies. Damien Kingsbury (this volume, Chapter 3) explains that the tsunami 'swept away much of the pre-existing political infrastructure in Aceh, and allowed the reconstruction of a new political framework' that 'better reflects the political aspirations of the people of Aceh as well as better corresponds with normative political values around representation, participation, accountability and transparency'. This chapter focuses on one particular aspect of Aceh's post-tsunami political regeneration: the rebuilding of village government in tsunami-affected areas. It is based on research conducted in 18 villages on Aceh's west coast in 2007, when the tsunami recovery effort had been under way for nearly three years.

Given the rather narrow geographic and temporal focus of this research, a number of caveats are in order regarding the extent to which many of these findings can be extrapolated to the broader Aceh context. First, the 'sweeping clean' in many of these villages was quite literal, with some communities forced to rebuild village government structures virtually from scratch. This is not the case, of course, in villages throughout most areas of the province not ravaged by the tsunami. Second, the massive tsunami recovery effort has created a unique 'institutional hothouse' with unusually high levels of capacity-building inputs, numerous 'imported' procedures and norms, and distinct constellations of incentives and rewards that again, largely do not pertain in villages throughout the remainder of the Acehnese hinterland. As well, the processes discussed in this chapter have only been under way for a short time, and thus should not be inferred as representing 'trends'. The extent to which they represent opportunistic responses to the particular context of the 'aid tsunami', and how deeply they will imbed in Acehnese society, can only be known with the passage of time.

The Aceh Community Assistance Research Project (ACARP)

The Aceh Community Assistance Research Project was a multi-donor supported qualitative social research project, aimed at identifying and better understanding the factors that supported or constrained recovery and redevelopment in communities in Aceh in the wake of the Boxing Day 2004 earthquake and tsunami. Field research was undertaken by a group of 27 Acehnese social researchers, led by a team of senior researchers from the provincial capital of Banda Aceh and from Jakarta and Australia. It took place over a three-month period between July and September 2006 in 18 tsunami-affected villages in the districts of Aceh Barat, Aceh Jaya and Aceh Besar.

The objectives of ACARP were to identify key organic and external factors that have influenced the success of communities in rebuilding their lives; to study the factors and conditions that contributed to the re-establishment and successful engagement of local community capabilities in the wake of major upheaval from natural disaster and conflict; to document and analyse the interaction between communities and external agencies in the reconstruction and recovery process, highlighting community perceptions of progress, constraints and the value of external assistance; and to train a group of Acehnese researchers in sound social research methods and build momentum for continuing social research initiatives and evaluative projects in Aceh.

Teams of three researchers spent a total of four weeks in nine 'matched pairs' of villages from sub-districts within the study districts. In each pair, one village was apparently recovering better than its counterpart, allowing for some comparative analysis. The researchers accrued a large quantity of data, including 533 household questionnaires, 298 interview transcripts, 54 focus group discussion transcripts and 87 case studies and family histories. Research teams also prepared village profile documents for each of the 18 villages, following a standard format. The project collected plans, reports and other forms of secondary data from donors, NGOs, national and provincial government agencies and the international and Indonesian media. The main part of the ACARP report focuses on village governance, particularly leadership, decision-making and problem-solving, transparency and accountability; women's participation; and social capital. The report also includes shorter sections on livelihoods and economic recovery and development and on housing and infrastructure.[2] Each village has its own story to tell, with specific composites of assets and constraints, achievements and frustrations. The analysis focuses both on the distinctions and diversity, as well as the commonalities between communities' experiences.

A final report from the research project, entitled *The Acehnese Gampong, Three Years On: Assessing Local Capacity and Reconstruction Assistance in Post-Tsunami Aceh*,[3] was published in Jakarta by AusAID in December 2007, and disseminated through a series of workshops and seminars in the three districts where the research took place, the provincial capital Banda Aceh and Jakarta. This chapter presents an overview of the ACARP report's findings on village governance.

Not surprisingly, leadership emerged as the key determining factor differentiating more successful from less successful village recovery, and this chapter begins with a discussion of findings related to leaders and leadership styles. This is followed by consideration of decision-making and problem-solving at the household and village community levels, then shorter sections on issues of transparency and accountability, women's participation and gender equality, and social capital.

The main findings discussed below derive largely from questionnaire data, which was then verified, supplemented and illustrated using interview and focus group transcripts, and the observations of research team members. The questionnaire itself employed a variety of different types of questions, primarily multiple-choice or open-ended. While this allowed for a richer collection of responses, it confounds neat statistical analysis. Responses for many of the questions were first sorted by frequency, then recoded into three columns: a) respondent's first response, b) respondent selected this as one of his/her responses, though not first, and c) respondent did not select this answer. This reclassification allowed for some simple tests for correlation with responses to other questions, using chi-square distributions. The more interesting correlations, however, are at the village level. Village-level analyses were performed manually (or visually), by ranking villages by frequency of positive or negative responses to particular questions, then comparing these rankings with how the villages ranked on other subjects. This proved a simple but effective means of identifying relationships between particular parameters, which were then explored further through in-depth analysis of transcript and observation data.

Findings and discussion

Leadership

Village Heads in Aceh are called *Keucik*, or *Geucik*. Many popular, media and donor descriptions give the impression of the *Keucik* as the wise and trusted keystone of Acehnese village society. According to prominent Acehnese scholar Syafii Ibrahim (2006), authority in Aceh derives from a variety of sources, including supernatural and spiritual powers (*kesaktian*), heredity (*keturunan*), knowledge (*ilmu*), and a combination of personal characteristics, including wise and just (*adil dan jujur*), courageous and decisive (*berani dan tegas*), generous (*dermawan*), kind and hospitable (*ramah tamah*). While popular imaginations envision a *Keucik* as protecting and upholding the interests of his community, historically, *Keucik* have acted as the agents of higher authorities (originally *Datuk* and *Uleebalang*, and more recently, district and national government).[4] Historically, the *Keucik*'s decision-making power was moderated by a permanent council of elders (*cerdik pandai*), known as the *Tuhapeut*. The *Tuhapeut* was independent of the *Keucik*, and functioned as the primary deliberative body in the village, that would make decisions then hand them over to the *Keucik* for consideration. The *Keucik* did not have power to change the membership of the *Tuhapeut*, and the balance of power rested with this council.

The office of *Keucik* has undergone numerous transformations over the past several decades. Beginning in the 1980s, with the implementation of the New Order government's Law on Village Government, the office of Village Head was incorporated into the national government structure. *Keucik* were directly responsible to the head of the sub-district government (*Camat*). These reforms also saw the important office of *Imum Mukim* in Aceh reduced to a largely symbolic role, while the *Tuhapeut* was replaced by a Village Assembly (*Lembaga Musyawarah Desa* or LMD) and Village Community Resilience Council (*Lembaga Ketahanan Masyarakat Desa* or LKMD), both under the leadership of the *Keucik*. The increased executive power of the *Keucik* was accompanied by a diminished role for village elders in deciding village affairs, and an increasing separation of powers between state authority and customary and/or religious authority (McCarthy, 2000).

During the conflict years, *Keucik* often found themselves targets of suspicion and intimidation by both Indonesian military and police and GAM forces. Precise figures of the number of *Keucik* killed or injured during the conflict are not available; however, in one instance during the height of the conflict, 76 *Keucik* from the district of Bireuen resigned en masse, stating that they were incapable of protecting themselves or their communities, much less of carrying out the duties of governing the village (Sinar Harapan,

2003). Scores more sought refuge in towns and cities, including one sub-district centre in this study. Under these conditions, it is easy to understand why individuals possessing the attributes described by Ibrahim above would choose not to hold the office of *Keucik*.

Further compounding the situation, local government in Aceh was seriously under-resourced in the years leading up to the tsunami. In many villages, 'government' consisted of the *Keucik*, and little more. In some more spatially dispersed villages, Neighbourhood Heads (*Kadus*) were more instrumental than the *Keucik* in assisting villagers with administrative affairs, with the *Keucik* functioning more as one of several *Kadus*, serving his own hamlet. Some more complete village governments included a few Section Heads (*Kaur*), for social and economic affairs and village administration. *Kadus* often served as *Kaur*, the rationale often being that *Kaur* were entitled to a stipend while *Kadus* were not. When the tsunami struck, these enfeebled institutions were ill-equipped to cope with the needs of their shattered communities – that is, if the officeholders survived the catastrophe.

In seven of the 18 villages surveyed in this study, the village *Keucik* was among the victims of the tsunami. Six more villages experienced the loss of one or more other key member of village government. Only five of the 18 communities came through with their entire village government structures intact. In the months following the tsunami, two more *Keucik* were unable to serve due to health reasons, and another two married outside their community, and took up residence in the villages of their new wives.

Temporary acting *Keucik* were appointed in the villages that had lost their leader. Sometimes, these were individuals who had shown leadership qualities during the initial days and weeks of the emergency, in other cases, surviving civil servants or teachers from the community were appointed – thus becoming 'part-time *Keucik*'. At the time of the research, direct elections had been held in many of the villages, and preparations were under way in several more.

Keucik in different villages in the study exhibited a variety of different leadership styles, and possessed varying levels of skill and ability. Some were sole leaders, others worked well with other members of village government and the community. Some were authoritarian and tolerated no dissent, others more inclusive and open to collaborative decision-making processes. A few, particularly those who were government employees appointed as temporary *Keucik*, were technocratic in their leadership style. Some were quite cunning and covert in their dealings with donors and government (and their own constituents), while others adopted open, transparent management and accounting styles. In a few villages, rumours of misallocation, nepotism, embezzlement and profiteering were rife, while most communities in this

Table I Keucik *most trusted*

	1st response	*Any response*
Total Overall	52%	66%
High Village Score[5]	97%	97%
Low Village Score	0%	0%
Median Village Score	45%	74%
Mean Village Score	51%	65%

survey gave their *Keucik* good marks for just and honest handling of aid resources.

A majority of questionnaire respondents listed the *Keucik* as the person most trusted in their community. 52 per cent of respondents selected the *Keucik* as their first response to the question 'who is most trusted in your community?'. The figure was as high as 97 per cent in one village, and zero in another. Respondents were allowed to list as many as five individuals in response to this question. 66 per cent included *Keucik* as one of their responses. Again, figures per village ranged from 97 to zero per cent.

Other figures who ranked highly in responses to the question of who is most trusted were the *Teungku Imum*,[6] *Teuhapeut* (see above), Village Secretary, and NGO or donor Village Facilitator. The *Teungku Imum* was more trusted than the *Keucik* in three of the 18 survey villages, while the Village Secretary ranked highest in one.

The *Keucik* scored slightly lower in response to a related question about who provides the most useful service in the community, though still rated highest overall. Other figures listed were similar to the question of who is most trusted, although the Village Facilitator moved up in rank ahead of the Village Secretary. *Keucik* also rank highest on the list of trusted and reliable

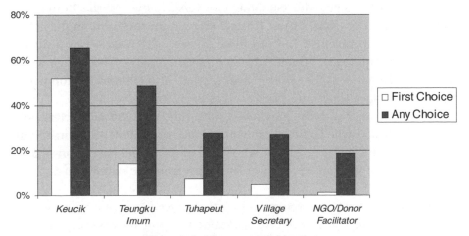

Figure I Most trusted leaders

Table 2 Keucik *solves problems*

	I st response	Any response
Total Overall	5%	23%
High Village Score	17%	84%
Low Village Score	0%	3%
Median Village Score	3%	20%
Mean Village Score	5%	23%

sources of information in the survey villages, with over 70 per cent of respondents listing the *Keucik* as their primary source of information. This was true before the tsunami as well.

The results of simple chi-square tests suggest a strong correlation between villagers' trust in the *Keucik* and certain other parameters, including a high frequency of village meetings (once per month or more), village meetings and consensus as a primary means of solving problems (in response to a question about how problems are addressed in the village), and generally high levels of trust within the community. Significantly, there is no such positive relationship between trust in the *Keucik* and 'the *Keucik* solves problems' as a response to the problem-solving question.

Ranking villages by frequency of the response 'the Keucik solves problems', while not a direct reversal of the previous ranking of '*Keucik* most trusted', produced a significant shift. When split into thirds (high, medium, low), three of the top six ranking villages for '*Keucik* most trusted' fell into the bottom third on the list of villages where the '*Keucik* solves problems', while only two remained in the top six. These latter two cases can be explained. In the first case, most villagers viewed the recent election of a new *Keucik* as the solution to their problems, while in the second, the *Keucik* was widely regarded to be a 'hero' who was responsible for turning that village's fortunes around since the tsunami. Conversely, two of the bottom six ranked villages for '*Keucik* most trusted' were in the top third on the list for '*Keucik* solves problems'. In both these villages, the *Keucik* was a district government employee, appointed as temporary *Keucik*. The village with a score of zero per cent for '*Keucik* most trusted' also fell into the top half of the list of villages where the *Keucik* solves problems.

Taken together with the previous results, this demonstrates a clear preference for *Keucik* who facilitate, rather than take control of, problem-solving processes in the village. *Keucik* who had adopted inclusive, consultative management styles gained much greater trust from the community.

Since we elected our young leaders, the village has been developing rapidly. They have been very successful acquiring the assistance we need. We are proud of them. Although still quite young, they are very responsible. Also, they value the ideas and opinions of the elders in the village. If there's a new initiative or aid programme, they always consult with the old people, and with the community. Everybody knows what's going on. (Khadidja, Focus Group DS-01, Darussalam)[7]

Two other factors that differentiated recovery outcomes were first, the depth and breadth of leadership within the community, and second, whether or not there were competing factions within the village leadership. While the former was often severely depleted by tsunami losses, in ten of 18 survey villages, multiple leaders survived, or new leaders emerged as the community began rebuilding. Those villages where a core group of leaders worked together well had clearly fared better than those with sole leaders. Co-leaders who played important roles in survey villages included the Village Secretary, Village Youth Leader (*Katua Pemuda*), *Teungku Imum* and other respected religious figures, NGO or donor-supported Village Facilitators, and a few village development cadre recruited and trained by NGOs or donors. In two of the villages, reintegrated GAM commanders and combatants had taken key leadership roles in the reconstituted village government. In three survey villages, customary (*adat*) functionaries and institutions – i.e., *Panglima Laut*[8] and *Keujreun Blang*[9] –played active roles in reassembling communities and accessing and distributing aid. In both these latter cases, communities exhibited greater cohesiveness, and less conflict or complaints over management and distribution of aid resources.

Most of the new *Tuhapeut* councils established since the promulgation of new provincial and district *Qanun*[10] on village government were still nascent; few had moved beyond the stage of forming committees to oversee direct *Keucik* elections. There is some concern that this traditional institution that once performed as a deliberative council of village elders – *cerdik pandai* – is to be transformed into a modern-day village legislature, and might sacrifice some of its authority and legitimacy as a result. Many people drew parallels between the *Tuhapeut* and the LKMD Village Community Resilience Council, a much maligned relic of the New Order period.

In some villages, factionalism plagued the recovery and reconstruction process. In three of the 18 survey villages, particular neighbourhoods (*dusun*) felt discriminated or left behind in the recovery process, and there was persistent discussion of splitting off and forming new village governments of their own. In each of these cases, these sentiments existed before the tsunami, though in two of these, divisions had been exacerbated by events since the tsunami. In the third, the recent direct *Keucik* election had led to some reconciliation between the factions, and greater inclusion of the previously disaffected *dusun* in village government and in aid allocation decisions. In other villages, the split was more personal, with different leaders vying for supremacy – and resources. The 'aid tsunami' of the previous three years provided fertile ground for these sorts of rivalries to flourish. This situation was more common in villages with authoritarian, non-inclusive *Keucik*, where a figure such as the Village Secretary or a particular Section or *Dusun* Head provided an alternative, often more sympathetic channel for villagers' hopes and grievances.

> *The Village Secretary resigned about a month ago. He could no longer see eye-to-eye with Pak Keucik. The Keucik no longer thinks about the people's needs, he's just looking after his own interests. The Secretary wrote so many proposals to donors, but they all just ended up on the Keucik's desk, because they were for the community. (M. Nasir, Interview BL-06, Bladeh)*

Direct elections for *Keucik* allowed several communities to transcend these schisms, and create a more united leadership structure. Direct *Keucik* elections had already been held in ten of the 18 survey villages, with preparations under way at the time of the research in five more. Of the ten elections, two were hotly contested and somewhat divisive, two were easily won by authoritarian (and disrespected) *Keucik* known for their intolerance of any challenge to their leadership (in both these cases, the elections were tainted by rumours of 'money politics'), while in the remainder of villages, the elections were congenial and harmonious, with a popular candidate winning by a large majority. In each of these latter cases, the election served as an effective community- and consensus-building experience, and led to a general strengthening of village government institutions, and an acceleration of recovery and development in the villages.

Decision-making and problem-solving

Questions about decision-making and problem-solving at the household and village level offered some interesting insights. Again, Aceh's specific historical context – particularly the last three decades of conflict and privation – inform how things are done in villages. On the one hand, communities were forced to be highly self-reliant, while on the other hand, the incomplete village government reforms of the New Order period, in combination with heavy surveillance and intimidation by security forces, led to the undermining of many customary community institutions, without providing effective alternative structures to replace them. The TNI-GAM conflict also made it risky and difficult to conduct public meetings in Acehnese villages.

At the household level, the majority of respondents revealed that husbands and wives are both engaged in household decision-making and management, with nearly 50 per cent of respondents stating that husband and wife consult on financial decisions, compared to less than 30 per cent who stated that the husband alone makes the decisions. The proportion of respondents who said that husbands and wives consult dropped a few percentage points after the tsunami, from 51 to 44 per cent, but this is largely offset by the increase in the number of single parent households since the tsunami. As for handling and managing household money, the wife played a much larger role, with 'wife' and 'husband and wife' each accounting for roughly equal proportions of nearly 75 per cent of responses to the question. These figures were the same for before and after the tsunami.

In terms of how families acquire resources to deal with emergencies or pressing needs, the highest number of respondents replied that they depend primarily on family and relatives (43 per cent before the tsunami, 24 per cent after), followed by selling jewellery or other family assets (36 per cent before the tsunami, 33 per cent after). Far fewer (9 per cent, both before and after the tsunami) sought loans from banks or other sources. The number of people who responded that they sought additional work to cover needs increased after the tsunami (9 per cent before the tsunami, 13 per cent after). The reduction in the number of households depending on relatives can be explained by the fact that many tsunami victims' relatives were in the same dire situation that they were, in combination with the availability of donor aid, particularly during the initial emergency and rehabilitation periods. Similarly, the increase in the number of people who sought additional work to meet pressing needs can be explained by the abundantly available jobs on construction and other tsunami relief projects, combined with the decreased ability of relatives to assist. That families who lost nearly everything in the tsunami continue to sell family assets to meet emergency needs seems curious, until one considers the practice of selling goods and equipment received from donors, government and NGOs – particularly livelihood assistance programmes.

At the village community level, there were a few significant shifts in decision-making and problem-solving practice. The most immediately apparent difference was the frequency of village meetings. Whereas 58 per cent of respondents answered 'less than six times per year' to a question about the frequency of village meetings before the tsunami, 51 per cent of respondents say that since the tsunami, they met more than once per month, with most of the remaining 49 per cent answering either 'monthly' or 'six to ten times per year'. Responses varied among villages.

'Village meetings' was the most common response to a multiple choice, multi-response question regarding how problems are solved in the village.

Interestingly, only one community reported any feelings of 'meeting fatigue', which emerged during discussions of community members' frustration over unresolved housing issues.

Figure 2 shows the overall ranking of villagers' responses to the problem-solving question:

While respondents were not specifically instructed to prioritize their answers, the order in which they listed their responses is indicative. For instance, nearly all respondents who answered 'request assistance from BRR[11]/donor/NGO', offered this as their third response, implying that they would exhaust other avenues first. Cross-checking questionnaire results against individual interviews revealed that respondents' first answer was their preferred choice.

Although 'village meetings' was the most frequent reply overall, it was not the leading response in every village. In two of the 18 survey villages, 'family and neighbours gather to solve problems' outranked village meetings

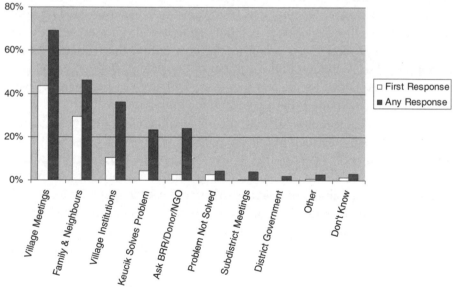

Figure 2 Problem-solving in the village

Table 3 *Village meetings to solve problems*

	1st response	*Any response*
Total Overall	44%	69%
High Village Score	71%	97%
Low Village Score	7%	43%
Median Village Score	43%	73%
Mean Village Score	44%	70%

as the leading response to this question, while 'village institutions' was a more popular response in two other villages, and '*Keucik* solves problems' was higher in one village.

As previously mentioned, there was a significant correlation between positive individual responses to this question, and respondents' trust in their *Keucik*. The same is true when aggregated at the village level. When the respective lists were divided into thirds, three of the top six ranked villages for 'village meetings to solve problems' were also in the top third of '*Keucik* most trusted', while three of the lowest ranked villages on each list were in the same block for the other. The correlation becomes even more striking when the list is split in half: seven of the first nine villages ranked by 'village meetings solve problems' fall into the top nine villages for '*Keucik* most trusted', and vice versa.

The opposite is true when 'village meetings to solve problems' is contrasted with '*Keucik* solves problems': Three of the top six responding villages to the first question fell into the lowest third on the second, while three of the lowest third for the former were in the top third for the latter. When split into halves, the rankings practically mirrored one another, again with seven of the top nine responding villages for 'village meetings solve problems' falling in the lower half on the list ranking villages by '*Keucik* solves problems'.

It is interesting to compare these responses with the response to the same question that 'problems are not solved'.

Of the six villages where respondents selected this answer, all but one fell into the bottom third of the list of villages ranked by 'village meetings solve problems'; all but two fell into the lower third of villages ranked by '*Keucik* most trusted' (and *all* into the bottom half); while three were among the top one third of villages ranked by '*Keucik* solves problems'. This further underscores community members' preference for participatory, deliberative decision-making processes.

We should discuss it first, get a consensus. Tell the people, 'There's some funding, let's have a meeting to decide what the money should be used for.' That's clear. Pak Keucik never says [this]. At most, he

Table 4 *Problems not solved*

	Ist response	Any response
Total Overall	3%	4%
High Village Score	37%	37%
Low Village Score	0%	0%
Median Village Score	0%	0%
Mean Village Score	3%	4%

*says, there was some aid funding and it was used for such-and-such.
After the money's already been spent, then he tells the people. It's not
that there aren't any other smart people in this village. But there's no
way to challenge Pak Keucik. He's powerful, and clever. Everybody
who matters, he's already got them in his pocket. Most of the clever
people here, they've already moved to the city, or to another village.
(Tgk. Muchlis, Interview SJ-03, Suak Jampok)*

The second most common response to the question of how problems are
solved was 'family and neighbours gather to solve problems'.

At the individual level, this response showed no strong correlation with
any other variables, save 'level of trust'. Ranking by village, as well, exhibited no strong patterns or positive relationships with other variables. A
pronounced negative correspondence between this response and levels of
women's participation in village meetings and decision-making will be discussed in a following section.

'Village institutions solve problems' was the third most common
response.

Aggregated at the village level, this response most closely correlates with
the response '*Keucik* solves problems'. No other clear patterns or correlations emerged. The accuracy of this particular response is considered
unreliable; attempting to corroborate these answers by examining interview
and focus group discussion transcripts indicated considerable variance in
respondents' interpretation of the term 'village institutions'. The other
answers to this multiple-choice question appear to have been less con-

Table 5 *Family and neighbours solve problems*

	1st response	Any response
Total Overall	29%	46%
High Village Score	48%	68%
Low Village Score	0%	0%
Median Village Score	35%	45%
Mean Village Score	29%	46%

Table 6 *Village institutions solve problems*

	1st response	Any response
Total Overall	10%	36%
High Village Score	50%	77%
Low Village Score	0%	0%
Median Village Score	7%	36%
Mean Village Score	10%	36%

founding, and cross-checking questionnaire results with interview, focus group and observation data affirmed the veracity of all other responses to this question.

Transparency and accountability

Although difficult to quantify – hence not explicitly addressed in the questionnaire – interview and observation data indicated a significant variation between different villages in the degree of transparency and accountability in the management of village government and aid programmes. Some programmes and activities, such as the World Bank-Government of Indonesia *Kecamatan* Development Programme (KDP) infrastructure projects, the AusAID Local Governance and Infrastructure for Communities in Aceh (LOGICA) Community Infrastructure Grants Scheme (CIGS) involved the establishment of dedicated management structures, and required transparent financial accounting and the use of public information display boards as an integral part of their implementation. They provided appropriate management skills training as part of the programme. Donor statements about the good governance objective of these programmes are unambiguous, as in the following examples from World Bank and LOGICA documents:

> *KDP is part of a broader effort by the Indonesian government and civil society to bring more transparency and accountability into development decision-making. The KDP's design principles point to a new way of doing business in Indonesia.*[12]

> *CIGS has funded small essential community facilities (where these are not already covered in other donor reconstruction plans), and has strengthened the skills of [Village Development Committees] to design and manage construction projects underpinned by transparency principles.*[13]

Many donors and NGOs also supported Community Economic Enterprises or Institutions (*Lembaga Ekonomi Masyarakat*, LEM, or *Lembaga Ekonomi Gampong*, LEGA), with a similar emphasis on transparency and accountability.

The degree to which these principles had taken root in different communities varied considerably among the 18 villages surveyed. A few village communities had enthusiastically embraced the principles of transparency and accountability, as exemplified by the following quotes from interviews and focus group discussions:

With the block grant project, we were all included from planning right through implementation. Then when it was completed, we were shown how much money had been spent, and how much still remained. The remainder went into the village government treasury, where it could be used for another project. It was a very open process. (Nasrul, Focus Group SM-02, Suak Manyam)

What the people in this village like about LOGICA is its trans-parency – everybody knows how much money has been expended because it's posted at the village hall, even in the dusun. The village government is starting to do this too. If there's a new programme, it is announced to the whole community, and then we discuss how to proceed. (Anwar, Interview JS-12, Jurongseuh)

All donors and programmes that come to our village, we have a meeting to discuss it and then appoint someone to be in charge. (Cak Ina, Focus Group CT-01, Cot Teumbon)

These statements contrast markedly with the following excerpts from interviews and focus groups in villages where the 'new way of doing business' had not successfully taken root.

If there are meetings to discuss assistance, we aren't invited. They need 20 people before they can distribute aid, but only five people turn up. It's not at all transparent. Everybody is very suspicious. (Ansari, Interview JB-17, Jabeuet)

Pak Keucik is not transparent when it comes to aid. If you ask him where the aid has gone, he always answers, 'I have distributed all of it to the community.' (Muchtaruddin, Interview UK-02, Uleue Karang)

Do the members know how much money has been collected? As head of the LEM, he has to be transparent with the members. How much money have we received from Oxfam, from Islamic Relief, from BRR? Have you been to the LEM office? Did you see any information about any grants? No, you didn't, because there isn't any. (Heti Kamala, Interview SJ-02, Suak Jampok)

There is a treasurer, but in name only. All the money is handled by the Keucik. You ask if there is a village account. Yes, there is. But nobody knows where the money is or what it's been used for. (Tgk. Norman, Interview BL-06, Bladeh)

Not all of the examples were as stark as those provided above. Based on data on villagers' satisfaction levels with aid programmes, frequency or prevalence of discord, evidence of public disclosure of financial information in the villages and the leadership and decision-making parameters discussed above, there emerged a sort of 'openness and accountability continuum' among the survey villages, wherein approximately one third (six) of the villages could be characterized as 'open, inclusive and accountable', and four as 'dominated by an individual or clique, with little or no accountability', with the remaining eight falling somewhere between these two extremes.

All of the villages surveyed had received more-or-less the same package of community engagement and village government skills training and support from the AusAID LOGICA programme, and all but one had implemented LOGICA CIGS Community Infrastructure Grants. Many have been recipients of legal rights and representative government training workshops from IDLO, as well as a number of other cadre training programmes. They were all subject to the same array of financial accounting and reporting requirements from district government, BRR and donors. Yet the outcomes had been very different.

It is a truism – and a tautology – that leadership and decision-making styles are key determinants in establishing the level of transparency and accountability in village government. As well, fair and transparent village elections had clearly contributed to improved governance in a number of the villages. Of the six villages identified as transparent and accountable, one of these was a recent convert, this being the direct result of a village election process that ousted an unpopular, domineering and unaccountable *Keucik*. The transformation of that community since the election had been quite remarkable. Several villages in the intermediate, transitional group appeared to be shifting in the direction of greater transparency and accountability. Again, direct *Keucik* elections or the preparatory process for elections was providing a strong impetus for this shift. In fact, people in one village in Aceh Jaya were so enthused about the outcome of their recent *Keucik* election that questionnaire results from there ranked among the highest for responses such as '*Keucik* most trusted', '*Keucik* solves problems' and 'level of trust' – despite the fact that this village had already had four *Keucik* since the tsunami, and lagged far behind its neighbours in terms of physical and economic recovery. The election had been held only a few days before the ACARP researchers began their survey of the village, hardly giving the new *Keucik* time to prove himself. Nonetheless, the people there expounded a profound belief in the capability and integrity of their new government.

Elections alone, however, do not guarantee positive outcomes. As previously mentioned, at the time of this research, ten of 18 survey villages had held direct *Keucik* elections. This included five of six villages where leadership was categorized as transparent, inclusive and accountable, but also two of four villages with uncommunicative, domineering and unaccountable leaders.

Women's participation

There was significant variability in the level of women's involvement in decision-making processes and assistance programmes among the survey villages. The survey questionnaire included a question about who participates in village meetings. Respondents were given a choice of several answers, including Husband/Father/Male Head of Household, Wife/Mother/Female Head of Household, Husband/Father *and* Wife/Mother, Child/Children, Adult Child/Children, and Entire Family. Combining responses for the second, third and sixth choices covered nearly all instances where females attended the meetings (the gender of children and adult children was not specified).

In many villages, respondents explained that women had difficulty attending village meetings because these were often held at night. As well, according to their culture, the concerns of wives and mothers were said to be represented in public fora by their menfolk. These same respondents explained that when women did participate in formal meetings and gatherings, they generally had a space outside the main meeting venue, or were there to provide catering.

In those communities where women were formally included in village meetings and consultations, their enthusiasm was highly evident.

> *In our village, men now listen to and consider women's opinions. When there is a meeting, for instance to discuss aid programmes, all the women attend. Often there are more women than men at the meetings. The women in this village really enjoy meetings. So long as there's an invitation, we'll be there! (Nuralia, Focus Group DS-04, Darussalam)*

Table 7 Women's participation in village meetings[14]

	Before tsunami	After tsunami
Total Overall	18%	29%
High Village Score	44%	64%
Low Village Score	0%	7%
Median Village Score	19%	23%
Mean Village Score	18%	28%

At the level of individual respondents, positive responses regarding women's participation in public meetings correlated with a fairly disparate assortment of other parameters, including '*Teungku Imeum* or other religious leader most trusted', 'Village Secretary most trusted', 'Village Facilitator most trusted', and 'frequency of village meetings'. They did *not* correlate with general high levels of trust in the community, nor with *any* of the responses to questions about problem-solving.[15] Aggregated at the village level, higher levels of women's participation showed relatively weak correlation with only a few of the variables discussed previously. When arrayed into thirds (high, medium, low), women's participation in village meetings showed a distinct negative correspondence with the response that 'family and neighbours gather to solve problems', i.e., three of six villages with the highest level of women's participation in village meetings fell into the bottom third of villages ranked by 'family and neighbours solve problems', while three of the lowest third in terms of women's participation in meetings were among the six villages where this practice was most common. This can be interpreted to mean that in those villages where women's participation in village affairs was not formally accommodated, they were more actively engaged in solving problems through more informal channels.

A stronger correlation existed between levels of women's participation in meetings, and the original classification of survey villages into pairs of more and less successfully recovering villages.[16] The perceived level of women's participation in meetings in successfully recovering villages was 35 per cent, compared to 21 per cent in the less successful group. Seven of nine successful villages fell into the top 50 per cent of villages ranked by level of women's participation (and vice versa), while among the matched pairs of villages, women's participation ranked higher in the purportedly successful village in six of nine pairs. It was higher in the successful villages before the tsunami, and had also increased in those same villages by a greater margin.

Women's participation in other types of activities similarly varied between villages. The activities with the highest level of participation by women included religious and ceremonial activities (75 per cent of respondents agreed that women participate), '*arisan*' revolving savings and credit associations (94 per cent, though the total number of *arisan* had declined since the tsunami), and training courses (60 per cent). The latter figure represented a slight (7 per cent) increase when compared to women's participation in training courses before the tsunami.

Many government, donor and NGO tsunami recovery programmes specifically targeted women, or stipulated a minimum level of women's participation or receipt of benefits. More than half of the village development cadre recruited and trained by the AusAID LOGICA programme in 203 villages in Aceh were female. In two of the survey villages, all ten village cadre were women (in one of these, a respondent explained that this was because men would rather seek paid work). With the LOGICA Community Infrastructure Grants, there were very specific guidelines about inclusion of women, including at least one woman member on the Village Development Committee formed to manage the project. (In almost every case, the female member was appointed Treasurer.) KDP, as well, had clear guidelines about including and targeting women in supported activities.

There is no doubt that the level of women's participation in planning, managing and implementing village development programmes in post-tsunami Aceh had increased, as a direct result of government, donor and NGO policies and guidance. The language of gender awareness and gender equity suffused much of the transcript data collected during this research. Women in those villages that had adopted some of these principles showed great enthusiasm for their new roles and responsibilities. This having been said, the data also showed a persistent bias about the limitations of women's public roles in Acehnese society. A simple text search of all the transcript data seeking the terms 'women' and 'activity' or 'women' and 'gathering' in proximity, yielded quite a large number of quotes. The majority of these quotes referred to *wirid yasin* (Koran reading) groups, while most of the remainder talked about the PKK Family Welfare programme A similar search for 'women' and 'meeting' or 'women' and 'planning' in proximity generated more material about women's participation in recovery activities, but almost all of this in response to direct questions from the researchers.

> *Don't you know, since the tsunami all the women in this gampong have been gendered! Aceh today is just like Medan, or Jakarta. Now women are doing men's work, like selling durian. Before, only men sold durian. But now, women can sell durian too ...*

> *As for meetings, to discuss housing, for instance, it's enough that just the men attend. After all, the decisions would be the same, and we [the women] are represented, right? And we women have meetings too. We hold them at the PKK centre, and no men are invited. That's fair, isn't it? (Keucik and Hasinah, Focus Group CK-01, Cot Kaleut)*

Social capital

Other studies have noted that social capital is relatively strong in Aceh.[17] Many of these same studies point out that the devastation wrought by the tsunami on the Acehnese community's social fabric and social institutions matches, if not exceeds, the physical destruction, and that the recovery effort is as much about re-establishing society as it is about reconstructing infrastructure and facilities and resuming production.

Previous sections have already examined important aspects of social capital in the discussions of household and community-level problem-solving, village meetings, trust in leaders and women's participation. These analyses indicated that levels of cohesion, inclusion and/or exclusion varied among the survey villages, and that village leadership had played a strong role in shaping that dynamic. Data indicated as well that donor approaches, and donors' relationships with communities and their leaders, can influence cohesion and trust. The terms 'social justice' and 'inequality' most frequently appeared in interview transcripts in reference to aid programmes that had engendered envy and jealousy within and between communities.

Trust is a key ingredient of social capital. Respondents were asked for their assessment of the level of trust in their community, and given a choice of four answers: Feelings of mutual trust are high; some people can be trusted while others cannot; feelings of mutual trust are low; suspicion and jealousy are high. Overall, the majority of respondents (55 per cent) selected 'some people can be trusted while others cannot'. The array of remaining answers produced the result shown in Table 8.

As previously discussed, a high level of trust correlated strongly with high frequency of village meetings, as well as the community's trust in their *Keucik*. There was an equally strong negative correlation with the villages where respondents answered 'problems are not solved': four of six villages where people selected this answer fell into the lowest six villages ranked by level of trust.

An important facet of rebuilding social capital is creating spaces for association and interchange, and re-establishing those activities and routines that bring people together. Clearly, communities that were spatially dispersed through the early months of the recovery process, had tended to recover more slowly than those where they managed to assemble – either in the same barracks, or in temporary housing in their own village or resettlement site. As well, early construction of *meunasah* or meeting halls provided an important venue for meetings and social and religious activities. For

Table 8 *Level of trust*

	High level of trust	Low trust; high suspicion and jealousy
Total Overall	25%	17%
High Village Score	83%	57%
Low Village Score	0%	0%
Median Village Score	20%	12%
Mean Village Score	25%	17%

example, as their first act after they had been allocated new land to relocate their village, the people of Cot Meukuta in Aceh Barat constructed a *musholla* (small mosque) from recycled materials salvaged from the barracks they had been occupying. In discussions and interviews, this rated as one of the most significant events of this community's post-tsunami history, and one of which they were very proud.

Most, but not all villages, had resumed many of their religious and ceremonial routines. Villages where this was not occurring were those at the tail end of the 'level of trust' spectrum. Almost without exception, women's activities, such as *wirid yasin* (reading of Koranic verses) and *seni rabana* (Koranic chanting with drums), had advanced more than men's.

> *If you ask me, the advantage of women is, when compared with the men, we still get together, all the women's activities little-by-little have all come back and progressed. Just look at our* wirid yasin, *each week it gets bigger. It's the same with other activities as well. We have our cooking groups again, and we've even got programmes going for the young women. (Cut Marhama, Focus Group KS-01, Kuwala Sagee)*

Several villages had also reinstated local *kenduri* (ritual feast) traditions, after a hiatus of one or two years.

Gotong-royong (community voluntary self-help) is another hallowed tradition throughout Indonesia. There was much discussion that the prevalence of cash-for-work programmes undermined this practice in post-tsunami Aceh.[18]

> *People here have become passive, they just wait for work ... They're used to cash-for-work now. There's been a shift in values, less unity in the community and the decline of gotong-royong. (Tgk. Salman, Interview UJ-10, Ujong)*

> *The youth here, most have been damaged by cash-for-work. They're spoiled, don't want to work, just wait for aid money. (Ledia, Interview LL-01, Lhok Leuhu)*

> *Maybe, in Aceh the* gotong-royong *spirit has been lost because of aid that wasn't well managed, the NGOs just handed out projects, used up their budget, not concerned about effectiveness. (Nusabilal, Interview KS-09, Kuwala Sagee)*

On closer examination, however, it became apparent that the spirit was still very much alive in most of the communities in this survey. Many respondents tempered their remarks about cash-for-work destroying *gotong-royong* by stating that neighbours still helped neighbours, with funerals, weddings, or taking turns shifting temporary houses to add rooms to newly-finished permanent houses. Informal, spontaneous *gotong-royong*, it seems, was still widely practiced in Acehnese villages. Indeed, despite the criticisms, anecdotal evidence also indicated that formal, routinized *gotong-royong* was still common as well, particularly in villages with popular *Keucik* or *Dusun* Heads, or for self-help projects – such as the *musholla* in Cot Meukuta – that were clearly in the community's interest. In response to a question about which household members participated in a variety of different types of activity, 89 per cent of respondents from the 18 survey villages answered that one or more household members participated in village *gotong-royong* activities.

> *The cash-for-work virus hit our village as well, but fortunately in our case, it was for a self-help housing project, and well managed by the NGO in a way that empowered people. (M. Ali, Interview BM-15, Blang Mata)*

This research was unable to establish a positive link between the amount, frequency and duration of cash-for-work programmes in particular survey villages, and the vigour of those villages' *gotong-royong* activities. This was due partly to the coarseness and unevenness of available data on cash-for-work programmes,[19] also a lack of quantitative detail in the interview data. The cash-for-work/*gotong-royong* lament did appear more frequently in transcripts from particular villages. However, these villages did not experience noticeably different levels of cash-for-work assistance than the others in this survey. Rather, the complaint that *gotong-royong* was in decline was more common in those communities where questionnaire data indicated ambivalence or dissatisfaction with village leadership.

Conclusion

It is no coincidence that much of the preceding reads like the pages of an NGO community development training manual. The sheer volume and intensity of the tsunami recovery effort created a unique situation with its own spatially and temporally distinct constellation of values, political structures and cultural vocabularies – a sort of post-tsunami institutional hothouse. To a significant degree, agendas and standards were being set by the international donors and NGOs that funded and administered much of the recovery effort. To what extent do the changes we witnessed represent fundamental shifts in Acehnese political structures and practice, or were they more of a circumstantial response to stimuli emanating from international donors and NGOs?

Located at an important crossroads between the Indian Ocean and Java Sea, the Acehnese have had economic, political and cultural links with a diverse range of regional and global polities dating back to the 14th century. Acehnese are adept at positioning themselves in relation to 'outside' powers, influences and cultures; sometimes resisting, sometimes subordinating themselves, sometimes cooperating, sometimes dominating and subsuming, all along incorporating aspects of these foreign entities into their own uniquely Acehnese identity. The international disaster relief community in Aceh was no exception to this pattern.

The most interesting questions arising from the ACARP research project involve the 'sustainability' of recovery inputs and institutional forms, and the future trajectory and velocity of the nascent 'trends' identified in the survey villages. Post-tsunami, post-MoU Aceh has witnessed an efflorescence of political inclusion and openness. At the same time, however, new constellations of patronage and privilege are forming, as the province's new political leaders consolidate their power and positions. It will be several more years before the contours, conduct and capacities of the institutions currently being constructed can be fully comprehended. This is as true of village-level institutions as it is of the relationships and structures presently reforming at the district and provincial levels.

The ACARP research showed that there is no single pathway to recovery and reform – different villages had combined different strategies, resources and actions to achieve their goals. Nonetheless, a few salient points can be extracted.

The finding that stands out most clearly from the village surveys is the correlation between good leadership and good recovery outcomes (and the corollary relationship between poor leadership and unsatisfactory outcomes). The role, and character, of the village *Keucik* plays prominently in this dynamic. Since the tsunami, donors and government alike have attached unrealistic hopes and expectations on the *Keucik*, needing them to be effective modern project managers, but who are also imbued with the supernatural and spiritual powers and attributes set out by Ibrahim above. If anything, this has only intensified since the new Law on Governing of Aceh and the provincial and district elections of 2007, the introduction of several new *Qanun* on village government, and the new governor's pledge to 'build Aceh from the *gampong*' (Sujito and Rahman, 2007).

According to the results of this research, communities' hopes and expectations vis-à-vis their *Keucik* were more realistic. Respondents were unambiguous in their preference for village leaders who facilitate and support, rather than command. 'Open', 'transparent', 'accountable' and 'just' were the adjectives most commonly attached to descriptions of a good *Keucik*.

As noted earlier, direct *Keucik* elections were generally contributing to a shift toward more accountable local leadership in Aceh. These elections served as effective community and consensus-building exercises in several of the survey communities, and probably strengthened nascent democratic institutions even in those villages where the contests were more divisive. However, the experiences of two survey villages where unsuitable candidates bullied and/or bought their way into (or held onto) power, indicate that this process can still be subverted.

It is a credit to BRR, the provincial and district governments of Nanggroe Aceh Darussalam, the exuberant print media that has grown in Aceh since the Helsinki MoU and Law on the Governing of Aceh, an increasingly savvy and intrepid local and national NGO community, and scores of international donor agencies and international NGOs that participated in the tsunami recovery effort, that the discourse of transparency and accountability had grown deep roots in Acehnese society in such a brief period. Its practice however, still lagged behind in some communities, to the obvious detriment of the people living there. Rather than deal with the obvious corruption and malevolent leadership in these communities, many donors and even government agencies elected to simply take their aid elsewhere. Those that were still operating in these villages seemed willing to turn a blind eye to the leaders' egregious behaviour.

Patronage and exclusionary behaviour can flourish in the superheated environment of post-disaster recovery situations such as post-tsunami Aceh. In a few of the ACARP survey villages, the actions of particular aid agencies or agents were found to have exacerbated factionalism and encouraged paternalistic empire-building. The expedience of creating special operational units at the village level, rather than working through the village government bureaucracy, can have the effect of creating a sort of 'multigate' decision-making and programme management structure with little or no downward accountability, often leading to confusion, frustration and suspicion in the community, and asymmetrical distribution of benefits.

This having been said, donor interventions such as the long-term placement of village facilitators; recruitment, training and support of village development cadre; and establishment of dedicated structures to manage community block grants, were shown to be effective means of empowering and enabling communities – village 'civil society' – to take control of the recovery process, and mould the type of village institutions and government they desire. One of the most positive outcomes in a number of ACARP survey villages was the incorporation by village government leaders of a number of participatory planning and collective decision-making, open and accountable financial management, and participatory monitoring and evaluation procedures and protocols, which were initially introduced as requirements of a particular donor block grant or economic development programme.

Those villages that had successfully incorporated ex-GAM combatants or commanders into village government and programme management structures were reaping prodigious benefits in terms of community unity, motivation and overall effectiveness of reconstruction programmes.

There were a number of examples as well from the survey villages of customary (*adat*) leaders and institutions playing active roles in the planning and implementation of recovery initiatives, significantly impacting the effectiveness of aid delivery and uptake in their respective communities.

Another stand-out finding of this research was the robust correlation between the frequency of village meetings, and a host of other positive values including mutual trust in the community, trust in community leaders, equity and harmony. While this may seem self-evident, the tremendous variability between villages as to how often meetings were held, indicates that this obvious truism is not always applied.

Conducive facilities for conducting meetings represented an important early priority in communities recovering from disaster, and the modest costs incurred in supporting community meetings resulted in significant increases in the efficiency and effectiveness of aid programmes. Those instances where village groups had been able to make collective plans or decisions and act upon them, had in each case provided a powerful boost to these communities' belief in their capacity to solve their own problems, and to the momentum and quality of recovery efforts there.

Regarding women's participation in village government and aid programme implementation, no strong correlation could be established between increased women's participation and significant shifts or patterns in other governance or social capital indicators. Clearly, in villages where women were more fully engaged in village meetings and recovery programme design and implementation, both women and men expressed satisfaction and confidence in the changes they had witnessed. Women in these communities showed great enthusiasm for their newfound 'voice', and revelled in their new roles as citizens and managers. It was also evident that in those communities where women were not formally incorporated into village community decision-making and problem-solving structures and procedures, they still played an active informal role, at the neighbourhood and household level.

The absence of any robust correlation between increased women's participation and other governance or social capital indicators was probably due to the fact that only a small number of the survey villages had fully embraced gender mainstreaming principles, and because this process had only been under way for a short time when this research was carried out. It is anticipated that these links may become more pronounced with the passage of time.

In the social, social welfare and small-scale enterprise spheres, anecdotal evidence indicated that women's groups and women's programmes were evincing stronger growth, and greater endurance, than their male counterparts. One factor that contributed to this was the fact that men had more options to work as labourers on various infrastructure and other recovery projects.

As stated in the introduction to this chapter, the Boxing Day 2004 tsunami and the massive recovery effort that ensued have created many new opportunities to craft more democratic, inclusive and accountable institutions of governance in Nanggroe Aceh Darussalam. This is equally evident at the village as well as provincial and district levels. The ACARP research demonstrated that different communities have responded differently to the disaster and availability of recovery aid, but that the general trend has been toward better local governance, and higher levels of participation and inclusiveness. The extent to which this nascent trend will continue after the tsunami recovery process ends remains to be seen.

The abundance of tsunami reconstruction aid had the unfortunate side effect of creating an artificial dichotomy between post-tsunami Aceh and those regions not affected by the tsunami – and hence not eligible for post-tsunami reconstruction assistance. This has generated some resentment among many inland communities, many of whom suffered extensive damage during the 30-year armed conflict. Post-conflict reconstruction assistance has been a mere trickle compared to the amounts of aid allocated for post-tsunami recovery and reconstruction. Nonetheless, many of the advances achieved in post-tsunami areas are being applied – albeit at a much smaller scale – in government and donor-assisted post-conflict recovery programmes. Awareness of the central role of village government and village community institutions in the success of the post-conflict recovery effort is widely acknowledged (MSR, forthcoming).

For both the 2004 tsunami and the 1976–2005 TNI-GAM conflict, it has been widely acknowledged that the damage to Aceh's social institutions and structures was no less severe than the devastation of the province's physical infrastructure and productive assets, and that the task of rebuilding the 'institutional software' would be more complicated and difficult than constructing new houses, roads and bridges. The findings of the ACARP research on post-tsunami recovery indicate that these predictions tended to underestimate the tenacity and ingenuity of Acehnese village communities.

References

Adams, L. and Winahyu, R. (2006) *Learning from cash responses to the tsunami. Case Studies*, London, Humanitarian Policy Group, Overseas Development Institute (HPG-ODI)www.odi.org.uk/hpg/papers/BGP_Tsunamilessons.pdf

BRR and International Partners (2005) *Aceh and Nias One Year after the Tsunami: The Recovery Effort and Way Forward*, Banda Aceh, BRR. www.reliefweb.int/rw/RWFiles2005.nsf/FilesByRWDocUNIDFileName/KHII-6K54EE-brr-idn-15dec.pdf/$File/brr-idn-15dec.pdf

Doocy, S.,Gabriel, M., Collins, S., Robinson C. and Stevenson, P. (2006) 'Implementing cash for work programmes in post-tsunami Aceh: experiences and lessons learned', *Disasters*, vol 30, no 3, pp277–296

DSF (2006) *GAM Reintegration Needs Assessment: Enhancing Peace through Community-level Development Programming*, Banda Aceh, The World Bank. www.conflictand development.org/data/doc/en/regCaseStudy/aceh/GAM%20Reintegration%20Need s%20Assessment2.pdf

Ibrahim, S. (2006) 'Kewibawaan dalam Pandangan Masyarakat Aceh' ('Authority in the Viewpoint of the Acehnese'), *Jurnal Ilmiah Administrasi Publik*, vol VI, no 1. http://publik.brawijaya.ac.id/?hlm=jedlist&ed=1125507600&edid=1135589533

KDP (2007) *2006 Village Survey in Aceh: An Assessment of Village Infrastructure and Social Conditions*, Banda Aceh, The World Bank. http://siteresources. worldbank.org/INTINDONESIA/Resources/226271–1168333550999/ AcehVillageSurvey06_final.pdf

Kenny, S. (2007) 'Reconstruction in Aceh: Building Whose Capacity?' *Community Development Journal*. vol 42, no 2, pp206–221

McCarthy, J. (2000) 'Village and State Regimes on Sumatra's Forest Frontier: A Case from the Leuser Ecosystem, South Aceh', RMAP Working Papers, no 26, Canberra, Resource Management in Asia Pacific Project, Research School of Pacific and Asian Studies, Australian National University

MSR (forthcoming) *Multi-stakeholder Review of Post-conflict Programming in Aceh*, Jakarta, Conflict and Development Programme, The World Bank

Sinar Harapan (2003) 'Para "Keucik" yang Terjepit antara TNI dan GAM' ('*Keucik* are caught between TNI and GAM'), 12 June 2003. www.sinarharapan.co.id/ berita/0306/12/sh02.html

Sujito, A. and Rahman, F.H. eds (2007) *Membangun Aceh dari Gampong: Catatan Ringan dari Riset Monitoring Pemilihan Keuchik Langsung (Pilciksung)*. (Building Aceh from the Gampong: Notes from Research and Monitoring on Direct *Keucik* Elections (*Pilciksung*)), Yogyakarta, Institute for Research and Empowerment (IRE)

Thorburn, C. (2007) *The Acehnese* Gampong *Three Years On: Assessing Local Capacity and Reconstruction Assistance in Post-tsunami Aceh*, Report of the Aceh Community Assistance Research Project (ACARP), Jakarta, Australian Agency for International Development (AusAID). www.indo.ausaid.gov.au/featurestories/acarpreport.pdf or www.conflictanddevelopment.org/data/doc/en/regCaseStudy/aceh/ACARP-report-lowRes.pdf

Thorburn, C. (2009) 'Livelihood Recovery in the Wake of the Tsunami in Aceh', *Bulletin of Indonesian Economic Studies* vol 45, no 1, pp85–105. http://pdfserve.infor-maworld.com/195614_751319832_909918760.pdf

Notes

* Parts of this chapter appeared in the report of the Aceh Community Assistance Research Project on post-tsunami recovery (Thorburn, 2007), written by the author and published by the Australian Agency for International Development (AusAID) in December 2007. Permission by AusAID to reproduce sections of the report is gratefully acknowledged. AusAID does not guarantee the accuracy, reliability or completeness of any information contained in the material and accepts no legal liability whatsoever arising from any use of the material. Users of the material should exercise their own skill and care with respect to their use of the material.

1   *Undang-undang Nomor 11 thn 2006 tentang Pemerintahan Aceh.*

2   For a summary of ACARP's findings on village governance, see Thorburn (2009).

3   Available at www.conflictanddevelopment.org/data/doc/en/regCaseStudy/aceh/ACARP-report-lowRes.pdf or www.indo.ausaid.gov.au/featurestories/acarpreport.pdf.

4   *Datuk* is a traditional Malay title for clan leaders. *Uleebalang* is an Acehnese term for local chieftain, or commander, dating back to the time of early Sultanates, but retained through the colonial era.

5   'Village Score' is the percentage of respondents in a single village that selected this particular response.

6   *Imam* of the village mosque.

7   All village names have been changed in the research report, also in this chapter.

8   *Adat* leader in the fishing community in charge of custom and traditional practices in marine fishing, including managing fishing areas and settlement of disputes.

9   *Adat* functionary responsible for assisting the *Keucik* in the management of irrigation for agriculture.

10   *Qanun* is Arabic for canon, and is used as the title of provincial and district regulations in post-MoU Aceh.

11   BRR is the acronym for the Executing Agency for the Rehabilitation and Reconstruction of Aceh and Nias, the agency established by the Government of Indonesia to facilitate and coordinate the implementation of rehabilitation and reconstruction programmes by the central and local government and foreign donor agencies and NGOs.

12   http://worldbank.org/faces/index.htm.

13   LOGICA 4th Six-monthly Work Plan and 6th Quarterly Report, September 2007, pp18.

14   These figures denote the proportion of questionnaire respondents who answered that women attend village meetings. They do not represent the percentage of women from that village who attend the meetings, nor the proportion of meeting participants who are women.

15   Exploring correlations between the questionnaire response that women participate in village meetings and other parameters does not actually tell us very much. These results should not be interpreted, for instance, to mean that women trust *Teungku Imeum* or Village Facilitators more, nor that women in villages where these figures are more influential participate in more meetings. The most significant insight to derive from this analysis is that the research did not find any strong correlation between women's participation in village meetings, and other leadership, decision-making, or social capital parameters.

16   As previously mentioned, the division of survey villages into '*bangkit*' ('awakening') and '*pra-bangkit*' ('pre-awakening' or 'problematic') villages was largely abandoned once data analysis got under way, as the distinctions between '*bangkit*' and '*pra-bangkit*' villages became blurred and indistinct. These designations were more useful in terms of initial site selection, than as analytical categories once data began to accrue.

17   See, for example KDP (2007); BRR and International Partners (2005); DSF (2006), or Kenny (2007).

18   A relatively recent innovation in post-disaster responses, Cash-for-Work (CFW) programmes are considered easier to administer than Food-for-Work (FFW) programmes, and can be less disruptive to local markets; they infuse cash into economies, and harness idle labour where people are no longer able to participate in their routine employment activities. CFW programmes were initiated in Banda Aceh within two weeks after the tsunami, and soon spread to outlying areas, reaching their peak intensity during the first three to four months of 2005. Total figures of numbers of participants or the amount of funds distributed are not available, but the vital role played by these programmes is widely acknowledged. For a discussion of CFW programmes' contribution to disaster recovery, see Adams and Winahyu (2006) and Doocy et al (2006).

19   All cash-for-work programmes had ended throughout Aceh by the end of 2005, more than 18 months before this research was conducted. Due to a combination of high staff turnover, decentralised management, and different reporting protocols among different agencies, it was difficult to collect and compare accurate data on the practice.

7

The Voices of International NGO Staff

Matthew Clarke and Suellen Murray

Introduction

The international response to the Indian Ocean tsunami was simultaneously immediate and significant. Between 160 and 400 non-government organizations and agencies were operating within Aceh within weeks of the tsunami occurring.[1] These international NGOs and agencies brought with them financial resources, materials and technical capacity. Given the resources available to them, expectations of affected communities, private and public donors, and the NGOs themselves that the relief and reconstruction efforts would be highly successful were high. However, while good work was undoubtedly done, the largest evaluation of the reconstruction efforts concluded that the overall effectiveness of NGOs was limited in a number of ways. After reviewing more than 140 evaluations from NGOs, donors, UN bodies and academic institutions, the Tsunami Evaluation Coalition identified a number of serious weaknesses in the international response. These included: organizations failing to work and support local communities; failing to coordinate and share assessment reports or other data; organizations using:

> *supply-driven, unsolicited and inappropriate aid; inappropriate housing designs and livelihoods solutions; stereotyping of options for women, small-farmers and small entrepreneurs; ... brushing aside or misleading authorities, communities and local organizations; inadequate support to host families; displacement of able local staff by poorly prepared internationals; dominance of English as the working language; misrecognition of local capacities resulting in inefficient implementation; applying more demanding conditions to national and local 'partners' than those accepted by international agencies; poaching of staff from national and local entities; and limited participation of the affected-population. (Telford et al, 2006: p19)*

How did these weaknesses occur, and why were these failures not recognized and rectified as they were occurring by those people implementing the responses?

This research is concerned with the experiences of those responsible for implementing these reconstruction interventions. International NGOs, such as this organization, were focused on providing for the immediate needs of those affected by the disaster, in the initial weeks following the tsunami. In this regard their efforts were traditional *relief* activities. However, soon after this relief phase, the actual physical destruction of the tsunami required international NGOs to refocus their interventions towards reconstructing physical infrastructure that had been destroyed – predominately houses and community buildings, such as hospitals and schools – and reconstructing communities that had been displaced and decimated. Reconstruction was therefore manifest in both material and non-material rebuilding.

This research is purposely qualitative. It captures the experiences of staff and short-term consultants employed by one international NGO[2] who were seconded for short periods to tsunami-affected areas. The purpose of this research is to hear the voices of those implementing reconstruction interventions immediately following the tsunami in order to distil lessons from their experiences. This chapter therefore draws heavily on interviews with some 21 staff who were deployed to Indonesia[3] during the period January to September 2005. These 21 interviews represent 80 per cent of all staff seconded for short periods to tsunami-affected areas by this international NGO.[4] Interviews with these staff were undertaken in two phases.

All interviews were semi-structured and guided by a schedule of questions. Interviews were each around 45 minutes to an hour in length. To ensure anonymity of participants, some identifying material has been removed from quotations used in the report. For this reason, all participants have been identified by number only (1 to 21). As indicated, the research participants represent the majority of interviewed staff who undertook work in the tsunami-affected areas between January 2005 and September 2005, and reflect a wide range of technical skills and time served with the international NGO. Approximately half of the participants had been involved in relief work prior to the tsunami; others had been recruited from elsewhere in the international NGO or were short-term consultants employed by this NGO. The differing expectations and experiences that resulted from this range of backgrounds are noted in the report where relevant.

This chapter, based on the words of the research participants, identifies three main areas of concern: management and leadership; infrastructure and systems; and preparation and support of seconded staff. Interviewed staff identified unclear management and a lack of leadership at the relief sites as the most significant problems they faced while undertaking their work. They reported a lack of clarity around the decision-making authority between the national offices, the regional rapid response relief team,[5] and other staff attached to international partnership offices. In addition to the lack of clear roles between differing arms of the international partnership, staff noted that they viewed the capacity of some expatriate staff sent into tsunami-affected areas as limited. Interviewed staff members noted that inappropriate staffing choices had been made and, among those selected for leadership positions, the skills required in an emergency situation were not necessarily present. There were also concerns expressed about the ways in which the NGO participated in seeking contracts without proper consideration of the circumstances, again reflective of poor leadership.

According to staff interviewed, there appeared to be a lack of clear systems and strategies in place, resulting in a lot of 're-inventing the wheel', as learnings from past experiences were not used. In addition, interviewed staff experienced difficulties in the provision of basic infrastructure in the early period-post-tsunami. It appeared that general disaster response strategies were not known about, or were not implemented, in some situations. This led to what was considered to be an undue focus on the organization rather than meeting needs. In addition, where strategic planning had taken place post-tsunami, there were concerns expressed that these plans had not been passed on.

In relation to selection and preparation of seconded staff members, participants expressed concerns about the level of briefings before and during their deployments. The majority of the issues identified by staff concern the broader international partnership, rather than the specific country office from which they were deployed; however, as part of the international partnership, this NGO could play a role in ensuring that its own staff members are better supported in future relief operations. In addition, the NGO could play a role in facilitating improvements in the policies and procedures of the whole partnership.

Those interviewed acknowledged that the Indian Ocean tsunami disaster had resulted in extraordinary circumstances: it caused considerable devastation, in some areas completely destroying local infrastructure; it affected numerous countries requiring many more staff than were readily available and, at the same time, there was limited availability of staff due to its timing during a holiday period; and there were financial contracts to implement relief interventions for which the international partnership were tendering. Despite these caveats, interviewed staff members believed that the organizational response (both for the deploying NGO and the international partnership) could have been of a higher standard. This chapter explores these constraints using the voices of those charged with the task of Aceh's reconstruction.

This chapter is structured as follows: Section 2 outlines the purpose of the research project, the methods used to conduct it, the main themes that emerged from the interviews, and broadly places them within the existing literature related to complex humanitarian emergencies, international development and organizational management. The next three sections outline the three main themes evident in the interviews: Section 3 discusses difficulties that staff identified with organizational governance and leadership at the relief operation sites; Section 4 considers the existence and implementation of infrastructure, systems and strategies and the extent to which interviewed staff reported that there were difficulties; and Section 5 discusses the selection of staff and their preparation and support. Section 6 concludes the report and summarizes recommendations to inform future responses to complex humanitarian emergencies.

Establishing the issues

While comments made by the interviewed staff indicate that their experiences of working in tsunami-affected areas were mixed and this report largely focuses on the more negative issues raised, many of those interviewed were keen to ensure that their positive experiences were also noted.

Interviewed staff highlighted several key areas where they believed the international partnership appeared to work well, including food distribution, the delivery of goods and services, undertaking assessments and designing programmes. More specifically, the provision of child-friendly spaces and early recognition of the need for helicopters in Aceh were noted as significant achievements. Many interviewed staff also reported positive relationships with the local national office staff in Aceh, at least at the day-to-day level at which they conducted their own work. Others acknowledged that they had worked with teams of people who had worked together well.

Overwhelmingly the comments of the staff interviewed reflected an organizational culture that was highly accountable and committed. All staff had gone to the tsunami-affected areas because they wanted to make a difference to the situation. The interviews clearly indicated that interviewed staff were characterized by a strong commitment to assist others and to be responsive within these particular circumstances. Despite some difficulties, the interviewed staff were pleased that they had been able to make some contribution.

Ironically, the high levels of desire to perform well and contribute to making changes could also have contributed to the level of concerns expressed. Some interviewed staff felt concerned because organizational issues thwarted them in getting the job done, a job that they felt highly motivated to undertake.

Approximately half of the staff interviewed had been involved in previous emergency responses. As a result, they knew that conditions would be difficult and that a certain level of disarray could be expected. They may also have been aware that organizational issues may inhibit their ability to contribute as effectively as they might have wished. For others who had little or no experience of emergency situations or had received little briefing for their deployment to a tsunami-affected area, their levels of concern may have been heightened due to their lack of knowledge of these usual difficulties. This is not to say that these difficulties could not be reduced but rather that some confusion was inevitable under the circumstances. The combination of commitment and a sense of powerlessness is demonstrated by a staff member who had not worked in an emergency relief situation before and experienced some difficulties in undertaking his work:

> *The worst things were just seeing suffering in refugee camps and never feeling like you can do enough in the circumstances ... you feel very incompetent and powerless and because the problem is so big and you're just so small ... everyone who I was working with felt that to some degree, perhaps to a lesser extent the more experienced persons but that was very difficult. (20)*

However, even among those who had experience in emergency situations, there was a sense that this emergency was exceptional in every possible way. Taking care to note that the tsunami relief effort was unprecedented because it required the international partnership to work in five different countries at once, several participants nonetheless noted that the international partnership's response to the tsunami was far poorer than they expected. For example, one staff member indicated that although he had faced less than perfect situations in his two previous relief experiences 'it was still something where all your effort was put into making a difference, not into trying to cope with administrative hassles'. (4)

The following three sections, based on the words of the interview participants and informed by the research literature, explores the reasons why some staff felt that the international partnership's response did not live up to their expectations or previous experiences. These are placed under three broad headings, although the three issues – (unclear management and poor leadership, lack of basic infrastructure and inadequate systems and limited preparation and support) are interrelated.

Governance and leadership

Management issues in international non-government organizations (NGOs) are well-documented in the literature (e.g., Lewis, 2001; Suzuki, 1998). In particular, the literature discusses some of the difficulties inherent in North-South NGO relations. However, there is limited literature concerned with management issues around authority and decision-making during emergency relief operations. In situations of emergency relief, expatriate staff work with national staff for short to medium periods. 'Northern' expatriate staff working in 'southern' agencies, and the implied power imbalance that this suggests, is the topic of some of the research literature. For example, Mukasa (1999) considers tensions with expatriate staff appointment which has particular relevance to emergency management which is heavily expatriate run. Related to this is that during emergency situations, the power that under the usual development circumstances is devolved to the national offices, becomes more centralized with greater involvement of international partnership staff in decision-making. While clearly attempts are made to operate as a partnership, the parallel structures can lead to confusion and conflict. In conclusion, Mukasa states that:

> *if they are to improve their effectiveness, international development NGOs will need to address this power imbalance in their internal organisational structures and confront the unequal relationships which may be created by the use of expatriates within their organisations. (1999, p27)*

Malhotra (2000) also considers the relationship or 'partnership' between northern and southern NGOs and describes the power imbalance driven by the resource transfer paradigm. Malhotra argues that resources and power rest with the northern NGOs in relation to southern NGOs and mitigates true partnership and suggests that northern NGOs focus on capacity building instead of operations in the south, that they embrace mutual (two-way not current one-way) transparency and accountability, and redefine policy and lobbying (for advocacy) roles, giving southern NGOs their own impetus, while northern NGOs focus on supporting southern NGOs rather than driving and informing.

The concept of capacity building has relevance to governance and leadership and is a topic addressed in the literature. Smillie (2001) notes that while capacity building can involve the development of technical and organizational skills and capacity, it also has wider dimensions. Capacity building can also mean building the capacity of a community and wider society over time. In its narrowest meaning, it could involve, over time, the development of skills around responding and managing emergencies so that, in this instance, national offices are less reliant on the contributions of support offices and the international partnership.

The need for awareness of and sensitivity to local customs and traditions was an issue raised by interview participants and is also acknowledged in the literature (e.g., Mukasa, 1999). In particular, the ways that expatriate staff experience leadership by local national office staff at the relief operation sites may be affected by their levels of cultural awareness. While also attributable to wider governance issues, lack of understanding of culturally-based conceptualizations of leadership may also have contributed to confusion and lack of clarity around decision-making processes. For example, Munene et al (2000) considers the national differences in values to development (not emergencies) in sub-Saharan Africa and uses data from two surveys in anglophone African nations. They suggest that there is a shared black African culture that emphasizes hierarchy, embeddedness and mastery, in contrast to alternative qualities of egalitarianism, autonomy and harmony. Hence, African managers stress reliance on formal rules and their superiors in reaching decisions. In contrast, Western European nations have a cultural profile in which managers stress self-reliance and consultation with subordinates. While Munene et al's discussion focuses on the implications of these characteristics for development in Africa, their research suggests the need to take into account specific cultural values around leadership and management.

Performance standards and accountability

Several sources provide guidance to international NGOs regarding accountability and performance standards. The development of professional standards in emergency relief for international NGOs emerged from reviews of operations in Rwanda during the mid-1990s which revealed significant difficulties and weaknesses.[6] The Sphere Project was a global NGO initiative to 'improve the effectiveness of humanitarian efforts and to enhance the accountability of the humanitarian system, primarily to those people who have a right to protection and assistance in disasters, as well as to agency members and donors' (Gostelow, 1999). This work resulted in the *Handbook of Minimum Standards*, the Humanitarian Charter and the adoption of the Red Cross Code of Conduct (Sphere Project, 2004), to which the international NGO under review is a signatory.

The research literature documents some concerns about the use of the Sphere minimum standards because of what is perceived to be an undue focus on technical assistance. Médicins Sans Frontières, for example, has taken the position that even though improved technical standards would save lives, more would be saved if international political will would address and prevent humanitarian disasters (Tong, 2004). As noted by Gostelow (1999, p319), 'humanitarian action cannot be a substitute for political action'. (For further discussion of these issues, see Hilshorst, 2002).

Also of relevance is the United Nations High Commissioner for Refugees' *Handbook for Emergencies* (2000) which, while providing direction specifically to United Nations staff, is applicable to others working in international relief operations. Adaptations of this material to the circumstances of NGO aid workers includes that produced by the Aid Workers Network (2002). The People in Aid Code of Good Practice provides guidance around management and support of aid personnel (People in Aid, 2003). These sources include material that is relevant to the discussions in this report regarding the provision of infrastructure, implementation of systems and emergency staffing, outlined further in the respective sections.

Quarantelli (1997) outlines principles for disaster management. While her paper is focused on disasters in developed countries (rather than in developing countries) and concerns responses undertaken by domestic staff, the framework provided offers relevant insights. She argues that good disaster management relies on the following ten principles: correctly identifying between response and organizational demands; adequately carrying out generic functions; effectively mobilizing personnel and resources; appropriately delegating of tasks; adequately processing information; properly exercising decision-making; developing overall coordination; blending emergent and established organizational behaviour; providing appropriate information for news media; and having a well-functioning emergency centre.

Management

A consensus existed among interviewed staff members that the tsunami response effort suffered from unclear management structures and poor leadership. Staff identified a lack of clear roles and decision-making structures across the international partnership as one of the most significant problems they faced while undertaking their work. For example, one experienced staff member deployed to Aceh suggested that the senior managers were in survival mode only: 'They held it together but there was no leadership or guidance.'(3) Another commented that: 'It was fairly chaotic there and ... for the next two weeks it was unclear who was responsible for leading the mission.' (7) During this time, this same staff member identified a 'lack of clear decision-making around who was in charge'. A consequence of this was that assessments were undertaken where community needs were identified, but there was no follow-up in response.

Indications of these unclear management structures and poor leadership were expressed in several ways. Firstly, there was a lack of clarity around the roles and responsibilities of staff from national offices, the international NGO, the regional rapid response relief team and the international partnership. There was also an Asian Tsunami Response Team (ATRT), established by the international partnership (initially based in Manila and later Singapore) whose role was to facilitate organizational decision-making, but interviewed staff appeared unaware of its existence in that they failed to comment upon it when interviewed. So while at the day-to-day level of their work the activities of the ATRT may not have been relevant to the interviewed staff, this lack of clarity around roles and responsibilities was manifested in difficulties in communication and collaboration between these various offices and their staff. Secondly, inappropriate staffing choices and a lack of certain skills among international partnership staff heightened leadership concerns. Two areas of particular concern reported by interviewed staff were strategic planning and technical expertise. In particular, this lack of expertise was evident in decisions that impacted upon longer term rehabilitation and surfaced when the international partnership sought contracts. At times, some thought the international partnership was more interested in its 'image', rather than implementing the most appropriate projects.

Concerns were also expressed about the difficulties experienced around the provision of basic infrastructure, the implementation of systems and strategies and the management of staff. While both of these topics have implications for leadership, they are considered separately in following sections.

Unclear management structures

Unclear management structures and the lack of clarity around roles and responsibilities were most markedly manifested in relation to decision-making process and lines of authority. Staff interviewed for this project described tensions between the national offices, the regional rapid response team and other staff (including themselves) who had been deployed in a relief capacity and were attached to the international partnership. The comments of several interview participants are given to reiterate the view that these were widely held views and raised high levels of concern.

Some staff did not know what protocols were in place, and some did not know that any existed. Others who were aware of the parallel governance structures (through experience, if not otherwise) reported that they failed to provide effective decision-making mechanisms, instead causing tension and confusion. As suggested by one interviewed staff member, 'that level of conflict and tension interplays all the way right down through the system, right down to the village and community level.' (16) For example, dual decision-making structures in Indonesia caused considerable frustration:

> *In terms of the structure, sometimes you didn't know who had the authority, whether it was because a lot of the stuff that we did had to be approved by the Indonesia office but they weren't necessarily on the ground with us, so the power base still seemed to be with [the partner NGO in] Indonesia but there were things happening here in Aceh that needed to happen quickly that were being sort of slowed down because of that need to sort of get approval from the Indonesia office. (3)*

Another staff member recounted the problems that resulted, despite protocols being in place:

> *I understand there's protocols in place, that they just weren't followed. Essentially we had situations where the relevant national director said 'I don't care, that's not how it's going to work' and then this sort of tussle ... I think if anything is a failure the very senior leadership of [the international partnership] to come in and pull [local senior managers] into line and their Boards and that's eventually what actually had to happen. It happened too slowly, which is a shame because it meant that our response, particularly in Aceh, was much slower than what it should have been and continues to be hampered particularly in Aceh. (1)*

Another interviewed staff member described this issue as an issue of sovereignty that needed to be resolved:

> *That's what being part of this partnership is and that comes right back to that whole question of sovereignty, who has sovereignty over what happens in a national context. (15)*

One of these problems was highlighted by a senior NGO staff member interviewed who believed that more briefing before going would have allayed some of these concerns:

> *It would have been useful to understand what the standard relationships and issues are in an emergency response between the international [regional] rapid response team and the national office because that proved to be a huge issue ... and how that plays out around the governance issues of who gets to make decisions and I went*

in completely unaware of the way in which that could go very seriously wrong. (7)

One interviewed staff member referred to 'operational imperatives' borne out of the ways that the NGO had continued to make 'the same organizational mistakes ... over and over again'. (18) The implementation of these 'operational imperatives' would mean that an emergency response would occur according to agreed principles and that, in doing so, some would give up their authority. According to this same staff member, 'they've not quite been signed on to in full yet'. The experiences described by interviewed staff during the post-tsunami response would support this view that operational imperatives are not yet in place.

Effects on staff in the field

Lack of clarity in regards to the roles and responsibilities of different arms of the international partnership had a direct effect upon interviewed staff assigned to tsunami-affected areas. For instance, decisions made by one person could be over-turned by another, leaving staff feeling very confused and frustrated. In some instances, interviewed staff reported having to work to several supervisors. For example:

> *You'll be working with one person and then come to an agreement and then somebody else will come in and say, 'that's not important'... you work with the relief manager or the IT manager and make a decision and then run with that, assume that's what been done and then find out a day or two later that the National Director has come in and said, 'no, we can't do that' for whatever reason. (18)*

This experience was shared by others, with one interviewed staff member reporting that she was 'there working in the local team in an emergency capacity so I had a local boss but then I had a regional boss and then I also had an international boss, so it was sort of confusion.' (19)

Yet, in some instances, confusion associated with multiple bosses was substituted for a lack of management and a complete vacuum of leadership. One interviewed staff member found that his first week in Aceh was highly unproductive because 'it was just too unclear who was responsible for what in that particular area'. (4) As a result, he identified a clear area of need where he could make a significant difference in his remaining five weeks and set to ensuring he achieved this goal. His success in Aceh was thus dependent on his own initiative, rather than direction given from appropriate leaders.

Others also took initiative in the absence of guidance and direction, but were less sure about their contributions. One staff member found a distinct lack of clarity around what was expected from her:

> *I ended up working ... for three or four days until the manager came back but it was really self-determined. It was really like going in and seeing what needs to be done and saying, 'well, shall I do this?' rather than anybody really being able to provide that guidance ... I probably wasn't that effective and I don't think that anybody was being effective. People were running around in circles because nobody was providing any leadership about what was to be done and who should be covering what and how it should be handled so I think it was a really difficult context for anybody to really do anything. (13)*

Despite these concerns by some, others felt that positive relationships had existed and they had worked together collaboratively. For example:

> *I had, what helped to get the job done, in the initial phases, the team from [the partner NGO in] Indonesia and the other support offices in doing the assessments ... there was a good culture of collaboration in being able to sit together and being able to nut out, 'okay, what will we do first? and how will we go about that?' and people were very prepared to just figure out 'how will we do this? what is our role?'... [We] were prepared to problem solve so when there wasn't a system for handing it over, we sat and we developed those systems. We set up databases, we wrote up notes, we shared that information, so there was a real sense of pulling in together and pooling our skills and working very, very long hours. (7)*

Another interviewed staff member expressed concern about the lack of appreciation of the perspective of the national offices:

> *I thought that the calibre of staff in [the partner NGO in] Indonesia was really quite high. I think they were treated with immense disrespect ... [A senior national manager] was concerned about the reputation of his programmes and so everybody saw that as him getting in the way or being obstructive and, from my point of view, he had every right to be concerned about the quality of his programmes because I thought the tsunami response was shocking and if that was poorly affecting on work they'd built up over years, then I would be concerned as well. (13)*

Taking into account both the difficulties experienced and the extraordinary circumstances, suggestions were made to improve these situations. After explaining how the partnership office teams appeared to fail to sufficiently communicate and collaborate with the national office they were supposed to be supporting, one interviewed staff member articulated his own opinion of how this situation could have been alleviated:

> *The country director and the international office who run this relief, they need to get together to say 'well, who's in charge of what' and let's, for the first three months of this disaster, have a structure in place that we use and you forgo some things and we will ... we will try to be sensitive to the cultural things as long as you can give your input ... it's either 'you're in charge as a country director and we'll give you the resources or we're in charge and you'll give us your resources,' either way, and I'm not sure what is the best way, but it needs to be just one structure handling it. (2)*

Lack of certain skill bases and inappropriate staffing choices

Interviewed staff raised two issues in relation to skills and staffing experienced within the tsunami response. The first was specifically about the staffing and skills of some international partnership staff. The second was a more general issue about the skill base of the international NGO. Some interviewed staff noted that they viewed the capacity of the regional rapid response teams sent into Indonesia as severely limited. Staff indicated an awareness of the difficulties of finding appropriate staff at short notice but felt that forward thinking could have solved the problematic issues that they identified with these pre-existing teams.

Interviewed staff also spoke of several cases where inappropriate staffing choices had been made. They noted some regional rapid response team members lacked experience and thus found it difficult to trust the decisions of the more experienced staff members with whom they worked. Others were well-known as 'very bad people managers. It was very unpleasant to work with them' (4), people who had no place in the relief response. As one interviewed staff member indicated:

> *There was clearly people who were put into the response who had had significant question marks over their performance in the past and yet they were put into again a very high stress, complex situation and performed very poorly as you would expect ... and the fact that we weren't prepared for that or hadn't actually done things previously*

to ameliorate that then I think we need to cop a bit of that on the chin. (1)

These views were collaborated by another interviewed staff member:

I think the issue was not looking at what is the sort of management that you need and what have you got rather than going back to, 'well, these people are in the [regional rapid response team]) so therefore we'll put them in charge even if we know that they're actually lacking in the skills that we need' and we knew with both the people who were problematic that they were lacking in the skills. One was just inexperienced and the other one had caused significant problems in lots of different environments and people were aware of that but they said we didn't have anybody else. My argument would be actually there was a whole range of people that could've been put into those roles and provided support rather than putting someone in that you know is going to create a whole lot of problems. (7)

An explanation for this poor staffing was that these decisions were made informally, 'through influence, relationships and networks' and on the basis of a 'very closed in group of people who get appointed to the senior positions'. (16) That is, they were selected from within the international partnership and on the basis of existing relationships, despite the likelihood of problematic, and some would argue, predictable, outcomes, as described. It was suggested that these processes of recruitment should be more formalized.

Interviewed staff also indicated that the regional rapid response team sent to Indonesia appeared to lack all the necessary skills required in an emergency situation:

They're supposed to be the experts in emergency and while they clearly had a lot of experience in that, my sense was that they lacked some pretty fundamental skills in a range of areas that you'd expect a senior person to be able to have, such as strategic planning. (1)

In particular, this staff member noted: 'You need a few people with some really broad skills and strong skills in people management, in strategy, in relationship and network building and I didn't see much of that on display.'(1) Another staff member highlighted that the regional rapid response team in Aceh did not appear to have a logistics specialist, yet logistics is crucial to any emergency operation. Others suggested that the operations directors did not have adequate skills bases.

According to some interviewed staff, the response to the tsunami revealed a wider lack of skills in the international partnership, and two areas in particular were identified: technical expertise and strategic planning. In relation to technical expertise, it was acknowledged an organizational skill base did exist but rather that it was 'overwhelmed':

> *what really showed up in with the national office in Indonesia ... was that our long time community development approach didn't actually have enough depth of technical expertise that could be swung into a different kind of response and so that raises questions about the quality of our technical approaches in the long-term development staff. (16)*

In relation to strategic planning, an interviewed staff member suggested that 'it is a skill set that we're deficient in ... and it was clearly lacking in ... in Aceh.'(1) Another interviewed staff member thought that the international partnership was 'managing as if it was a $5 million programme in five countries instead of $350 million' and that there was 'a lack of critical analysis'. This 'critical analysis' would have meant much greater consideration of:

> *what we're doing there, what's our role, what's going to be most sustainable... people focus on the wrong things and are running around in circles instead of standing back just a little bit. (16)*

Addressing these skill gaps could require recruiting staff from outside the international partnership or to capacity build within the organization. In some areas, at least, this was noted by other interview participants as happening, and is addressed further in Section 5 (page 174) in relation to international NGO staff and their involvement in relief situations. In particular, one interview participant spoke about the capacity building of local staff:

> *Emergency response planning should start months and months, years and years in advance. There should be a part of every local non government organization of a considerable size ... preparing for that sort of thing should be owned by local staff more than international. Of course that wasn't the case in the country I was in, it had to be run by outsiders ... I think the kind of money that's spent flying people in, if that was spent on local preparedness for the disaster, I think that would be really helpful. (20)*

A problem both caused and compounded by the poor experience or skills of some staff, was the high turnover which in turn led to considerable instability and incoherence in the international partnership's tsunami response. Interviewed staff acknowledged that it is common in emergency situations for many staff to spend only a few days or weeks in a relief area before being replaced. However, they also indicated that in some situations, replacements had to be made due to inappropriate staffing choices. In addition, they were frustrated by the way in which decision-making structures changed each time new staff members arrived. For example, one interviewed staff member deployed to Aceh indicated that he started with one boss but then, as two more senior people arrived, this manager was relegated to other areas, yet:

> ... *would start doing things that he wanted and then these other people would countermand that and you'd be half way through something and someone would say 'oh no, we don't want to do that any more, we need to do something different'. There's a lot of what I call wheel spinning going on. There were just too many competing demands for our time. (4)*

Another interviewed staff member had four bosses over the eight weeks he was there, as well as almost as many role and title changes during this time.

Taking into account the unfavourable and unprecedented conditions produced by a tsunami which affected many countries at one time, interviewed staff still felt that there had to be ways to ensure that the capacity of the regional rapid response teams were far better than they were. For example, it was suggested that if a specialist in one crucial area is not available for a regional rapid response team, there should be some prior agreement that an appropriate person be sourced in one of the international partnership offices. This would mean that there could be a pool identified of potential strong leaders who were flexible and understood cultural perspectives. Alternatively, staff could be recruited from outside the international partnership, as another interviewed staff member suggested:

> *We need to have some other systems and we need to very quickly be able to assess the need to go outside. There were a whole lot of people who offered their support through the support offices which weren't taken up because they were outside the system ... we always look internally for our leaders ... the fact is that people may not necessarily have leadership experience in an humanitarian emergency, but you can make an assessment that they have the skills to lead various aspects and we need to be able to look more flexibly at the workforce that we have and we need to have a database of people that we can call on. (7)*

Too much emphasis on NGO's 'image', rather than meeting need

Interviewed staff members raised the notion of 'image' in relation to two contexts; first, in relation to international partnership's relationship to other international relief organizations; and, second, to the wider general public. In both contexts some interviewed staff were concerned that there was too much emphasis on maintaining a particular perception of the international partnership rather than attending to the work that needed to be done. Other staff were less concerned. Their view was that this work was a part of what needed to be done; in the first instance, in terms of securing contracts and, in the second, to inform donors of the work that the international partnership was undertaking and to encourage further donations.

Several interviewed staff indicated that they felt the international partnership had been overly concerned with its own image as an international NGO in the competitive world of international development and relief. This sense of competition with other NGOs led, in the opinion of one staff member, to too much focus on 'planting your flag' (3) on projects just for the sake of having some, rather than identifying where the international partnership's skills and expertise lay (and this is related to the previous discussion regarding areas of expertise). What was important was to be seen to be doing the right thing to maintain the international partnership's impressive international reputation:

> *It was only through our external signals to the rest of the NGO community that made [the international partnership] look like we knew what we were doing but behind the scenes we were in a bit of a mess ... I'd say the real organization kicked in about four weeks after we were there. But in the early days the pressure was on to move from 18th place out of 20 to first, second or third but it looked with the helicopters and the vehicles like we knew what we were doing. (6)*

A third interviewed staff member agreed that: 'it was certainly that sort of turf war stuff going on' but explained that the international partnership was feeling particularly vulnerable when compared to other NGOs because of poor staff selection:

> *I don't think we were very good at that turf war and, again, it goes back into relationships and being in the right venues and being externally focused and all that sort of stuff, so again a skill set deficiency within [the international partnership] more broadly. So, I know, particularly in Aceh, they recognized that and some time after I left, sent*

in someone who they thought could better 'muscle in' on some of those opportunities, but I would have thought again it was a skill set that you would normally expect a senior leader in the emergency relief team to be able to display. (1)

Again, others located these experiences within its context:

There were a lot of pressure from the support offices to spend and it's very difficult to spend in an immediate relief situation. The government isn't ready to start signing on the dotted line about which schools it wants fixed up. If you imagine the whole of the west coast, all of the roads, the ports, the infrastructure was gone, these were isolated communities and you're dealing with hundreds of thousands of people at the raw edge of grief that just had their whole world ripped apart, so you can't go in there and start talking to them about what do you need to rebuild your business, they haven't buried their dead yet. (12)

In addition, working with much larger sums of funding created unique circumstances:

I feel that we cannot blame anyone if I am appointed for a $1 million project and then in six months or in two years suddenly, for whatever reasons, I'm asked that I have to deal with $100 million. We are going to have gaps and those are the gaps that we are seeing. People are used to their vision only restricted to $1 million or $4 million or $5 million or whatever, then suddenly you've got to expand your horizon to an unimaginable lot … the pressure to show things on the ground, to get something physically out there and everyone is struggling to get things done in a society and a situation where everything is very slow pace, government systems are not very effective … just taking things to another level. (12)

But at the same time, another staff member provided a reminder of the nature of this kind of work and situation:

If you don't claim something quickly you're out. And that's pressure and that's the real world. That is the real world of this stuff, you have to do that and it can be very competitive and it's very uncomfortable for many of us but there is that pressure … every one of these agencies, not just [the international partnership] … they've got money and they're competing for the opportunity to find a community and authorities or local partners to work with in that kind of crisis. (15)

Other staff expressed concerns about what was involved in presenting the international partnership's image to the wider community. In undertaking this image-making, the immediate needs identified out in the field were not being addressed as quickly as they would have liked. This is highlighted by a senior and long-term staff member responsible for logistics in Aceh, who was compromised by the competing demands of various partnership offices. In indicating how he had to off-load important supplies to free-up helicopter space for those whom he referred to as 'development tourists', he noted:

> *I had a three-way death wish here, the helicopter pilot that wanted to do everything like they just walked out of 'Good Morning Vietnam', the organizational structure that was telling me 'we need to get the goods down the coast line'- there are emergency things - and the partnership saying to me 'we have to put on the best face that we can, we have important visitors coming, we have to look professional'. (6)*

He suggested that if there had been sufficiently strong leadership in the tsunami response, controls would have been put on the number and type of visitors allowed to monopolize resources in this way.

Another staff member commented on the effort expended recording and transmitting images to the outside world of the work being undertaken in responding to the tsunami, and this was also of concern because she believed it tied up valuable resources:

> *[The international partnership] was ... more worried about media, they were more worried about sending cameras down to me to get pictures of little kids than sending down stuff that was actually going to help those little kids. (13)*

In contrast to this view, other staff members acknowledged that there is pressure to have media coverage so that the donors can receive information about the work being done, and to encourage further donations. However, one interviewed staff member who worked in communications argued that it could have been done better. She noted the lack of organization around the collection of media images and developed policies and protocols to deal with film crews. She identified a need to know:

> *where they're going and not going to the same place five times because you're putting so much pressure on the local field staff who are just trying to order food and save lives and you're shoving a camera in their face all the time ... there needs to be some kind of order and structure*

*and responsibility to manage the mayhem so it's not cowboys running
in with cameras and running out with photos and footage. (19)*

Partnership governance issues are not unique to this NGO, as debates in the
research literature concerning northern and southern NGOs structures tes-
tify. This research clearly points to difficulties that were experienced by staff
throughout the organization in undertaking their work during these emergency relief operations.

In addition to the lack of clear roles between differing arms of the international partnership, interviewed staff were concerned about the capacity of
some expatriate staff sent into Indonesia. Interviewed staff members noted
that inappropriate staffing choices had been made and, among those
selected for leadership positions, the skills required in an emergency situation were not necessarily present. There were also concerns expressed about
the ways in which the international partnership participated in seeking contracts without proper consideration of the circumstances, again reflective of
poor leadership.

Infrastructure and systems

Many interviewed staff reported difficulties in accessing basic infrastructure
early in the tsunami response and not having in place standard systems that
would facilitate their work. The apparent lack of infrastructure and systems
and implementation of strategies in tsunami-affected areas is associated
with leadership issues but is worth exploring separately given the considerable concern interviewed staff members expressed about this situation.
These systems and strategies were of two kinds: first, a general international
partnership plan put in place at times of disaster to deal with immediate
ways of working and, second, the strategies developed to deal with both the
local crisis circumstances and over time. There was some disagreement as
to whether the international partnership actually had systems and strategies
in place or whether they were just not filtered down to the field. As discussed
in the previous section, there was also the concern that the international
partnership did not have staff with expertise in strategic planning. Either
way, interviews highlighted several issues which illustrated this concern with
the existence of the international partnership's systems and strategies and
their implementation:

*It was just chaotic in a sense that there was a massive job to be done
and they had plenty of money to do it and the systems in place and
the structures required to make that machine work weren't there. (20)*

Lack of basic infrastructure

Central to difficulties early in the international partnership response, and critical to both general plans and also specific localized responses, were the lack of basic equipment and infrastructure to respond effectively. These problems were more acute in Aceh than other places affected by the tsunami:

> *In Aceh, it was more difficult because of the lack of infrastructure ... I was certainly surprised that the first plane load in didn't have satellite dishes so that we could get satellite broadband ... and a range of other systems that I would have thought pretty common across a category 3 disaster ... When you can't get internet and access to some of that sort of stuff weeks after the disaster, then there's something wrong. (1)*

Access to adequate telephone services in Aceh was crucial but not straightforward, as another interview participant described:

> *The concerns for me were not having adequate mobile telephone coverage ... The Jakarta office gave us pre-paid mobile telephones. Now I had my phone which would work but it was so expensive to dial ... so the issues of the telephones were a concern, especially when we ran out and we found we had pre-paids. We had to ring down to Jakarta and we got this 20 digit number to plug into the telephone but all the instructions were in Indonesian so we had to get staff to help. These small frustrations in a very pressured environment compound into bigger issues than what you think they are. (6)*

Another staff member suggested that systems should be in place to ensure that all the international partnership relief workers come with a laptop computer, have a common email account configured in the same way and, where security measures are in place, passwords should be available.

The lack of infrastructure had an impact on the work of one interviewed staff member in Aceh. Poor communication and lack of information and resources thwarted his efforts to establish a temporary regional office. He was unable to communicate with his manager until later in his deployment, as he did not have the proper equipment. However, he remarked: 'even in the last ten days when I had the communications equipment, things were not getting that much better because they still could not bring the support because they could not recruit people quick enough.' (8)

Inappropriate or poor systems put in place

Interview participants expressed dissatisfaction about the lack of systems put in place. The international partnership has resources for establishing systems for emergency relief work which covers a range of areas including finance, commodities, food monitoring and human resources. While some knew about these resources and used them, others did not:

> *Those CDs which go through every single aspect of programming and how to run your assessments and how to set up your finance systems, how to set up your admin systems, it's all there and [the regional rapid response teams] have all that … It wasn't used. Like thousands and thousands and millions of dollars they spent at the partnership level developing these tools and there's emergency relief databases with all this stuff on and people knew that, I don't know whether that means, I don't know the material intimately was my first response, but I don't know whether that just means that the material is not good or adequate or useful or whether it's just that people aren't trained in how to use it properly. (13)*

Another interviewed staff member described the effect of not having suitable systems in place:

> *People had individual responsibility and they were doing their own thing as best as they could … we put people out in various areas in zones to set up the response there and then they were saying 'I need to have an engineer,' and 'I need to have the tents for school classrooms' and 'I need to have child friendly spaces with school books.' The systems to actually enable that to happen weren't really there. They were very hit and miss and they relied more on individuals going to all links rather than their own systems so when they got employed and they needed money to be sent down to locations it really required someone who would ring someone who would then run around and try and make it happen rather than clear systems which just worked for us to support the programme. (7)*

In this case, these difficulties were attributed to a lack of leadership in the first weeks after the disaster struck and then, later, poor prioritization by the programme director: 'establishing the organizational infrastructure rather than focusing in on what we need to do to make this response effective for the community.' (7)

But even when systems existed, or were put in place, there were concerns about their usefulness in the extreme conditions post-tsunami. In particular, several interviewed staff indicated that 'Some of the processes that they put in place were not relevant to a relief situation' (3), resulting in one interviewed staff member finding that things she had asked to be supplied in her first week still had not arrived when she left five weeks later. Another interviewed staff member similarly highlighted that accountability systems which might be appropriate in a development situation, simply hindered his work in Aceh in a relief situation:

> *The Jakarta staff were wonderful people but their mind was in development mode, their mind was saying 'well, we normally get three quotes. Can you nick down the street and get three quotes?'... then you go down and get three quotes and the finance people would say 'hang on one of these quotes is not for the same item, you've got to go and get it again'. (6)*

Another staff member indicated that while the provision of mobile telephones that only work on a geographically limited, pre-paid network might be appropriate in a development situation, it caused huge headaches in an emergency situation. He stressed the need for a different set of emergency protocols to be established by all national offices so that these simple frustrations do not hinder the effort of future relief efforts. Another argued that emergency protocols around basic issues that are standard to any relief operation, such as the provision of water or United Nations endorsed treated mosquito nets, should be established. In addition, she suggested that all national offices need to have standardized databases, such as for the tracking of food and non-food items, to ensure a quick and efficient response. This lack of connection between local needs and international supply meant that 'there was an over-supply of everything'. (4)

Furthermore, two interviewed staff members were concerned that qualified people were not put into the field quickly enough or in sufficient numbers to deal with the crisis. One noted (and this also relates to the discussion previously about recruitment):

> *I would have thought it was a laid down procedure on how to attack this kind of disaster, you'd assess the situation, you'd bring in experts, you try to get the projects, it seems to me – and again I'm not in the project area, so I'm only speaking from what I heard and what I saw and how – we were actually in a situation where we nearly lost a lot of the projects that we should have had, and we were in a situation where we might not have got projects and that meant that we wouldn't*

have something to actually spend the money on and I think a lot of that was because we had a lot of people in the office doing the organizing but we didn't have the actual technical experts out in the field making assessments and grabbing hold the projects. (2)

Poor communication

According to staff interviewed, there were a number of occasions when crucial strategic planning and other documents were not handed over, adding to frustration and wasting time:

People at a very senior level knowing what's going on across the whole programme and being able to guide you and coordinate and know where you're heading. Now that changes in a relief situation quite quickly but there should be some basic things that sort of remain and I know that some strategy documents drawn up which weren't published and then when we did our strategies it was brought to light that well, hang on, we've got a strategy document, it was written up, someone spent a heck of a lot of time doing it so why are we re-inventing that? So that was, a few things like that got lost and just again standards, no hand over notes. (3)

Those staff members who were experienced and already had strong networks across the international partnership believed that they had achieved some important goals while they were assigned to a tsunami-affected area, but were concerned that without this background they may have felt quite differently. Others new to relief work, however, still felt that they did some good work but were less certain about having 'made a difference'. For example, this reliance on personal experience and relationships put newer staff in a vulnerable situation. An interviewed staff member indicated that part of his frustration was that: 'it was sort of expected that I knew these people and knew where all these things were coming from but I had no way of knowing that.'(4) In noting how important the existing relationships he had with international staff were to his day-to-day work, a senior staff member predicted how a less-experienced employee might have coped: 'It could have killed you … I had no preparation or briefing. I was basically told when you get there you're going to be pointed in a certain direction and off you go.'(6)

Policy and procedures developed by the international partnership and others (e.g., UNHCR, 2000; Sphere Project, 2004) provide clear guidance regarding emergency infrastructure and the implementation of systems in emergency situations. The responses of the interview participants suggest that some of these guidelines were not followed. While the circumstances of the deployment post-tsunami were unusual, it is an opportunity to reiterate the need for good practice.

Preparation and support

Although related to the broader systems and strategies highlighted previously, interviewed staff members also spoke specifically of the apparent lack of preparation demonstrated by the international NGO when it offered its own office staff to assist with the tsunami relief effort. In particular, they noted that there had been an insufficient assessment of what roles needed filling, what projects should be developed and, thus, what people would be suitable to send. As indicated previously, the UNHCR advises:

> *There should be no delay in committing personnel. However, solely adding personnel will not meet the organizational needs of an emergency ... Experience shows that for a given operation, smaller teams with clear allocation of responsibilities are usually more successful than larger teams whose members have less clearly defined roles. (UNHCR, 2000: p292)*

In addition, staff indicated that the international NGO could have better prepared its staff for potential involvement in relief situations. While they acknowledged that a high staff turnover in the industry makes this a complex task, a pool of trained staff on standby could have resulted in a better response.

Once deployed, some staff were concerned that there was inadequate support, partly, as a result of communication difficulties and a lack of appropriate supervision on site. Debriefing was also noted as an important part of their deployment. The following discussion highlights the issues raised in relation to the preparation and support of interviewed staff who were deployed to tsunami-affected areas.

Training in and experience of emergency relief by deployed staff

As noted, about half of the interview participants had had experience working in emergency relief settings prior to working in the tsunami-affected areas. While one other staff member interviewed had been involved in an overseas secondment programme that had enabled him to experience a relief situation prior to an emergency occurring, all others had no formal training or experience in a relief environment. It is acknowledged, however, that many had experience of working in a development setting. But, as suggested below, interview participants noted the differences between the two situations:

> *I didn't know exactly what to expect because I hadn't been to an emergency before ... similar rules apply on how to do the job but it's in a slightly different environment. I had the skills but probably not the experience for an emergency. (19)*

For those staff without prior experience of an emergency situation, to firstly make sense of the conditions under which they were working was a priority. As one interviewed staff member with field experience said: 'I've done it all when I've hit the ground' but 'we should be given an opportunity to be trained so at least when we go in we can hit the ground running.' (6) He suggested that such training should be extended to many more long-serving staff.

Briefing of staff prior to or at the commencement of deployment

Interviewed staff were well aware that it is difficult to provide sufficient briefings in emergency situations, simply because of the speed at which aid organizations must respond. It was also acknowledged that the international staff who arrived earliest in the tsunami-affected areas had left their own country at a time of year when many people were away or otherwise on holidays for Christmas and New Year, hampering the organization's capacity to provide briefing. It was also acknowledged that, particularly in Aceh, the scale of the disaster was initially unclear.

However, there were inconsistencies in the level of information different staff members were provided with; some were provided with a reasonable level of background information prior to leaving their own country, others reported that they went without any briefings. More importantly, staff members highlighted the importance of having a briefing session in the field or being able to talk to someone who had just left the field as crucial background to being able to 'hit the ground running'. In particular, some staff stressed the importance of briefing around cross-cultural awareness:

> *When we are going into a country it is their operations we are going into and, mind you, these guys have their own constitutional agreement, their own board and suddenly the tsunami comes and the*

tsunami brings with it a tsunami of foreigners and, at one point of time, we were from 15 different countries ... one has to recognize that we are going into a completely different culture, different sensitivities have to be followed and to be aware of those sensitivities, cultural protocols, and just the expectations, the tensions, the social political expectations. (12)

As reiterated by the Sphere Project (2004, p40): 'Aid workers should have relevant technical qualifications and knowledge of local cultures and customs and/or previous emergency experience.'

Health of deployed staff

Only one staff member mentioned that the currency of vaccinations could be an issue, but he highlighted a broader lack of health preparedness. The international NGO currently has no system in place to ensure that staff on standby for emergency situations routinely update their travel vaccinations and undertake medical examinations. The latter is important, given that in an emergency situation there is often no time to visit a doctor prior to deployment, yet it is hard to assess any changes in a staff member's medical condition without a baseline.

The Sphere Project (2004) advises that all staff should receive vaccinations prior to deployment, and appropriate briefings on health issues, both prior to their deployment and when they arrive on-site. The Sphere Project also recommends that, upon arrival, staff should be briefed on water safety, prevention of HIV/AIDS and other endemic infectious diseases, medical care availability, medical evacuation policies and procedures, and workers' compensation.

Under more usual emergency conditions all these issues may well have been addressed; in the chaotic conditions post-tsunami and with a contingent of staff who were less experienced, briefings may have been less than comprehensive. While it is unclear whether or not these briefings occurred in all cases, it is a timely reminder, especially as at least two interview participants reported experiences of serious ill health during or immediately after their deployment. In one case, at least, even though there were procedures in place to receive medical support locally, closer supervision might have meant that this staff member was evacuated sooner.

Supervision and performance management

A lack of guidance in relation to the work of some interviewed staff has already been discussed in relation to the effects of poor leadership. Here, the focus is more on the supportive aspects of staff supervision. A senior staff member expressed concern about the poor level of supervision and support provided in some settings:

> *People were put in very insecure vulnerable positions that they should not have been … sitting here in [in the deploying country] you can't actually look after them appropriately and we are trusting our colleagues to manage them. (16).*

One staff member said that as a consequence of poor leadership and, in her case, the absence of a field manager, she was unable to receive feedback on her performance. She felt that this was a significant downfall, because she would have liked to have had the opportunity to learn more from her experiences. Receiving feedback on staff performance is noted by the Sphere Project (2004) as a key indicator of a common standard of supervision, management and support of personnel.

Support and debriefing in the field and upon return

It is well-recognized that aid workers require debriefing (Omidian, 2001; Wilson and Gielissen, 2004). Interviewed participants reported that, generally, the post-tsunami conditions were stressful and such debriefing was necessary. However, particular additional stresses may have been experienced by those who felt that organizational issues thwarted them in getting their job done. As noted before, interviewed staff reported high levels of commitment to do their job and feeling unable to work effectively may have added to the difficulties that they experienced.

Much of the debriefing undertaken by interviewed staff in the field appears to have occurred informally. Interviewed staff members relied on their own networks including colleagues and families or personal faith to deal with the emotional and work-related issues that surfaced during their time in a tsunami-affected area. Some of this support relied on access to telephone or other forms of communications to contact people back home. However, not all staff were aware what financial or other support was available to facilitate these contacts.

The extent to which emotional support and debriefing in the field was provided by the international NGO seemed to vary. One interviewed staff member suggested that it would certainly have improved his experience if such support had been more formalized. Importantly, he noted that for someone with less experience than himself in relief situations, this would be essential to their coping in what would always be a trying environment. Another said that, while he did not feel unsupported, it was mostly his own personal resources of having had previous experience of working in these kinds of circumstances that got him through.

In contrast, other team members described themselves as having been well supported by the deploying country office during their time in tsunami-affected areas. Debriefing after returning from the tsunami-affected areas has been made available to interviewed staff and some staff acknowledged its value. Others did not feel that they needed to take advantage of the offer; others appeared unaware that it was available.

Policy and procedures developed by the UNHCR (2000) and aid agencies (Sphere Project, 2004; Aid Workers Network, 2002) provide clear guidance regarding the preparation and support of aid workers deployed to complex humanitarian emergencies. The responses of the interview participants suggest that some of these guidelines were not followed. While the circumstances of the deployment post-tsunami were unusual, it is an opportunity to reiterate the need for good practice.

Conclusion

The purpose of this research was to document the experiences of international NGO staff who participated in the response to the Indian Ocean tsunami. In doing so it aimed to inform future responses to complex humanitarian emergencies. This research involved detailed interviews with twenty-one staff who were asked about their experience of deployments in relief operations in tsunami-affected areas, in particular, in Indonesia.

In undertaking reconstruction efforts in Aceh, short-term deployed staff from this international NGO worked under difficult circumstances. In the initial period following the tsunami, these staff sought to meet the basic needs of those affected in terms of health care, shelter, food and water. Following this, these staff re-focused their work to consider reconstructing both the physical destruction wrought by the tsunami as well as rebuild shattered communities. In trying to deliver these reconstruction efforts, staff experienced three distinct difficulties in terms of their own organization which affected their ability to effectively respond to the tsunami crisis: management and leadership; infrastructure and systems; and preparation and support of seconded staff. These issues constrained these short-term deployed staff's reconstruction efforts.

It is incumbent upon NGOs to continuously seek to improve their operations and improve the capacity of their staff to successfully implement relief interventions. NGOs must learn from the experiences of these staff to improve their own capacity to respond effectively in the future. Three main concerns were raised during these interviews: unclear management structures and poor leadership at the relief operation sites, inadequate provision of basic infrastructure and difficulties in the implementation of systems and strategies; and concerns about the preparation and support of these staff. While the reconstruction efforts in Aceh were significantly larger than any other response undertaken by the international community, international NGOs do have considerable experience in responding to complex humanitarian emergencies. Further, policies and procedures have been prepared and development that provide clear guidelines when responding. The responses of those surveyed indicate that these guidelines were not always followed and this constrained their effectiveness in responding.

International NGOs are accountable to their donors (both private and public) but also the communities with whom they work. The major evaluations of the tsunami response (primarily those undertaken by the Tsunami Evaluation Coalition, TEC – see Telford et al (2006) and Cosgrave (2007) as examples) have indicated that the reconstruction could have had greater impact than it did on the lives of those affected by the tsunami. International NGOs ought to learn the lessons of the Aceh reconstruction to ensure that future responses to complex humanitarian emergencies do not repeat these same errors. Part of learning these lessons are listening to the voices of those deployed to implement the reconstruction interventions.

References

Aid Workers Network (2002) *Emergency staffing.* Online at: www.aidworkers.net/management/people/staffing.html accessed 21 September 2005

Cosgrave, J. (2007) *Synthesis Report: Expanded Summary. Joint Evaluation of the international response to the Indian Ocean tsunami,* London, Tsunami Evaluation Coalition

Gostelow, L. (1999) 'The Sphere project: The implications of making humanitarian principles and codes work', *Disasters,* vol 23, no 4, pp316–325

Hilshorst, D. (2002) 'Being good at doing good? Quality and accountability of humanitarian NGOs', *Disasters,* vol 26, no 2, pp193–212

Lewis, D. (2001) *The Management of Non-Governmental Development Organisations,* London, Routledge

Malhotra, K. (2000) 'NGO's without aid beyond the global soup kitchen', *Third World Quarterly,* vol 21, no 4, pp655–668

Mukasa, S. (1999) *Are expatriate staff necessary in international development NGOs? A case study of Uganda,* International working paper no 4, Centre for Civil Society, London School of Economics

Munene, J., Schwartz, S. and Smith, P. (2000) 'Development in sub-Saharan Africa: Cultural influences and managers' decision behaviour', *Public Administration Development,* vol 20, pp339–351

Omidian, P. (2001) 'Aid workers in Afghanistan: Health consequences', *The Lancet,* vol 358, no 9292, p1545

People in Aid (2003) *Code Good Practice in the Management and Support of Aid Personnel,* London, People in Aid. Online at www.peopleinaid.org/code/index.htm, accessed 10 October 2005

Quarantelli, E.L. (1997) 'Ten criteria for evaluating the management of community disasters', *Disasters,* vol 2, no 1, pp39–56

Smillie, I. (2001) *Patronage or Partnership: Local Capacity Building in Humanitarian Crises,* Bloomfield, Kumarian Press

Sphere Project (2004) *Humanitarian Charter and Minimum Standards in Disaster Response,* Geneva, Sphere Project

Suzuki, N. (1998) *Inside NGOs: Managing conflicts between headquarters and field offices non-government organisations,* London, Intermediate Technologies

Telford, J., Cosgrave, J. and Houghton, R. (2006) *Joint Evaluation of the International Response to the Indian Ocean Tsunami: Synthesis Report,* London, Tsunami Evaluation Coalition

Tong, J. (2004) 'Questionable accountability: MSF and Sphere in 2003', *Disasters,* vol 28, no 2, pp176–189

UNHCR (2000) *Handbook for Emergencies,* 2nd edn, United Nations High Commissioner for Refugees. Online at: www.unhcr.ch/cgi-bin/texis/vtx/home accessed 21 September 2005

Wilson, J.P. and Gielessen, H. (2004) 'Managing secondary PTSD among personnel deployed in post-conflict countries' *Disaster Prevention and Management,* vol 13, no 3, pp199–209

Notes

1   See Cosgrove (2007) for the low estimate and (www.wordmag.com/Analysis/analysis_2005.12_tsunami_part1.html) for the high estimate.

2   To ensure the anonymity of these interviewed staff, the international NGO will not be identified. Also, even though most participants did not request anonymity, identifying information has not been used in this report to preserve the anonymity of all interviewees. As most interview participants are still employed by the international NGO minimizing the possibility of identification was considered paramount.

3   Some interviewed staff also had experiences in Sri Lanka, India and Thailand.

4   This international NGO is part of an international partnership with offices in both developed and developing countries.

5   This is a standing team of relief specialists employed by the international partnership that can be deployed within 24 hours of a complex humanitarian emergency occurring in the Asia-Pacific region.

6   As discussed though, the largest evaluations of the reconstruction effort suggest that these weakness and difficulties were repeated (see Telford et al, 2006 and Cosgrave, 2007).

8

The Role and Experiences of Badan Rehabilitasi dan Rekonstuksi (BRR)[1]

Fuad Mardhatillah

Introduction

Disasters have marred almost the whole of modern Acehnese history. They have included natural disaster (such as the tsunami) and the traumas resulting from them, and also the 'disasters' resulting from man-made conflict. The significance of conflict has often been overlooked in efforts to develop Aceh in the wider context, not just in terms of physical infrastructure but also in terms of human capital. The conflict between GAM and the Republic of Indonesia, which raged from 4 December 1976 (following the Banda Aceh Proclamation at Bukit Tiro) to the signing of the Memorandum of Understanding in Helsinki on 15 August 2005, resulted in the destruction of infrastructure, community demoralization, and significant loss of life.[2] The resulting destruction of the social infrastructure has been an important impediment to the successful development of the region.

The earthquake and subsequent tsunami on Boxing Day 2004, that measured about 9.0 on the Richter scale, destroyed everything that stood along a major portion of the western coast of the province of Nanggroe Aceh Darussalam (NAD). Another earthquake, on 28 March 2005 struck Aceh again and crippled the communities of the nearby Nias Archipelago. Efforts to reconstruct these two regions were immediately begun by the government of Indonesia and its partner organizations. Two and a half weeks after the Nias earthquake, President Susilo Bambang Yudhoyono (SBY) announced a master plan for the reconstruction of Aceh and Nias that had been developed by the *Badan Perencanaan Pembangunan Nasional* (National Development Planning Agency, Bappenas).[3] A day later, SBY formed the *Badan Rehabilitasi dan Rekonstruksi NAD-Nias* (NAD-Nias Rehabilitation and Reconstruction Agency, BRR).[4] In the following two weeks, BRR's leadership was sworn in. From that time, the wheels of rehabilitation and reconstruction began to turn.

More than halfway through its term of operation, it was not easy for BRR to carry out its assigned duties. There were successes, but there were also a significant number of impediments as well. BRR approached these occurrences as individual challenges to be addressed and transformed, to the extent possible, into opportunities more in line with the most wide-ranging interests of the public as beneficiaries. The experiences of BRR in this effort will be considered here and will focus on NAD, as limitations of space do not permit a detailed analysis of the situation in Nias as well.

To this end, it is vital that we critically consider the nature of the context within which BRR was formed and operates. The interplay of physical factors and human nature and behaviour must be taken into account in discussing the various tasks associated with the rehabilitation and reconstruction effort. For this reason, the historical context that has served as a backdrop for the reconstruction of Aceh and its people to date will be considered briefly below.

The paradox of harmony

Common ideals, which exist in the life of a people and nation, often face the threat of destruction in the effort to achieve them. Communities are often forced to accept an overarching common orientation, but this may not address various individual and group orientations within the community that are smaller in scope. These threats arise from an intensification of narrow conflicts of interest. For example, influential individuals or groups that exist in the community are not handled fairly or in a way that satisfies their interests by the national system of political management.

Discrimination and injustice in various sectors of national and social life, including all the interconnected processes of development which are planned and carried out by the government, are often the cause of a loss of ideals. When the threat of disintegration emerged in Aceh, for example, it seemed to have been caused by the absence of opportunities for free and substantial self-actualization for the people of the region, as a result of a forced interpretation of the nature of a nationalism, that was top-down, unitary and uniform, and that eliminated a dimension for dialogue and debate. The potential for diversity, in which each entity demands the opportunity for appreciation, actualization, and participation, exists everywhere, including in Indonesia and in Aceh. Yet governance that is closed to participation and tolerates the existence of exclusionary social discrimination and the widespread use of force tends to give rise to serious injustice in the distribution of the results of development. When this occurs, it is fitting that the public question the need for a nation if its existence only devastates them and drives them into despair. In other words, the existence of a nation is ideally supposed to give rise to harmony in the collective life of the public. What has happened in Aceh and what its people have experienced is disharmony. It is apparent here that a paradoxical situation has resulted in discord whose impact has increasingly distanced each individual from the common ideals that were implicit when the nation was founded.

In Indonesia's history as a nation, violent and bloody conflicts have taken place over a long period of time. Specifically, these conflicts were a result of the centralistic, authoritarian, bureaucratic, symbolic and militaristic New Order government, that used force as a means of control. Its systems robbed the public of its right to self-actualization in many spheres of social, economic, political, and cultural life. In addition to stifling the ability of individuals to engage in critical analysis, the creativity, imagination and productivity of the public were destroyed.

So, the societal diversity that should give rise to culture and civilization, that would enhance mutual understanding and respect, has not been a positive force in Indonesia. In fact, there should have been opportunity and potential conducive to the development and innovation. Yet most of Indonesia's rich cultural potential has been totally unusable, while its diversity has been made uniform by a normative political ideology of symbolic social harmony that is deceptive and opposes the natural plurality of society.

For the period when the New Order government was in power, Indonesia was envisioned as a peaceful and harmonious family whose father, Pak Harto, never tired of showing his smile and gentle side to the public. But in attack mode, that regime built a network of force and violence that terrified and strangled its own people by silencing those who were critical, and brutally cracking down on certain elements of the public as well as extremist and separatist groups. This included its most sadistic behaviour toward the Free Aceh Movement (*Gerakan Aceh Merdeka*, GAM) when Aceh became a region of military operations, from 1989 to 1998. This is the paradox of the New Order's version of the 'harmonious family': soft on the outside but hard underneath. National behaviour that suppressed and threatened then became an experience that was recognized as a form of truth that was internalized by the public to the extent that it penetrated and formed their mentality, acting like a brake on the flow of sociocultural and political awareness. People became closed, unwilling not to conform (in their opinions and so forth), because difference was the enemy. They developed an oppressive nature, with the strong overrunning the weak, and they tended to put their own personal interests, security, and enjoyment above everything else, rather than work together for larger aims and interests they had in common.

It is apparent that this internalization was a means of accommodating experiences that occurred continuously over a long period of time, eventually becoming commonplace or ordinary, and finally becoming simply the way of things. Over time, this contributed to the development of a way of thinking and a type of awareness within the community, which in turn gave rise to the behaviour observed during this time. Experiences of injustice and violence, for example, may have turned the attitudes and behaviour of the public towards discrimination, achieving by force, a culture of violence, and other irrational acts.[5]

That was Indonesia's modern past, which framed two types of historical awareness among the public that are different and diametrically opposed. There are those individuals who wish to create from the past a tradition that should be factored into future development. These are the people who benefited from the political system and institutions of the past. On the other hand, there are a few people who wish to make the past no more than a subject of study; they seek change because they are aware of the scale of marginalization and crisis that have overrun almost every aspect of life. This seems to be indicated by the growing number of the poor and the widespread mental and physical suffering of the public for which there almost seems to be no remedy. This is the result of the compounding nature of an authoritarian national governance using force and violence since the founding of the nation.

The experiences of the past always contain lessons that will give us reason to hope that we will not become mired in the same mistakes for a second time. Historical analysis is, for this reason, extremely important in planning, designing, and carrying out better and more realistic development for the future. It is unfortunate that the members of the first group are much more numerous than those of the second and are found in all our social strata. Further, the groups that are resistant to change are increasingly dominant in determining societal behaviour, especially within the ranks of the elite. They then strengthen the status quo and reinforce resistance to change.

This resistance is extremely counter-productive in the effort to make common progress and to raise the level of prosperity of society as a whole.

This type of behaviour has become endemic in Indonesia. Nonetheless, it often manifests as actions that seem to be (pseudo) democratic or critical and seem to be in the public interest. In fact, because we lack practice in democracy and acquired it prematurely, and because it is imitative and often opportunistic in nature anyway, it embodies an attitude of self-promotion that is quite extreme. The practice of always putting one's own self first has the potential to cause conflict that can erupt at any time when the narrow interests of an individual or a group cannot be accommodated or fulfilled. This is the paradox of 'false democracy'. The GAM separatist movement was one embodiment of public opposition in Aceh to the false democracy that existed for almost the whole period of the New Order government. The reality of the situation is that those who protest against false democracy are not necessarily the most democratic. As a result, democracy that seems to represent the demands and needs of everyone has been impeded by the individual desires of those who fought for it and who have failed to consider common goals.

The aftermath of conflict

While it is beyond the scope of this chapter to analyse historical events, it is impossible to understand the development situation in Aceh today without considering the effects this prolonged period has had on the public. Continued rebellion and uprising by the people indicate that the people must be an important element in the process of conflict resolution. Up to now, their role has often been ignored. The central government has only recently accepted GAM as part of the local political elite. In fact, the whole decision-making process for Aceh will in the end rest on how the members of the public respond, form attitudes, and choose to participate.

On the other hand, conflict has left many negatives. Basic economic infrastructure was destroyed, damaged, or allowed to fall into disrepair and is not available for public use. This swelled the ranks of the poor. Governance structures and traditional institutions, that were crippled by a centralized political system that was intended to create conformity and hegemony, sapped societal institutions of their initiative, creativity, and productivity. In addition, the conflict resulted in the physical destruction of houses, schools, and other educational facilities. Teachers were silenced and fearful. The educational process was disturbed down to its roots. In short, the quality of life in Aceh fell to a nadir and will no doubt take time to return to a productive level. Special attention must be paid to the survivors and their families. In some cases, conflict has crippled their moral sense, left deep traumatic wounds and led to a distrust of other individuals and groups, and a latent or even overt desire for revenge against others. Finally, trust has been lost by society as a whole. Trust in the central government by the region and trust in government officials by the public have been destroyed. Worst of all, the Acehnese no longer trust each other. One result of this is the phenomenon of the 'wolf in sheep's clothing' that has already preyed on many citizens.

The experience of continuing conflict has created a specific type of character among the Acehnese. To outsiders, the Acehnese personality continues to be seen as extreme, critical, hard-headed, coarse, flexible, steadfast, determined, wary, and strongly Muslim. But is this characterization still accurate now? Because we cannot tell exactly how the public's psyche has been affected, real comprehension of the psycho-social situation of the Acehnese is vital. Without an in-depth understanding of the situation, no development effort will have the hoped for results. The heart of the problem here is that acknowledgement of and an effort to address societal paradoxes are required for reconstruction and rehabilitation to be effective but are very difficult to elucidate and comprehend.

The tsunami

At the turn of the century, the peace process involving GAM and the Republic of Indonesia had failed, and martial law was declared in 2003. This became a State of Civil Emergency in 2004. Then, on the morning of 26 December 2004, an event took place that shocked the world. An earthquake measuring 9.0 on the Richter scale shook the Indian Ocean and created a deadly tsunami. Tsunamis are unusual in the Indian Ocean, occurring more frequently in the Pacific. The tsunami shocked and saddened the whole world and created a sense of human solidarity, once the impact of its extraordinary and crippling destruction was known. Aceh was the region that was most severely stricken.[6]

The damage to Aceh was described by President SBY as follows: 'This is the biggest natural disaster in Indonesia's history. The local government is crippled, infrastructure is massively damaged, there is no electricity, there is no fuel, clean water is scarce, communications and transportation are dead.' Even though the great wave 'only' struck a small part of Aceh, it was there that the centres of community life were located, including the cities of Banda Aceh, Calang, and Meulaboh. Because of the *ie beuna* ('flood', the Acehnese term for the tsunami), the region, which had already been damaged by social upheaval, was now ruined.

Soon after, three important steps to remedy the situation were taken by the Indonesian government. First, it declared the situation a national disaster. Second, it mobilized nationwide resources in an effort to cope with the disaster. During this phase, international support was extremely helpful with, among other things, medical teams and transport in the form of ships and helicopters. Third, the national government returned to the local authorities the right to run relief efforts through the mechanism of Satkorlak (*satuan koordinasi pelaksana*, operational coordinating units) as the basic units that would coordinate aid and deal with victims. The concern of the international community was shown by the size of their commitment.

Especially during the emergency phase, more than US$700 million was remitted to the Indonesian government as tsunami aid.

The government then divided the handling of the disaster among three groups: emergency relief workers, reconstruction planners, and reconstruction workers. The reconstruction phase, which was preceded by the formulation of a master plan, aimed to restore public services and rebuild the societies of Aceh and Nias as well as their physical surroundings. Efforts to recruit aid commitments from donor communities were made by seeking information on pledges and commitments that were given at the meeting of the Consultative Group on Indonesia in January 2005. These commitments were one source of funding for later reconstruction activities.[7]

The master plan that was formulated by the reconstruction planners would later be formalized in law and would then act as a general guide as well as an operational plan for BRR in managing reconstruction activities for the length of its term of operation. According to the master plan, reconstruction programmes would cover the short and medium term. Short-term programmes ran from the fourth month following the tsunami up to two years after the event (2006). This phase was referred to as 'rehabilitation' and had as its aim restoring public services to a significant level. Middle-range programmes, termed 'reconstruction', would last until four years following the tsunami (2009) and were intended mostly to rebuild social, economic, cultural, and political infra- and superstructure in the regions of Aceh and Nias.

For the nation of Indonesia as well as GAM, this disaster seems to have generated momentum for changing the dominant paradigm in attempting to solve the long-running conflict in Aceh. It made both sides more serious in seeking a win-win solution at the discussion table.[8] After six rounds of discussion over seven months, the Indonesian government and GAM finally reached a historic agreement, the Helsinki MoU, just four months after BRR was established.

The peace was a very important factor that would greatly simplify and facilitate the reconstruction activities in Aceh that were assigned to BRR. The situation today, now that fear, insecurity, and vulnerability have become 'old news', is like a new beginning for the long process of the rehabilitation and reconstruction. This will require the building of a societal structure that is fair and equitable through a dual recovery process. Healing of post-conflict wounds has been assigned to the *Badan Reintegrasi-Damai Aceh* (Aceh Reintegration-Peace Agency, BRA)[9] while BRR is charged with post-tsunami reconstruction.

BRR present and operating

The socio-political situation and conditions discussed above that existed when BRR was founded were less than ideal. Public trust in government agencies was long gone. The impetus for creative and productive participation on the part of the community was weak as the public had been ignored in government development processes for too long. When opportunities were created for this kind of participation, what ensued was in fact counter-productive as the parties tended to focus on their individual interests and, in the end, were not able to reach an agreement that was acceptable to everyone. There were many problems with human capital, and narrow individual interests were more dominant in determining the motivation and aims of the participants. Socio-political patterning that the public had experienced led to many instances where orientation was towards the needs of individuals. It is not surprising that a concern for joint development in approaching a common future was very hard to find. A number of development processes had been running for some time but never really crystallized into a collective movement, to be worked on together and whose results would be owned and utilized together.

The trauma and psychological effects on the public as a result of conflict and the tsunami also gave rise to a range of other problems like apathy, a tendency to be dependent, a lack of seriousness in thinking and working and a weak work ethic that acted to impede reform efforts in the rehabilitation and reconstruction of the region. Moreover, the widespread damage and increasing poverty also presented a paradox at a time Aceh was overrun with aid funding.

These were the complexities of the situation that BRR and its Board of Operations had to consider, even though its staff was very limited at the start and, for the first six months of its operation, did not have a substantial and representative office.[10] From the start, the agency already faced the demands of the public that BRR immediately carry out all its duties in rehabilitation and reconstruction. At the same time, however, BRR could not use its own initiative as it thought best. It had to abide by the requirements of *Keppres 80/2003 tentang Pengadaan Barang dan Jasa* (Presidential Decree 80/2003 on the Provision of Goods and Services). In addition, BRR was required to carry out its functions in accordance with the relevant regulations, even though the detailed and accurate statistical data needed for its rehabilitation and reconstruction programmes was still scattered among a number of agencies that had collected information in the past. Data sets on the same topic often varied and often contained very significant differences. There was no single data assessment that could be used in programme implementation that enumerated socio-economic and political issues and that would indicate priorities. In the meantime, there were numerous local, national, and international organizations that were involved in the rehabilitation and reconstruction process and had to be coordinated by BRR. They demanded their own privileges and displayed their own forms of arrogance. In addition, organizations that were formed by law very rarely operated in regions where a state of civil emergency was still in operation, and this had political implications that affected the presence of foreign workers.[11] A further paradox was that BRR had to operate within the context of laws that had been passed under normal circumstances but that were being implemented under conditions of disaster and crisis.[12]

The atmosphere of dilemma and paradox that BRR faced at that time has continued into the present. Its situation has been likened to 'building a ship for an immediate launch and having only a compass that is hard to use and can't be trusted'.[13] For this reason, as Kuntoro Mangkusubroto, the head of BRR, has said, in general, it will be impossible for Aceh and Nias to recover without strong and wide-reaching authority. Finally, by mandate, BRR was given independent authority, free from intervention by other government agencies.[14] Nonetheless, the programmes in its budget must be approved by the national parliament. The agency has broad authority but is not free to improvise dynamically in response to the unpredictable and constantly changing demands of the community. Moreover, its internal management has continued to search for the best format for its work, and in accord with challenges in the field, it needs a system of work that is conducive to running of its programmes and achieving its aims in rehabilitation and reconstruction.

As noted above, the public's trust in the activities and integrity of public institutions, especially those associated with the government, is limited.[15] In fact, BRR has a mission to coordinate 561 international organizations working on the rehabilitation effort and around 40 domestic ones. Moreover, BRR must ensure that these funds effectively reach their targets and do not leak away. In order to restore public trust and adhere to organizational aims, the agency has needed management that does not take a 'business as usual' approach.

BRR attempted to offer a new organizational ideal. It embraced professional, transparent, accountable, and responsible work practices.[16] BRR has also employed many young people, who have potential, energy, dynamism, and a new outlook. The agency maintains a commitment to aid recipients to encourage their participation and the involvement of the community (community driven development).

While BRR has taken community demands seriously, including the elimination of corruption, collusion, and nepotism, it has not been possible to achieve 'zero corruption' in the confused socio-political environment of the present in a short time. It is most realistic to reduce and anticipate the occurrence of corruption by expressing an attitude of 'zero tolerance'. For this reason, BRR encompasses structures like its Board of Directors, Board of Supervisors, and Anti-Corruption Unit (Satuan Anti Korupsi, SAK) and has developed an Integrity and Capability Pact for all its employees. BRR has also encouraged cooperation and even invited other agencies, like the Commission for the Elimination of Corruption (*Komisi Pemberantasan Korupsi*, KPK) and the Financial Auditing Agency (*Badan Pemeriksaan Keuangan*, BPK), to conduct a public audit of its financial management. Efforts of this kind are new to government organizations in general. In this context, from its inception, BRR set itself up as an institutional role model that has tried to establish systemic changes that might serve as an example for other government bodies. This has not been easy to put into practice as resistance, both within BRR and from outside, has been high. Often, it has not been possible to carry out beneficial and important plans because of lack of support from various parties.

BRR's relationship with local elements, like the regional government, local NGOs, and other social organizations, has generally been good, even though there have been problems and impediments to productive, transparent and accountable cooperation with some of them. Several examples have related to inclusion of local elements (participation) in planning and implementing BRR's programmes for the public good. The agency, and other rehabilitation organizations, has used a great deal of local manpower, including former GAM members and priority has also been given to local stakeholders.

Empowerment is demanded by the people of Aceh, and BRR has involved the regional government from the first. Almost all of its heads of work units (*kepala satuan kerja*, KSK) and much of the staff under them are employees of regional government from a variety of offices. They are always involved in coordination meetings, including in the Consultative Meeting on Development Planning (*Musyawarah Rencana Pembangunan*, Musrembang). In addition, in 2005, the list of activities and programmes covered in BRR's budget originated almost entirely from the recommendations of the relevant sector/local office, even when not supported by complete and valid data.[17] In its own operations, BRR has always coordinated its activities with those of the regional government, even though the results obtained have been far from significant. The involvement of local elements from BRR's earliest days is extremely important. These individuals and groups will be the ones to take over and manage BRR's assets (infrastructure and programmes) and run the programmes and activities still deemed to be of importance by the government of Aceh through its sectoral offices when BRR's term of operation ends. For this reason, the lack of synergy between BRR and local government is now viewed as requiring attention in anticipation of April 2009 when BRR will cease to exist. This goes along with the statement of President SBY calling for the transition from BRR to the provincial government of NAD to be handled carefully and seriously.[18]

One institutional and programme asset that has been built up by BRR is its Coordinated Team (*Tim Terpadu*), which was formed in December 2005. This team is a support unit within the agency that coordinates the activities of relevant government offices working to serve and facilitate foreign organizations/personnel who are involved in Aceh-Nias rehabilitation through an 'under one roof' service approach. Formed under Perpres No 69/2005, this ad hoc team is expected to continue post-BRR and will still act to facilitate the involvement of foreign organizations that wish to assist in the development of Aceh in the future.

In the period that BRR and a number of foreign agencies have been working on the rehabilitation of Aceh, many new buildings have been erected. The community's economy is moving forward, with the restoration of centres of trade and the appearance of coffee houses and restaurants open until late at night. This was never seen during the years of conflict. Shops, travel agents and airline representatives, furniture dealers, microfinance institutions, sidewalk vendors and supermarkets are crowded with shoppers. The records of Bank Indonesia (BI) in Banda Aceh show that, notwithstanding an inflation rate in 2007 of over 24 per cent,[19] the amount of money in circulation has increased significantly. Aceh's economy is growing. The per capita gross domestic product based on current prices not including gas and oil was around 3.7 per cent in 2004 but has now reached 25.4 per cent.[20] The effect of this improvement has influenced every aspect of the life of the public in Aceh.

These facts underscore the fact that the region and the life of the people of Aceh have changed a great deal over a relatively short period of time. The Indonesian President and Vice-President have expressed their satisfaction. Other nations that have provided aid are pleased and have offered additional support. The UK, the Netherlands, Germany and the European Union have made a commitment to increase aid. In total, the nations of Europe have contributed US$1.9 billion, or 32 per cent of the total US$6.1 billion available (from the US$7.2 billion needed). The UK has even called for BRR to serve as an example to others of post-disaster management.[21]

From this, it is apparent that opinions of BRR among international donors tend to be positive. Nonetheless, the impression that has developed among the public, and especially among those who have received its services, and that is often reported in the media has tended to be negative, cynical, and unappreciative of the difficulties. This may be due to delays in programme implementation and problems in targeting recipients who were truly victims of disaster and hence eligible to receive assistance. It should be noted that the social variables directly and indirectly influencing BRR's processes are numerous and complex compared to the technical issues it has faced. Many impediments have related to its rehabilitation and reconstruction programme operations. Reconstruction in the field has been affected by a lack of accurate and valid data, while what exists has often been subject to manipulation; problems with the availability of land that is appropriate for use and ready for development; problems with the level of commitment on the part of those involved in carrying out projects in accordance with the guidelines in effect and agreements that have been made; a lack of active and productive participation on the part of stakeholders in cooperative efforts to facilitate programmes and activities; and also issues in the provision of goods and services, necessary logistical requirements, and staffing problems.

Because of the numerous societal impediments in the field, many of BRR's programmes have been behind schedule, off target, or otherwise less than effective. Even though BRR has engaged in monitoring and evaluation up to a point, its efforts are still felt to be inadequate. Even so, with all its shortcomings and systemic weaknesses, BRR continues to move forward with the implementation of programmes. Despite the agency's mixed record, it is possible that evaluation when the agency is no longer in existence will show evidence of concrete benefit.

Coordination, participation and transparency

For three decades, Aceh was known as a 'hot' and dangerous region. Yet, when the tsunami struck, the flow of aid donors and foreign volunteers, who were moved by the massive destruction, could not be stemmed, even though Aceh was officially closed to foreigners and the state of civil emergency was still in effect. This was the time the calls for openness gained momentum and an exhausted and suffering public became ready for peace. Hundreds of organizations arrived to assist, along with thousands of volunteers and workers. Some came from non-governmental organizations or the military, others were doctors, activists, students or other professionals.

This rapid and urgent process was not easy. To the people of Aceh, the relationship and conflict between their traumatic past and their hopes for a better future gave rise to a number of paradoxes that linked the two. These connections were not easy to elucidate in a short time and hence had to be dealt with while moving forward – not in passing. The paradoxical conditions within which BRR was established and had to work will be discussed below.

At the level of relevant local concerns, a most apparent problem was coordination. Good coordination requires open, intensive, and effective channels of communication between parties, the existence of active and productive participation and a shared perspective and willingness to commit a significant amount of time. These principles are not easy to apply when each party puts its own needs first and does not share a common perspective based on mutual interests and the public good. In the Consultative Development Planning Meeting, for example, for reasons of its own, the regional government and its sectoral offices were reluctant to inform BRR of the content of the List of Budgeted Projects (*Daftar Isian Proyek Anggaran*, DIPA) it had compiled and planned for. In actual fact, openness was required in order to coordinate efforts and avoid duplication and overlap in programmes and locations and to create a more detailed mapping of who was doing what in what location to facilitate an understanding of the gaps that still existed and in assigning duties and roles.

To ameliorate the situation, BRR tried to act as a role model. One of these was its 'DIPA Analysis', something that had never been done before.[22] In November of 2005, the Office of Social Affairs, the Regional Office of Religion, the Office of Culture, the Office of Youth and Sports, the Women's Empowerment Bureau and the National Family Planning Agency took part in the DIPA analysis conducted by the ASB section of BRR in the presence of stakeholders in the programmes. In an effort to update data on the effects of rehabilitation and reconstruction, BRR set up a database called Recovery Aceh-Nias Database (RAND). Through RAND, making use of the internet, all parties, including those in donor nations on other continents, could quickly and easily access information on the rehabilitation/reconstruction effort and its progress. In addition, they could monitor the implementation of aid funds and find out where work was being carried out by a given organization. Unfortunately, this valuable resource was not fully used because the parties involved did not keep their data up to date, and interruptions to internet service often occurred.

At the level of the public, a serious paradox related to transparency and participation. In relation to participation, in addition to the fact that BRR called for it, the public's demands came as a reaction. Everyone involved understood that participation was necessary to create a sense of ownership among those who would benefit from programmes and their results. With the growth of this sense of ownership, the continuity and maintenance of programmes would be guaranteed. But it often happened in the field that the participation that did occur was counter-productive or pseudo-participation. This was a result of the public's minimal social awareness of the need to consider the broader needs of the wider community.

Many people asked to be invited to participate but, when the moment arrived, changed their mind. Many also changed their mind even before an opportunity arose. There were several reasons for this. Perhaps most significant was the fact that the public often based their decision to participate on the availability of incentives. This was likely an effect of the Cash for Work programmes that were initiated early in the rehabilitation process by a number of foreign agencies. The Cash for Work programmes were intended to ease the situation of victims by busying them clearing land, restoring fields, and building new roads so that remote rural areas could be reached. This was normally carried out simultaneously with programmes to build either temporary or permanent housing.

What was initially hoped was that the Cash for Work programmes would not only encourage participation but would also provide income for poor families that had lost their means of livelihood. The participation of the public in these programmes over time – but rapidly – created a counter-productive tendency of dependence and a perception that their participation would be paid for, and finally, that this was the actual meaning of the initiative. If BRR announced a participatory programme that did not offer incentive payments, then most of the public would not take an active role or become involved in the initiative in question. For this reason, participation was not generally seen as active involvement to address joint concerns and then feel a sense of ownership of the results of development which, from the beginning had involved everyone in the process of planning, implementation, monitoring and evaluation.

It may be true that the culture of cooperation (*meuseuraya*) and consultation (*duek pakat*) had increasingly vanished from the lives of the people of Aceh after the implementation of UU No 5/1974 on Regional Autonomy, which served to strengthen the enculturation of socio-political principles across the nation and suppress the unique features of traditional law, regional cultural awareness and the different cultures and their values that existed at the time. Additionally, various local conceptions of Acehnese culture have been lost from the social memory of the public and are at risk of disappearing. With the disappearance of local culture as a result of laws that were put into effect by the nation's leaders, a longing to return to traditional culture has now arisen in Aceh, as the traditions of the past are believed to have been more harmonious, more beneficial, and better. The traditions and culture of recent years are not seen by the public as having benefited them. Ironically, the means to return to something that was considered better in the past is not conceptualized in a way that can be put into practice. On occasion, the people of Aceh have fallen into the trap of romanticizing the past, but no longer have a working knowledge of the traditional institutions that structured community life at that time. The loss of traditional values within what is seen as having been a culture of cooperation is manifested in the lack of enthusiasm on the part of the public for group activities, like cleaning mosques and other public facilities, maintaining irrigation channels for the rice fields and inter-village harvesting. This suggests that people's longing for the past is not realistic. As is the case in other parts of Indonesia, cooperation is one important avenue to achieving a sense of ownership and common aims within a community that will serve to create a more unified future.

Another factor is that participation is increasingly demanded for programmes requiring physical work, while overlooking participation of a more substantial nature such as generating alternative solutions and finding answers to shared problems in the community. Based on this conception of participation, the community driven principles espoused by BRR in the implementation of its programmes have often not been effective and have not succeeded in creating a sense of ownership by the public to jointly continue and maintain the results of development.

In relation to transparency, BRR has been called for from all sides to operate in a transparent manner. From the beginning, the agency has published complete information on its financial status as well as the details of its projects on the internet and in its own newspaper *Seumangat*. But now, for unrelated reasons, that newspaper is no longer being published. The agency's experience suggests that the culture of transparency has not yet become part of a set of public expectations requiring that all handling of public funds, in both government and community organizations, be carried out in a manner that allows for general scrutiny. In Indonesia as a whole, transparency, while desirable, remains largely outside of reasonable expectations.

It should be noted, however, that there will always be issues that are open and others that must remain closed to the public. The euphoria following reformation has taken openness in Indonesia to an unprecedented level of understanding and which seems to be all-encompassing, but in fact only relates to financial management, which has been a central problem in this nation. The dissemination of information about a given organization, to the public, for example, is not considered to be an aspect of transparency. This phenomenon is closely related to the tremendously closed culture of the nation, especially in relation to money, such that government organizations and individuals who manage programmes and public money are not yet willing to be transparent.

In Aceh, issues like these have caused a fair amount of tension. As might be imagined, the experience of conflict has led to a high degree of distrust, which has become normal, even though it encompasses wariness and suspicion. People do not trust other Acehnese, much less outsiders. It should not be surprising then, if BRR, as an outside party, has often been caught in the middle, criticized but praised, hated but needed. Some developments have exposed a sorry state of affairs. For example, a number of community leaders, including those in traditional positions of authority (*keuchik, tuha peut, panglima la'ot,* and so forth), have been found to have misused aid or abused their authority for their own benefit or for the benefit of their cronies. This has clearly damaged the public's trust and its perception of fairness.

Creating a climate of mutual trust requires change at a basic level. Conscious recognition of the need to change the system is required, and it is the government who must do this and then give the public a chance to observe, oversee, and evaluate. If not, the price to be paid will be extremely high. The culture of secrecy will continue across generations. BRR has tried to be open as a function of its status as a role model, which it was expected to be by the president, who hoped it might set an example and a precedent and act as a reference for the public in pressing the regional government about the need for a system of administration that demands openness of information from all parties that manage programmes and public funds. In this way, the public's trust in the government will be restored along with the implementation of responsible openness.

BRR and foreign NGOs

It is worth considering the relationship between BRR and the 500 foreign NGOs involved in the rehabilitation and reconstruction of Aceh. These foreign NGOs had to be coordinated and facilitated by BRR, which first had to determine who was doing what. In its coordinating role, BRR set up a mechanism called 'concept notes'. This served as a template for elucidating the issues and questions that arose as well as information that had to be provided by foreign agencies that wished to be involved in rehabilitation and reconstruction activities and programmes in Aceh. This concept was introduced to BRR and then workshopped with a number of representative stakeholders involved with the proposed programmes, who would discuss, analyse, and evaluate the concept notes provided by a particular NGO. From the results of these workshops, BRR would then decide to approve the programme described in the NGO's concept notes, postpone it, or whether more work on the project was needed. Once the NGO's concept notes were approved by BRR, then the proposed project would be carried out by the organization that formulated the plan. In practice, there have been almost no concept notes that have been turned down. If anything was unclear, improvements would be suggested. If a programme was good but no funds were available, BRR would recommend that funds be requested from the Multi Donor Fund (MDF) containing new money from foreign sources. Using this mechanism of concept notes, BRR could also study the field and determine whether there was overlap between organizations and also ensure no duplicate budgeting took place. If there were still gaps in dealing with the needs of disaster victims, BRR would step in to fill them.

All the relevant information regarding the name of an organization, its location of operation, the amount of money it had used, and the type of programme or project it was involved in was entered into BRR's RAND database. All the organizations whose programmes had been approved were requested to update the data on their work and its results up to the time they were finished. Using the RAND database, all interested parties, including the international community outside of Indonesia, could access information about rehabilitation and reconstruction activities carried out by foreign organizations in Aceh. Using this coordination mechanism, all donors who had made aid available through specific organizations could also oversee operations.

In addition to this coordinating function, BRR played the role of facilitator, helping to find a solution if an NGO encountered difficulties in the field. In addition, in issues relating to handling the impact of the disaster in specific sectors that involved multiple organizations, BRR would undertake to form a working group. This would allow the exchange of information, experiences, and problems in the hope that the parties could learn from each other and find ways of addressing any problems that had not been solved.

Conclusion

To the public that was to benefit from aid, the disaster at first made them the objects of recovery. But when that phase passed, this provided an excellent opportunity to ensure that they will be able to help themselves in the future.

Recovery programmes present a challenge to humanitarian programmes and have been instructive to BRR. As a new agency charged with carrying out rehabilitation and reconstruction, BRR has had to adapt to the dynamics of change in the face of criticisms and pressures that have arisen in the field. It has had to act as a coordinator and also as a sensitive, quick, and flexible implementer. BRR's handling of various problems in a disaster situation often required creative breakthroughs. Its efforts have been praised by Bill Clinton, former President of the USA, serving as tsunami ambassador for the UN Secretariat General, who noted that the agency's formation was a successful experiment.[23] But the agency has not only needed a new set of rules but also time and manpower so that its staff could learn the system. Almost none of them had experience dealing with a disaster as severe as the tsunami in Aceh, and some were themselves from Aceh. The disaster at least provided an opportunity for local involvement in matters essential to the communities' own welfare.

BRR has tried to correct basic problems, including addressing negative ideas that formed over many years as a result of Aceh's experience in the past. Re-evaluating the basic values that underlaid participation and implementing measures to improve transparency were among the actions it took. For example, it held that by expanding community participation to include the lowest levels, it would be possible to productively encourage initiatives on the part of the local public in an effort to restore community life to a functional state. In addition, it would indirectly strengthen public participation in efforts to find a meaningful solution for the region.

One action that was taken by BRR was joint land titling (JLT) between husbands and wives. This proved to be one link in the chain of gender issues and encouraged the participation of women in rehabilitation. Village planning was used as a means for local residents to design the sort of settlement they wanted. Even so, village planning still required a coordinated effort by all sectors so the results of development could be seen and enjoyed by the residents of a particular location. Development had been sector-based in the past, and a change in approach and perspective was needed. The old method was converted to a village-based system, where the settlements in question would be developed by all government sectors available.

Among those with the authority to carry out development projects, the most competent party to take over the role of NGOs and BRR after 2009 is the government of Aceh itself. For this reason, beginning in 2006, BRR initiated the process of transition to those concerned with local needs to develop their capabilities. BRR has already turned over a large part of the role of implementation to its regional offices so that they can work with the *kabupaten* or city governments. A Joint Secretariat involving BRR and the regional government has been set up to synergize joint activities and to facilitate knowledge transfer and the eventual handover of authority. BRR's programmes for 2008 have been developed in conjunction with the local government. Nonetheless, it cannot be denied that BRR still has important work to finish at this halfway point in its term of operation. Land ownership, for example, is impeding the construction of homes, and the problem of land release still requires the full attention of the National Defence Agency (*Badan Pertahanan Nasional*) at the central as well as regional level.

In a broader perspective, there has been pressure over how recovery through rehabilitation and reconstruction following the tsunami and reintegration following the conflict can be unified. A means by which the government of NAD can reconcile all the achievements of the ad hoc agencies involved (BRR, BRA, and so on) is needed. A case in point is BRR's economic aid programme This aid has been viewed as discriminatory because it seems to favour victims of the tsunami and overlook victims of conflict. This can lead to friction at the community level. On another front, social, economic and cultural problems that have the potential to lead to conflict must be identified with the aim of mitigating them so that destructive behaviour on the part of the public does not eventuate.

The realization of economic empowerment in the region has also been an issue of wide concern. The question is how the concept of economic empowerment can be put into practice and its benefits felt by all the victims in Aceh, including victims of the tsunami (natural disaster), victims of conflict (social disaster), and the destitute, marginalized, and poverty-stricken public, who are victims of unfair policies and the existence of structural oppression. In this context, the nations of Europe have pressed BRR to assist the less developed regions in Aceh.[24] The President and Vice-President of Indonesia have expressed the same sentiment, and the post-tsunami process must aim to benefit the whole community of victims as well as the destitute, without discriminating among them.

To this end, by 2009, BRR had achieved a number of concrete results, including the construction of 127,000 houses; the rehabilitation of 97,000 hectares of arable land (this figure exceeds that damaged by the tsunami); the construction of 2500km of road; the repair of 11 airfields; the rebuilding of 1000 schools, 787 health centres, 1600 mosques; and the training of 2600 teachers. Additionally, thousands of projects were implemented to improve the capacity of public and social institutions, including government, the economy, law, culture and religion.

Discussion of BRR's activities arose from various segments of the community. Negative comments from the international community were few, and many felt the organization was praiseworthy. Among these international organizations, this may have reflected a comparison with other disaster locations around the world. At the national level, criticism and praise were about equal. Among the people of Aceh, however, comment was almost entirely negative and showed almost no appreciation for BRR's efforts. On 21 March 2009, a number of local organizations in Aceh presented an award to BRR at a conference. This was completely unexpected, but the views of the public are worth considering for the insight they might provide into local perceptions of the redevelopment effort.

First, BRR was accused of employing more workers from outside Aceh than from the local population itself. This was especially predominant during the first year of the organization's operation when it was forced to recruit a significant number of personnel from Jakarta, who were required to set up and run programmes. For positions that did not require a high level of training, Acehnese were given priority and the opportunity to work on the reconstruction of the province. In 2007, when BRR's employees numbered 1500, approximately 60 per cent of staff were Acehnese.

Second, BRR was accused of promoting Christianization, that was supposed to be part of the mission of a number of foreign organizations. BRR tried to address this by producing a leaflet outlining a series of do's and don't's for organizations operating in Aceh as well as a code of ethics and information about Islam. This document was written to reflect the views of a number of members of society who were surveyed for this purpose. The leaflet was distributed to all the foreign organizations in Aceh, but this did little to change public opinion that BRR was protecting the agents of outside organizations intent on proselytizing to the population. This criticism tended to come from a small group of religious elite who used the local media to foment hatred of foreigners within the community. BRR was quick to investigate and set up meetings with members of the community in the interest of stopping continuing rumours of apostasy. Eventually, this issue died down, but it was not possible to determine exactly where it had originated.

Third, BRR was felt to lack transparency, despite efforts to publish its financial status and funding breakdowns online for all to access. The organization had involved its stakeholders in planning since its inception, and tendering was conducted openly and freely. In fact, BRR was much more transparent than many government bodies, in Aceh as well as elsewhere in the country and was highly rated in both 2007 and 2008.

Fourth, it has been suggested that many victims have not been rehoused, even to the time of this writing, after BRR's term has ended. This perception is largely due to the dynamic nature of information on the matter that changed constantly and rapidly grew in volume. BRR had great difficulty collecting data, and many were contradictory. Nonetheless, the organization did put in place mechanisms to ensure no one was disadvantaged, but there are always gaps in any endeavour where corruption might occur. This is especially the case in a community where manipulation has been a way of life as it has in Aceh following three decades of centralized, authoritarian control.

Fifth, there were accusations of corruption within BRR itself that appeared constantly with a number of different interests at their heart. Organizationally, BRR attempted to close off all the avenues where corruption might occur. The presence of its Anti-Corruption Unit, its commitment to integrity and high moral standards, its maximal levels of remuneration to its employees, and its cooperation with international auditors like Ernst and Young and Price Waterhouse all attest to the seriousness of its aims in the midst of a corrupt community. In the period 2005–2008, 123 cases of corruption were referred to the appropriate body for causing a loss to the state of some Rp120.3 billion. The corruption BRR anticipated did indeed occur, but it should be noted that the sum of Rp120 billion is small in comparison to BRR's total budget of Rp21 trillion.

Despite these attacks on BRR, the organization did not fight back or trade accusations. In this, it represented a forum for the practice of democracy for a public that had lost its nerve to criticize the government more than 30 years before. It is hoped that, once BRR is dissolved, the ability of the public to criticize the government will continue to evolve and its criticisms will become more objective. BRR was also successful in penetrating the complex system of bureaucratic rules and defying the saying that 'if it can be made difficult, why should it be made easy?'. Finally, despite its shortcomings, BRR attempted to do the best work possible and act as a role model for the post-conflict, post-disaster people of Aceh, including its elite who are most resistant to change.

The rehabilitation and reconstruction movement must now continue. Success will not be easy, but the results of the development process will be enjoyed in the future, by one or several future generations. Peace, the implementation of Islamic law, the translation of UUPA No 11/2006 into an institution framework (*Qanun*), and reform of the system and governance in Aceh are all challenges that remain to be faced by the local government in a critical and innovative manner.

In addition, new challenges will emerge and will have to be faced in a participatory manner. Aceh has reached a crossroads where dilemma and paradoxes abound. Unless addressed immediately, the mistrust of the government by the public will begin to grow again. This time, it is likely it will take a more sinister form because now it is more horizontal in nature, in addition to its vertical aspect directed at the government of Aceh itself. For this reason, the government's attempts to make changes in Aceh will be the key to success in creating prosperity for the people of the region. This is the most important task for the government of Aceh now that BRR has begun the changes. It is hoped that everything BRR has done will serve as capital in creating a better future for Aceh that is more just, more democratic and more respectful of human values.

Notes

1   The editors would like to thank Dr Rebecca Fanany for her assistance in the translation of this chapter, which was submitted in Indonesian.

2   According to official data from the Badan Reintegrasi-Damai Aceh (BRA), the conflict between GAM and the Republic of Indonesia resulted in the loss of 20,114
people through death or disappearance, 550 disabled, and 5228 homes burned or
destroyed. See '*Fakta Seputar Reintegrasi (2)*', 22 June 2007, http://bra-aceh.
org/details_news.php? bra=new&id=292.

3   The master plan was developed in Jakarta on 15 April 2005 based on Presidential
Regulation No 30/2005.

4   The legal basis for the formation of BRR is Government Regulation to Replace Law
No 2/2005 (dated 16 April 2005) which, on 25 October 2005, passed into law as
Law No 10/2005.

5   Another example of an act habitually carried out by the New Order regime that
came to be internalized into the awareness/cognition of the public, for example, was
the branding of 'communist' that the New Order used to mark groups or individuals that criticized or protested against the government. Its aim was to discredit the
group in question. This strategy remained in use to the end of its power. Now we
see that this strategy of stigmatization and labelling is still common and is frequently
used by individuals or societal groups to discredit their political rivals. This strategy
of stigmatization continues to be repeated with small variations.

6   The tsunami killed 300,000 people (almost 7 per cent of the population) in Aceh.
With the earthquake in Nias, about 120,000 homes, some 3000km of road, 120
large bridges, 1500 ordinary bridges, 28 ports, 11 airports, 2800 hectares of coastal
jungle, 35,137 hectares of mangrove swamp, 29,175 hectares of coral reef, 2000
hectares of fish farms, 4717 boats, and 100,000 small and medium sized businesses
were damaged or destroyed. Tragically, this all took place in about 10 minutes. For
figures on damage assessment, see *Memperkokoh Hikayat Kehidupan: Laporan
Kegiatan Dua Tahun Badan Pelaksana Rehabilitasi dan Rekonstruksi Nanggroe Aceh
Darussalam dan Kepulauan Nias*, August 2007, pp14–17.

7   Funds for the reconstruction of Aceh and Nias came from the international debt
moratorium for Indonesia.

8   It was no less a personage than the head of the Iskandar Muda Military Command,
Major-General Endang Suwarya who said: ' . . . the additional humanitarian duties
required following the tsunami meant that the "military operation" almost ceased
by itself'. A GAM spokesman, M Nur Djuli, expressed a similar sentiment: 'We saw
the impact the tsunami had, with so many Acehnese dead and also members of the
military. We thought, why are we still at war?' *Buku Presiden Dua Tahun Tsunami*
(in press).

9   BRA was set up in February 2006 following the Decision of the Governor of the
Province of NAD No 330/032/2006 (dated 11 February 2006) and No
330/213/2006 (dated 19 June 2006). BRA is charged with providing social support
for those who have been disadvantaged by conflict by making funds available for
economic empowerment to various parties. These include former *Teuntra Nanggroe*

Aceh (TNA) (Acehnese military) members, former political prisoners and those accused of crimes against the state, and members of the public adversely affected by conflict (including GAM members, non-TNA members, members of GAM who surrendered before the MoU was signed, and members of anti-separatist groups). BRA has opened offices in all the regions and cities of Aceh. In addition, a number of international and national aid organizations that support the reintegration and reconstruction process are present in Aceh. The operational director of BRA is M Nur Djuli. (http://bra-aceh.org, accessed, 24 September 2007).

10 BRR, based on Perpu No 2/2005, clause 7, section 3, is to have three sections. They are its Board of Directors, Board of Supervisors, and Board of Operations. This last section, because of its close contact with the public, is generally known as BRR.

11 Aceh's state of 'Civil Emergency' was instigated by President Megawati Sukarnoputri on 18 May 2004 with Keputusan Presiden No 43/2004 which was officially revoked by SBY on 18 May 2005. He issued Peraturan Presiden No 38/2005 which returned the region to 'normal civil' status.

12 The implementation of Keputusan Presiden No 80/2003, for example, had to be carried out as standard procedure in the provision of goods and services by the government in order to avoid legal consequences. Because this regulation was made with the assumption that normal conditions applied, there were several crucial matters that became very difficult to handle despite the disaster conditions that required immediate action. For this reason, the Indonesian Parliament is now working on a Plan for Laws on Disaster Management, one of which will offer a solution to this problem.

13 For example, the master plan, because it was developed prematurely (in only about three months) based on a weak assessment of need, has finally been acknowledged by many to be almost impossible to use.

14 BRR's status is comparable to a ministerial office. BRR can use funds from the national budget through its own special KPPN (*Kantor Pelayanan Perbendaharaan Negara*, National Treasury Services Office) that was set up by the organization. This is a mechanism that has not been used before. Further, in relation to the authority of the Board of Operations of BRR, see clause 17 of Perpu No 2/2005.

15 As a responsible step to overcome the lack of public trust, BRR intentionally does not use the usual government logos (such as the Garuda Pancasila or the motto '*Bhinneka Tunggal Ika*') and uses the map of Aceh instead.

16 BRR's full commitment is contained in a clause of the regulation that established it, Perpu No 2/2005, clause 6, which states: 'rehabilitation and reconstruction shall be carried out on a basis of transparency, accountability, participation, and responsibility, giving priority to the general welfare and avoiding corruption, collusion, and nepotism.'

17 This is observable in the initial data available, some of which related to the Religion, Social Affairs, and Culture Section of BRR and concerned the number of refugees, orphans, and so forth.

18 This statement was made at a meeting with the head of the Operations Section of BRR, Kuntoro Mangkusubroto, at SBY's residence in Puri Cikeas, Bogor, West Java, in May of 2007. See '*Presiden Minta Proses Transisi BRR ke Pemerintah Aceh Segera Dilakukan*,' www.kapanlagi.com, 25 May 2007.

19 World Bank (2007) *Laporan Perkembangan Ekonomi Aceh*.

20 *Laporan Pemerintah Nanggroe Aceh Darussalam*, www.nad.go.id.
21 President SBY stated: 'This has rarely happened and is proof that trust in Indonesia internationally continues to grow.' See *'Presiden Minta Proses Transisi BRR ke Pemerintah Aceh Segera Dilakukan'*, www.kapanlagi.com, 25 May 2007.
22 This was considered a breakthrough because, in the past, such things were considered taboo, especially an analysis and discussion of a list of budgeted projects (DIPA).
23 'This agency [BRR] is playing an important role in coordinating the recovery effort and ensuring the process is led by Indonesians. President Yudhoyono's decision, that led to the establishment of an organization specifically to handle these difficult tasks and that is headed by Mr Kuntoro, was a correct one. This will be recorded in history.' *Aceh dan Nias Setahun Setelah Tsunami*, December 2005, p4.
24 This statement was made during the visit over several weeks of the head of BRR's Board of Operations to the European nations that contributed to the recovery effort in Aceh and Nias.

9

Remaking Neighbourhoods in Banda Aceh: Post-tsunami Reconstruction of Everyday Life[1]

Annemarie Samuels

Three years after the devastating tsunami of 26 December 2004, a lot of visible reconstruction was taking place in Aceh's capital, Banda Aceh. Its coastal neighbourhoods, that had been swept away by the tsunami waves, were replaced by hundreds of almost uniform houses built by aid agencies. Signs and billboards indicated which aid agency was responsible for which building, and houses differed accordingly. Some neighbourhoods were even referred to in relation to their donor, such as 'the Turkish houses', the 'Buddha Tzu Chi neighbourhood' or the 'Jackie Chan houses'. Government buildings were rebuilt and roads were improved. Reconstruction seems to equal 'constructing' or rebuilding the urban environment, and this has been the main focus of the authorities as well as aid organizations from the time they started to plan the post-tsunami reconstruction of Aceh, a couple of weeks after the disaster. However, apart from the visible, built environment, 'reconstruction' is also a less visible social, psychological and everyday process. Banda Aceh's residents did not sit and wait for their society to be reconstructed. Indeed, because people form the society they live in, only they themselves can rebuild it. Or, as Dorothea Hilhorst proposed in her inaugural lecture (2007): 'Societies reconstruct, they are not being reconstructed, even though most writings make us believe that reconstruction is a project to completely renew and fix a country, like the Marshall Plan planned and driven by external aid.' In the same line of thought, this chapter will argue that the efforts that affected people themselves undertake to remake their society are the most crucial part of the reconstruction process; and that without them any form of reconstruction is not possible.

Grass-roots activities directly after the tsunami were numerous, as becomes clear from the survivors' stories. These activities ranged from sheltering homeless family and friends, to cleaning houses and gathering and burying dead bodies. Immediate post-disaster coping mechanisms have received considerable attention in the social science literature. As a consequence, the disaster mythology – that affected people are helpless victims – has been corrected before (see for example Fischer, 2008). However, up till now, little attention has been paid to longer-term[2] grass-roots reconstruction activities.[3] This chapter will address reconstruction practices of survivors in Banda Aceh, three years after the tsunami. The people's reconstruction efforts can be found both in activities that can clearly be labelled as 'reconstruction', such as rebuilding houses and (re-)starting women's groups, as well as in the remaking of everyday life. In the post-disaster city the practices of everyday life (de Certeau, 1984) continuously make and remake the urban society. Furthermore, it is in everyday life that people deal with 'reconstruction' as planned and directed by government and aid organizations.

It is impossible to separate everyday practices according to what is 'reconstruction' and what is 'normal', since making and remaking continuously overlap, and reconstruction and everyday life are so much interlinked. It is also undesirable to strictly separate crisis and normalcy analytically. On the one hand, many social and cultural assets stay 'normal' during a crisis (Oliver-Smith, 1992). On the other hand, past experiences of dealing with crises become part of cultures (Bankoff, 2003). Because of these interrelations of crisis and normalcy as well as reconstruction and everyday life, a good way to look into the long-term post-disaster reconstruction process is by studying what is going on 'on the ground', where people reconstruct society from their rich experience and where 'normalcy' is continuously recreated.

An ethnographic approach to the post-disaster reconstruction of society gives insights into the way everyday practices shape society. It gives insight into the everyday use of space and it shows the way the social and built environment influences people's vulnerability and resilience. It also shows how reconstruction and development projects influence daily life. These insights can lead to a better understanding of the way society reconstructs. Finally, they may also improve the reconstruction projects that are directed 'from above'.

The sections below explore some of the longer-term, everyday aspects of grass-roots reconstruction in Banda Aceh. Most of the people whose stories are told here live in neighbourhoods in or near Banda Aceh that were partly or totally destroyed by the earthquake and the tsunami. In all of these places many people lost their lives. However, three years after the tsunami these neighbourhoods had again become lively places, where many returned survivors and newcomers lived. The next section will deal with place attachment and the importance of the neighbourhood as a social (reconstruction) space. The second part of the chapter will focus mainly on the remaking of everyday life in Banda Aceh's neighbourhoods. The last part will address the question of what 'reconstruction' can mean, while the conclusion returns to the main question: who is 'reconstructing' Banda Aceh?

Remaking relations with people and places: The neighbourhood as a social space

Tsunami survivors often said that they did not think they would ever return to live in their former neighbourhoods again, after seeing the scale of destruction immediately after the tsunami. Yet, three years later they had come back to these places, together with many of their neighbours who survived the disaster. Some survivors chose not to return to their former neighbourhoods, often because of fear and trauma, or because they owned a house elsewhere. The majority of people, however, did return. Often they had little choice, as they could not afford to buy or rent a house elsewhere, and economic needs tied them to the city. But interestingly enough, many commented that even if they had been given the choice, they would have returned to their own place. Many better-off people, who could have afforded moving away, eventually chose to return.

When discussing this eventual wish to return, survivors often mentioned that it felt better to live in 'their own place'. Dewi,[4] a young woman who lost a child during the tsunami, said: 'Acehnese people say, "it's good in other people's neighbourhoods, but it is even better in one's own neighbourhood".' Later she explained: 'Although it was said "do not move [back], you have to go away from the coastal areas", I did not feel so. There is no way I would move [away]. This is called the ancestral ground [*tanah turun tenurut*].'[5] Nova, a middle-aged woman from a neighbouring street, told me how, together with her husband, she had built their house over a period of 20 years. When the tsunami struck, they had just begun to build a garage. At first she did not want to return either, but later on she started to feel sorry for the remains of the house and they decided to reconstruct it, because it had taken them so long to build it.[6]

Neighbours and friends are also mentioned as a reason to return to one's own place. Lina is a student who used to live in the same neighbourhood as Dewi and Nova, together with her parents and other family members. Before the tsunami her parents rented a house, and they had not yet received a new house at the time of the interview. It was still uncertain whether they could return to their neighbourhood. Since the barracks her family now lived in were far away from the city and university district,

Lina temporarily stayed with friends. She hoped they could come back permanently:

> *We love our neighbourhood. Although it is near the sea, we still [want to live] here. This place is close to the city [centre]. We are not used to live far from the sea and the city. All our friends are from here, so if we would move we would again experience a loss. We already lost family members, now perhaps we would lose our neighbours too. We just [want to] live here and accept what Allah has given us.*[7]

Others specifically mentioned that they wanted to return because of the memory of their disappeared family. As one of them said:

> *Here, I am safe, and it seems as if the people that disappeared did not disappear ... I want to be close to all those who already died. [Close to] my child, my grandchild and my mother. I could not be in another place. It is here that we have to live again.*[8]

Place attachment, the affective bonding between people and places (Altman and Low, 1992), was one of the reasons to return to the recovering neighbourhoods. However, as has been mentioned above, many people had little choice, as they could not afford to live elsewhere. Furthermore, the strong belief that one has to accept Allah's will and that everyone's time of death has already been determined was often mentioned as a reason for not being scared of living so close to the sea. Many people said that 'death can come anywhere'.

Apart from attachment to a specific place, the neighbourhood in general is an important space for social activity and social relations in Aceh. As a consequence it is a central space of remaking social life. A few months after the tsunami, barracks were constructed in or near many neighbourhoods. Many of the survivors that could not (yet) return to their houses and did not live with family came to live there, together with their former neighbours. Some of them participated in the 'Cash for Work' programmes that were used to clean up the neighbourhood. While living in the neighbourhood barracks, they could keep an eye on the construction of their houses and participate in activities of NGOs and community meetings.[9] Three years after the tsunami, most barracks were demolished and most of the survivors lived in their rehabilitated or newly constructed houses. Both people who had lived there before the disaster and newcomers participated in re-established community activities such as the *arisan*,[10] studying the Koran and praying in the mosque. Neighbours are invited to attend each other's family celebrations, such as marriage and the birth of a child. When the celebration takes place at home, neighbours are traditionally called upon to help prepare the food.[11] Next to organized activities and events, neighbourhood relations are continuously remade during many informal daily activities. For women, these include among others, going to the neighbourhood market in the early morning and chatting together in the late afternoon, while men hang out together at the local coffee shop or kiosk and chat informally before and after the evening prayer in the mosque. During the celebratory activities after the fasting month, neighbours visit each other, and often a neighbourhood community collectively organizes meals to celebrate the birth of prophet Mohammed and the new year of the Islamic calendar. Not only celebrating, but also mourning is partly a public neighbourhood affair. Significantly, during the years after the tsunami, collective meals have been prepared and used in many neighbourhoods on the date of the tsunami, as a way to collectively commemorate the disaster.

Of course, neighbourhood relations also involve gossip and conflicts. Gossip often relates to behaviour or activities of other neighbours, and social status depends to a large extent on whether one's family is 'originally' from the neighbourhood or has come to live there in recent decades. During the reconstruction process, quarrels have arisen about distribution of aid. For example, people in charge of allocation were accused of unfair distribution and keeping too much for themselves. The Aceh Community Assistance Research Project even found that local leadership is 'the key determining factor differentiating more successful from less successful village recovery.' (ACARP, 2007: pviii). The order in which people received houses, their quality and the number of houses received,[12] could lead to social jealousy and was a major source of frustration expressed against the authorities in charge of the process. For some, the lack of spontaneous community activities, because of residents' preoccupation with their individual problems, was worrisome. However, even these kinds of conflicts and gossip show the importance of the neighbourhood as a social space.

Although attachment to their own house and neighbourhood was one reason to return to the tsunami-affected parts of Banda Aceh, some people also mentioned that moving to another place would just mean establishing the same kind of social relations with new neighbours. Examples of the creation of new neighbourhood structures could be found in relocation neighbourhoods. People who had lost their land during the tsunami or who had rented a house that was destroyed by the disaster were relocated to these new places. They frequently mentioned the importance of having good relationships with one's neighbours. Furthermore, the quick remaking of everyday social life in these neighbourhoods signals the importance of the experience of social structures before the tsunami for remaking 'normalcy'.

It illustrates how post-tsunami reconstruction is a process of both change and continuity.

Recreating livelihoods: The creativity of everyday life

Ria lost her husband and children during the tsunami, while she herself was severely injured. During a difficult recovery process she stayed temporarily with family in another town. They urged her to stay with them, but she felt she had a reason to come back to Banda Aceh because her sister and brother-in-law, who had also lost all their children, still lived in the city. Together with them she stayed in the barracks and in early 2008 she lived with them in their newly built house. Ria said how sad she was and that the memories of the tsunami would always stay with her. She was often scared, especially when the weather was bad. She was also making plans for the immediate future. In February 2008, she said she wanted to build a small kiosk in front of the house, where she would make and sell fried bananas. Only a month later, the kiosk was there and some neighbours were chatting, sitting on the small bench next to it. A year later her business was still running and in the late afternoon many neighbours would gather at her kiosk.[13]

Another widow, Ros, lived in a neighbouring area. During the tsunami she lost her four children and her husband. Three months later she returned to her neighbourhood, because tents and food were provided there. Because her family had lived in that place for generations, many other surviving neighbours were part of her extended family. Although food was provided in the camp, she was in need of cash to buy other basic needs. That is why a couple of months after the disaster she started to work in a restaurant in the city centre, although she had never had a job before. After six months she tired of the job and quit. She found work in one of the 'Cash for Work' programmes that were meant to clean up the destroyed neighbourhoods. Through these programmes, organized by several aid agencies, residents were paid a small amount of money per day for cleaning up their own and other neighbourhoods. In Ros's own neighbourhood she was one of the first to receive a new house, because of her status as a widow. When she had moved in there she asked some men to build a small kiosk in front of her house with materials found in the debris. With a small amount of borrowed money she bought a few products to sell in her kiosk: 'I started with Rp500,000[14] that I borrowed from someone to fill the kiosk. I bought packs of cigarettes, two packs of this, two packs of that. I bought one bag of sweets for the children, like that, very small. After a while I started to save a little and I could expand little by little. I returned the money I had borrowed.' Later she participated in a project in which groups of women prepared snacks and gained a little income. But after the manager ran away with the money, she focused on the kiosk. Just before she remarried in February 2008, she was able to buy a motorcycle with her own money.[15]

Remaking everyday life is a creative process (Das and Kleinman, 2001). Many people in the parts of Banda Aceh that were destroyed by the tsunami created new forms of living and sharing together with family, friends and neighbours. As Oliver-Smith shows (1992: 16), the ways in which people react in a post-disaster situation are mainly derived from their previous experiences. At the same time, however, they find new ways to shape their new situations. Some widowed women and men chose, like Ria, to stay with brothers, sisters, parents or grown up children. Some lived on their own. Two widows in Ria's street lived on their own in their own houses. They both said that they were often lonely in the house, especially at night, but they also enjoyed each other's company in many daily activities. Many others, like Ros, chose to remarry. Younger as well as middle-aged widows and widowers remarried within years after the disaster. For them, to have a family again seemed to be the best way to go on with life, even though the memory of the ones that did not survive was still strong.

Like Ria and Ros, many people took on work and other daily activities that they had not done before the tsunami. For most of them, work was a financial necessity, but many also mentioned the psychological benefits, saying that 'having something to do' meant some distraction from disturbing memories. Furthermore, small-scale businesses such as selling cakes or prepaid phone airtime increased social interaction with neighbours. Although some people did receive credits or grants (in money or in kind) from an NGO, many others put in their own money, or money they borrowed from friends. People with a low income, however, more than once mentioned that they had a great need of access to credit to restart or improve their businesses. Although more NGOs started to focus on economic recovery programmes near the 'end'[16] of the reconstruction process, many people were not reached by any of them.

One of those people was Iskandar, who could not take up his former job of selling fish, because his health had deteriorated as a consequence of the tsunami. Having lost his wife and children, he temporarily returned to the village of his extended family, but came back to Aceh in search for work. Because he did not own land and had rented a house before the disaster, he did not receive a house in his village. Although many other former tenants received houses in relocation neighbourhoods, more than four years after the tsunami he had still not received one. After his return to Banda Aceh he borrowed money from friends to rent a small wooden building and start a shop, which he later turned into a coffee house. He slept in the back of the place. His social life centred around his friends from the neighbourhood, with whom he spent much time and on whom he depended to take care of his business when he had to go out for a moment. He wanted to marry again, but said he would need to have a house first.[17]

However precarious the situation may be, and however welcome external assistance would be, people often have other options to manage to get by. These options often depend on social relations, which are an important asset in the reconstruction of communities and livelihoods (see also ACARP, 2007). Economic and employment policies as well as post-disaster economic assistance play an important role in stimulating the urban economy. However, again, the fact that actual work is done and new businesses are started is mainly thanks to the effort of the affected people themselves. At the same time the eagerness with which people started to rebuild their livelihoods provides a strong argument against the idea that disaster survivors quickly become aid dependent and do not want to work any more.

Religion, grief and coping

[The tsunami] is a test that we can pass in the eyes of Allah. After a while I came to understand that my child and my house were not owned by me [but by Allah]. If Allah wants to take them, He takes them ... I am still sad, I still cry, but I have to accept it with my whole heart. Every day I feel better now. The tsunami came because I had forgotten Allah, but now I understand ... The sadness is still there however; if I meet with my friends here it is still there; if I tell the story now, I still cry ... I do not know where [his daughter's] grave is. Or if she is still alive. But if I think about that I will go crazy. So I surrender to Allah. And I am convinced that He owns my child. I am sure she is with Allah.[18]

The loss of life as a consequence of the earthquake and tsunami in Aceh has been enormous and three years after the tsunami grief and the memory of the tsunami were a part of daily life for many survivors. At the same time, strong religious convictions help people to accept the disaster and go on with their lives. For many, their belief in Allah was the only thing they could hold on to during the tsunami that, as was often remarked, seemed to be the end of the world. Survivors tell of praying together on rooftops or even of people praying to Allah while being in the water. After the tsunami, religious interpretations of the disaster became the most important framework to give meaning to what happened. Religious as well as administrative leaders called the disaster an act of Allah. The interpretations of local people for example include explaining the tsunami as Allah's punishment for committed sins or as Allah's will to 'clean' the province because of the conflict. Others call the tsunami a test or a warning, given by Allah to make the Aceh's people stronger in their beliefs. Many religious interpretations are future oriented as they see the tsunami as Allah's way to make Aceh a better place and the Acehnese better people. And many tsunami survivors said they could only surrender to Allah's will and accept their fate. In individual interviews, but also during informal conversations among each other, people said that Allah had already taken their loved ones who were safe in heaven and that the only thing they could do was to accept His will and rebuild their lives. Most often people said that if it is your time, you will certainly die wherever you are and that apparently they had been given more time in this life. The religious interpretations of the tsunami are articulated in individual stories and in informal discussions among survivors. Moreover they form part of broader public narratives and are a very important aspect of social and psychological reconstruction.

Similar attitudes to disaster have been noted in other parts of Asia. Bankoff (2003) shows how the concept of *bahala na* in the Philippines implies both a passive acceptance of fate, and a sense of risk-taking and courage. This attitude of acceptance and courage enables people to return to places that are repeatedly affected by disaster. Schmuck (2000) describes the case of people's reaction to returning after floods in Bangladesh. There, hazards were seen as an act of Allah against which one cannot and should not do anything. In both the Philippines and Bangladesh, outsiders often describe these attitudes as fatalistic and problematic. However, they are actually coping mechanisms that help people to face repeated hazards (Bankoff, 2003) and to return to daily life as quickly as possible (Schmuck, 2000). Schmuck shows that the belief that Allah has not only given the floods but will also help believers to survive them, helps people to go on with life.

In a similar way, the social and psychological force of religious explanations of the tsunami and the belief in predestination are a crucial part of coping and reconstruction mechanisms in Aceh. Grief is an aspect of daily life for many of Banda Aceh's residents, but at the same time their individual and shared beliefs form an important stimulus for going on with life and remaking their world.

Reconstruction

What is 'reconstruction'? For the governmental reconstruction agency, BRR, as well as for many international aid organizations, reconstruction seemed to be in the first place a technical effort of literally constructing or rebuilding places; if possible even 'building back better'.[19] Especially housing has become a very popular field of assistance for many NGOs and foreign donors, even though some of them did not have any experience in construction work (Steinberg, 2007). Three years after the tsunami, government and aid agencies started to pay more attention to social and economic assistance, but still to a much lesser extent than to the built environment. For most tsunami survivors, the external assistance consists mainly of physical private or communal assets, such as houses, roads and sanitation. Although rebuilding houses and infrastructure is obviously a primary need, there may be other reasons that explain the abundance of attention to these aspects of the post-tsunami society. Arguably, the popularity of physical reconstruction activities over more socially oriented programmes has much to do with issues of visibility, measurability and short-time results. Because aid agencies have to present results to the donors abroad and because evaluation reports are often caught in a language of quantitative results, physical reconstruction projects are often more easy to account for than socially oriented projects. For the tsunami survivors, housing has become an entitlement. As houses have been promised to all tsunami survivors, they could claim the right to a house,[20] in contrast to social and economic assistance, to which individuals and neighbourhoods were not formally entitled.

Different dimensions of reconstruction, including the social and built environment, are very much interrelated. Also, the many social actors, their actions and the effects of those actions are connected in the complex arena of reconstruction. It would be a mistake to classify the remaking of everyday life as purely a grass-roots affair, separate from reconstruction projects of government and aid agencies. These projects have many effects on society, both in positive ways, as they for example include making possible a quick return to people's neighbourhoods and everyday lives, and in possible frustrations arising from corruption, unequal distribution of aid, and a lack of coordination and accountability (see Telford et al, 2006). It is important to note that local people are not passive receivers of aid but are very much part of the aid distribution process, which can result in corruption through unequal power relations but also in the community deciding that priority should be given to the most vulnerable. Furthermore, reconstruction should not be seen as just a technical process, but at least as much as a political and social process.

Although reconstructing the built environment has been the priority of many aid agencies and the BRR, Banda Aceh's residents also engaged in it immediately after the tsunami and continue rebuilding and remaking places. In some cases specific types of houses could be negotiated with aid agencies and some projects even asked people to build their own houses (while money and materials were provided). In case the house was only partly destroyed, the owner would receive a standard amount of money for its rehabilitation and had to add his or her own money if this was not enough. However, most survivors whose houses were completely destroyed received a standard house without any consultation. Many people started altering their houses and gardens quickly, if they had the means to do that.

The discourse of 'reconstruction' as primarily literally 'building back' seems to be widespread in Banda Aceh, among aid agencies, government and local populations. Apart from the literal construction, aid agencies have programmes that focus, for example, on micro credit or the training of teachers or midwives.[21] However, this chapter argues that reconstruction includes much more. If we look at the society that 'reconstructs', reconstruction includes, for example, buying a new motorcycle or television, reviving neighbourhood activities and growing flowers in front of one's house as well as dealing with the memories of the disaster. Also, 'reconstruction' should not be seen as a process that can be finished in a limited amount of time. It is important to pay attention to its long-term effects. In Banda Aceh the reconstruction process directed by government and aid agencies and the money that came with it has many unintended effects. The city saw exorbitant increases in housing rents and continuously inflating prices of basic needs. The influx of hundreds of NGOs as well as the governmental BRR provided economic investment and jobs with high salaries to some. However, when the NGOs and the BRR were leaving, the economic situation was worrisome. Another effect was that many immigrants came to the city after the tsunami, in search for work, to live with family or because of a marriage. In the end, although 'reconstruction' is often seen as a technical effort of 'building back', it is important to recognize that remaking a post-disaster society has many more dimensions, at the individual and community level as well as for the larger society, some of which have been discussed in this chapter. Moreover, the effects of both the tsunami and the reconstruction process, ranging from problems with the distribution of housing to a lack of employment opportunities, do not end after 'building back'. They could be anticipated and acted upon earlier in the process.

Conclusion

Who is 'reconstructing' Banda Aceh? After the tsunami, a range of social actors participated in Banda Aceh's reconstruction process, creating a complex arena of different and overlapping activities and actors. However, even though this was one of the largest post-disaster reconstruction operations ever, it is still mainly the people's activities that remake society. Reconstruction is a long-term process that affects the whole society and in which local people are the main actors. Taking an ethnographic approach to the study of this process makes us deal with the important question of how people remake their daily lives. It also takes us to less visible dimensions of reconstruction such as religion, emotions and social relations. Asking how affected people cope and remake daily life after a disaster teaches us, as Oliver-Smith already noted (1992: pxiii), about capacities to survive and ways of dealing with loss. In Banda Aceh the neighbourhood is an important, flexible unit for remaking daily lives. The social aspects of places, through neighbourhood social relations and activities and people's emotional attachment to their own place, are especially important for rebuilding everyday life in the reconstructing city. Also, after the tsunami new social relations between friends, neighbours and family members become more important as people decided to form households together or share meals and other daily activities.

Taking the perspective of reconstruction at a local level leads us to ask different questions about reconstruction as directed by the government and aid agencies. For example, instead of discussing 'participation' of affected people in aid agencies' projects, we may ask how aid agencies can participate in the people's reconstruction. At the same time, humanitarian assistance projects may profit from paying more attention to the people's activities. Looking at the ways in which people cope and start rebuilding may help to get clear where and how to assist their activities (see also Telford and Cosgrave, 2007). When one takes this more integrated approach, it takes time to find out how to contribute to societal reconstruction. It also takes time and organizational will to coordinate the process and see to it that not every organization is struggling for itself or is competing with others; leaving some places and people with an abundance of aid and others with almost nothing. Recognizing that reconstruction as well as its effects are part of a long-term process, more participation of aid agencies is both desirable and possible.

The local people are the main actors in remaking their society; a reconstruction process without a definite end. Society is continuously made and remade, also in Banda Aceh's neighbourhoods that were destroyed by the tsunami. Their inhabitants are remaking their lives every day, in new ways as well as based on experiences before the disaster. Both the memory of the tsunami and the general discourse of accepting fate and going on with life figure strongly in their narratives and actions. As one of the survivors said: 'This life is a part of us. We have to lead this life, whatever it brings.'[22]

References

ACARP (2007) 'The Acehnese gampong three years on: Assessing local capacity and reconstruction assistance in post-tsunami Aceh.' Report of the Acehnese Community Assistance Research Project

Altman, Irwin and Setha Low (1992) *Place Attachment*, New York, Plenum Press

Bankoff, Greg (2003) *Cultures of Disaster: Society and Natural Hazard in the Philippines*, London and New York, Routledge

Das, Veena and Arthur Kleinman (2001) 'Introduction' in: Veena Das et al (eds) *Remaking a World: Violence, Social Suffering and Recovery*, Berkeley, Los Angeles, London, University of California Press, pp1–30

de Certeau, Michel (1984) *The Practice of Everyday Life*, Berkeley, University of California Press

Fischer, Henry W. (2008) *Response to Disaster: Fact versus Fiction and its Perpetuation. The Sociology of Disaster*, Lanham, University Press of America

Hilhorst, Dorothea (2007) Inaugural lecture: *Saving Lives or Saving Societies: Realities of Relief and Reconstruction*, Wageningen University

Mantel, Carola (2008) 'Post-tsunami housing reconstruction in the Indonesian province Nanggroe Aceh Darussalam: Two case studies in comparison', unpublished MA thesis, University of Zurich

Oliver-Smith, Anthony (1992) *The Martyred City: Death and Rebirth in the Andes*, Prospect Heights, Illinois, Waveland Press

Schmuck, Hanna (2000) ''An Act of Allah': Religious explanations for floods in Bangladesh as survival strategy', *International Journal of Mass Emergencies and Disasters*, vol 18, no 1, pp85–95

Steinberg, Florian (2007) 'Housing reconstruction and rehabilitation in Aceh and Nias, Indonesia – Rebuilding lives' *Habitat International* vol 31, pp150–166

Telford, J. and J. Cosgrave (2007) 'The international humanitarian system and the 2004 Indian Ocean earthquake and tsunamis', *Disasters*, vol 31, no 1, pp1–28

Telford, J., J. Cosgrave and R. Houghton (2006) *Joint Evaluation of the International Response to the Indian Ocean Tsunami: Synthesis Report: Executive Summary*, ALNAP, London, Tsunami Evaluation Coalition

Notes

1   The fieldwork for this contribution was conducted with support of the Stichting Fonds Catherina van Tussenbroek and the Aceh Research Training Institute.

2   'Long-term' is used in this chapter to denote the period starting when the emergency phase of a couple of weeks starts to come to an end. As 'reconstructing' a society is conceptualized here as part of the everyday 'constructing' of society, 'long-term' reconstruction does not have a clear end (in contrast to the 'reconstruction' as planned by the government). In the long-term, reconstruction will become more and more 'construction' as an ongoing process connected to the memories and agency of the survivors. As the data for this chapter were gathered between three and five years after the tsunami, they mainly deal with the situation at that time and the period up till then.

3   But see for example Oliver-Smith (1992) and Bankoff (2003).

4   The names used in this chapter are pseudonyms unless agreed differently with the respondents.

5   Interview 15 February 2008.

6   Interview 22 February 2008.

7   Interview 29 January 2008.

8   Interview 6 January 2008.

9   This part of reconstruction was far more problematic for communities that were housed far away from their neighbourhoods/villages or communities that lived dispersed over different places (ACARP, 2007; Mantel, 2008).

10   The *arisan* is usually a monthly gathering of women from one street or neighbourhood, in which they put money together, which is won by one of the members through a lottery. Everyone will win the lottery once, until after a few years every member has had her share (which means that she has her whole input back). Other forms of *arisan* are gathering money to be used by members in case of illness or to pay for funerals. Apart from neighbours, families and groups of friends also can have *arisan*.

11   Calling upon neighbours to prepare celebration meals seems to become less prevalent nowadays among the urban middle class, as more and more people decide to rent a public party hall and hire catering.

12   Sometimes survivors could get extra houses for married or unmarried children if they owned land. Policies as well as practices concerning receiving houses have been non-transparent throughout the reconstruction process, resulting in some people 'illegally' receiving extra houses, while others who would have a right to a house did not receive one.

13   Interview: 19 February 2008.

14   About $50.

15   Interview: 20 March 2009.

16   The BRR (Bureau of Reconstruction and Rehabilitation, the governmental agency organizing the reconstruction process) as well as many NGOs envisioned the reconstruction process as limited in time. After four years, BRR's mandate ended and many NGOs finished their projects and left the province.

17   Interview: 28 December 2007.

18   Interview: 18 December 2007.

19   'Building back better' was one of the progressive phrases often used by BRR.

20   The right to receive houses has turned into one of the most important social and political issues of the reconstruction process. Apart from the fact that at the end of BRR's term in April 2009 still more than one thousand people had not received a house yet, there were frequent controversies about the quality of housing and about people illegally receiving one or more houses meant for tsunami survivors.

21   However, as mentioned before, these programmes do not reach everybody.

22   Interview, 18 November 2007.

CONCLUSION

10

Lessons from Aceh

Sue Kenny and Matthew Clarke

The chapters of this volume have reflected upon the reconstruction of Aceh following the Indian Ocean tsunami. They reveal the ways in which different perspectives provide different understandings of the reconstruction, and it has become apparent that there is no single or 'correct' interpretation. While this multiplicity of views might be considered a constraint to learning from the experiences in Aceh, examining the reconstruction response from numerous viewpoints can actually enhance the depth of comprehension and the lessons that can be learned. Rather than being purely an instrumental evaluation, for example solely interested in the mechanics of the response (for example the. number of houses built, number of health clinics established, number of unaccompanied children reunited with their families), this approach allows a more encompassing suite of lessons to be identified.

In the number of countries and people affected, the Indian Ocean tsunami has been the largest natural disaster to occur in modern times, and while its enormity made it particularly unique, there are general lessons that transcend this specific event. Natural disasters do occur frequently and it is possible this frequency will increase as a direct result of climate change (Clarke, 2008; IPCC, 2007). Preparedness to respond to complex humanitarian emergencies is important for all countries. Natural disasters occur in developed countries (e.g. Hurricane Katrina in the US in 2005) as well as developing countries (e.g. Cyclone Nargis in Myanmar in 2008). Certainly an interesting and recent phenomenon has been the flow of aid from 'poor' countries to 'wealthy' country in response to such events. For example, Papua New Guinea donated A$65,000 in response to the 'Black Saturday' bushfires in Australia in February 2009, while the government of Indonesia donated A$1 million for the fire reconstruction efforts, as well as sending a forensic team to Victoria to assist with identifying the dead (AusAID, 2009). The lessons that can be identified from analysis of the post-tsunami reconstruction of Aceh will therefore have wide relevance.

It is important to note that the lessons from Aceh reconstruction are not simply a diatribe of errors and mistakes made during the reconstruction.

While poor decisions were undoubtedly made (see Cosgrave, 2007), there were also examples of successes (many of which are discussed within this volume). Therefore the lessons described below are drawn from both good and poor practices displayed within the reconstruction. They focus on cultural sensitivity, community engagement, political regeneration, participatory practices, government planning and international responses. It is expected that these lessons, while mired in a very specific event, will be more widely applicable to future complex humanitarian emergencies.

The overarching lesson that this volumes identifies is that *reconstruction is not a one-dimensional process. 'Reconstruction' must refer to multiple aspects, involve multiple players and allow for multiple perspectives and experiences.* A one size fits all cookbook does not work. It is inappropriate to consider that a single approach or a single 'view' is sufficient when responding to a disaster. It is necessary for local and international agencies, host governments, donors and local communities to purposely seek out different perspectives and different voices to ensure that the response is inclusive and encompassing.

This overarching perspective on what we can learn from analysis of the reconstruction of post-tsunami Aceh sets the framework for other lessons.

1 Contextual factors are critical to designing appropriate responses

Not only is every reconstruction multifaceted, it occurs within a particular context. For example it is not possible to understand the dynamics of change and intervention in Aceh's reconstruction without grasping how the often tortuous political history has set the backdrop for political regeneration after the tsunami, or how Islam is a key part of the social and cultural context. Such understandings are reminders of the folly of analysing post-disaster reconstruction as abstracted technical procedures.

2 Disasters result in physical and non-physical destruction

Disasters and reconstruction are not just 'natural events', as some of the media tend to portray them. They impact on the emotional and spiritual psyche of individuals as well as the physical infrastructure. As Wisner et al (2004) point out, disasters are a complex mix of natural hazards and human action. It is therefore necessary to address political, cultural and social dimensions and importantly, the 'whole' person, not just the physical manifestation of the destruction wrought by the disaster. However, addressing non-physical needs is not linear or easily planned. Nor does it allow for stringent reporting. The international community needs to learn more about psychological reconstruction as reconstruction of the psyche is just as important as reconstruction of infrastructure.

3 Participation of all stakeholders (with primacy given to affected communities)

As Cornwall (2008) points out, participation is always a political process. All stakeholders need to be involved, and as far as possible, ownership of responses has to be ceded to the community. Aid is more effective if its intended recipients are involved in every stage of its provision. During periods of reconstruction, especially in the relief phase, the delivery of aid can be ad hoc and extremely fast. It is therefore important that the method of recipient participation should be organized as quickly as is practical. Many survivors of the tsunami spoke critically of being passive observers. It is necessary to recognize the 'principle of mutuality' and interconnectedness when working with disaster-affected communities. It is also important to remember that affected communities do NOT have to accept aid as offered or work with whatever NGOs appear. The purposes and dimensions of participation need to be articulated, including why people should be involved, what powers they will have and for how long they will be involved.

Participation of communities is very important. However, the practical expression of this participation can cause tensions. It is common for initial responses to a disaster to include 'work-for-cash' (food, shelter, etc.) schemes in response to disrupted livelihoods. However, the use of such schemes must be managed carefully, as it can lead to a counter-productive tendency of dependency and perception that participation must be paid for. Cooperation and coordination between NGOs on this issue is necessary, as the practices of a 'generous' NGO can have repercussions for 'less generous' NGOs.

Disasters that result in large loss of life necessarily mean that some of those who die will be community leaders (formal or otherwise). Communities must be supported in replacing these leaders (including teachers, spiritual leaders) at the earliest stages of reconstruction efforts so that they have representatives capable of protecting and projecting their interests in the reconstruction planning. Good leadership is correlated with good reconstruction outcomes, strong participation and 'buy-in', transparency, joint decision-making, frequent meetings and recovery outcomes that deliver trust, equity and harmony.

4 Communities have strengths that must be recognized and their participation prioritized

A deficit approach to reconstruction is ineffective and inappropriate. International NGOs must recognize assets and strengths of affected community when 'building capacity'. They should avoid constructing or validating survivors as victims and the ensuing victim entrepreneurship. This focus perpetuates disempowerment. In the initial stages after the disaster, it is often local survivors who are best able to respond immediately to the material and emotional needs of other survivors. Local survivors both give and receive assistance in the initial phases and excluding these stakeholders from subsequent phases of reconstruction is inefficient. Later phases of reconstruction ought not overlook the contribution the survivors made in the initial response.

5 Understanding key stakeholders

Disasters often bring together key stakeholders with little or no prior contact (i.e. international NGOs and local communities). Relationships must be built or established in short timeframes due to the urgency of the response required. Overall coordination is essential if these relationships are to cohere. However, stereotypes that might form the basis of these initial relations may hinder effective responses to natural disasters. Stereotypes of donors as self-serving and publicity-seeking, OR as selfless and willing to do whatever it takes to assist those affected, are unhelpful. Stereotypes of affected communities as innocents grateful for any assistance offered, OR as self-interested and seeking only to extract as much as they can from donors, are equally unhelpful. Interactions between these two types of stakeholders based on any of these stereotypes will therefore be sub-optimal. A rational appraisal of each stakeholder is needed on a case-by-case basis. This of course takes time, but will result in more efficient partnerships and effective outcomes.

Sometimes international aid agencies face a choice between pleasing their donors in their home country by expedient actions, managerial control and forcing 'Western' ways of doing things on recipients, and a slower process of recovery involving participation of recipients and 'local' ways of doing things. It is important that all stakeholders understand this tension and that international agencies are transparent in the choices they make.

6 Religious and cultural beliefs cannot be excluded from consideration

Religious and cultural beliefs of the affected community are often central to any reconstruction effort. Religious beliefs can impact on the affected community's understanding of why the disaster occurred and this therefore informs how it ought to be responded to. An affected community's spirituality is vital and cannot be separated from the response. Local, national and international aid agencies must recognize and understand the religious and cultural contexts in which they are working, and adapt their procedures accordingly.

Holding a neutral position on the affected community's expression of religiosity by donors and aid agencies can be difficult. While it is necessary to work within local cultural environments, religious belief can become more firmly held by communities after a disaster. Criticisms of religious activities (including, for instance, sharia law in Aceh) can be difficult to make by both locals and external agencies, even if these expressions of religiosity entrench powerlessness of certain members of the community.

Affected communities are vulnerable due to the destruction they experience, and 'proselytizing' organizations can raise significant tensions. 'Proselytizing' organizations can be found in different religions and can use disasters as opportunities to 'seed' churches or attract converts. They can jeopardize the work being undertaken by other faith-based organizations of the same religious persuasion.

7 Communication is central to effective responses

In large disasters it is very difficult but important to maintain some overall communication strategy as part of coordination efforts. This minimizes errors and the extent to which activities are replicated. Limited and basic communications complicate such coordination. Certainly a databank of how international NGOs are responding is necessary to aid coordination. Strategic options need to be clear, as do criteria for choosing specific strategies. Exit strategies, in particular, need to be developed and communicated to all stakeholders.

The media also play a key role in communicating various aspects of disaster responses. This includes raising public attention to suffering, brokering aid, documenting use of aid, and editorializing on the delivered response. It is important to be aware of the tensions between each of these roles. The media and aid agencies are also responsible for another tension that surrounds the arrival of 'CHE tourism' (celebrities and ordinary people visiting sites of disaster). Often such visits take considerable effort to manage and can be at the expense of including locals in communication efforts and strategies.

8 Needs assessment

The politics of needs assessment in very important in any reconstruction process (Fraser, 1989). It involves issues around who decides what the needs are and what needs should be prioritized. Needs assessment must be approached carefully. If it takes too long people become disaffected and cynical. If it is too brief, then aid is often poorly directed and undermines faith in the whole reconstruction process.

9 Reconstruction cannot be a reinvention of the 'past'

Communities often view reconstruction as 'getting things back to normal', whereas donors and governments often see reconstruction as 'building back better'. Getting back to normal might require small (unfunded) projects and may be very attractive to survivors. However reconstruction does not mean a return to the 'original normal'. A 'new normal' is required. Building back better requires substantial funding and results to maintain donor support. While not mutually exclusive, tensions between these two approaches arise when one is prioritized over the other, or where communication and consultation between the key stakeholders is sub-optimal. It is not possible to quickly restore or return to a culture that has been destroyed due to the enormous loss of accumulated intergeneration sociocultural wisdom.

10 Gender analysis must underscore responses

While disasters affect communities indiscriminatingly, the fact that societies are often organized by gender roles means that the impact of death and injury can have a gender bias. For example, many communities affected by the tsunami were fishing communities. Men traditionally fished in boats, while women worked at home. There was therefore a greater proportion of women killed by the tsunami, as many men were at sea when the tsunami hit, while the women were on land. In this absence of women, men are now assuming the roles that women traditionally filled of family carers and social networkers. This gendered impact must therefore be considered and support tailored to assist both newly female-headed households and female-absent households. Disasters can also provide women with space to provide leadership and direction for their communities that was traditionally not possible. They should be supported in this new role.

11 International NGOs must be fully prepared for work in complex humanitarian emergencies

Large disasters often attract large amounts of funding, with some NGOs successfully raising millions of dollars from generous public donations (see Feeny and Clarke, 2007). However, there is no correlation between funds raised by international NGOs and their preparedness and competence in effectively expending these funds. Indeed, too much funding can lead to too much pressure on NGOs, which in turn leads to duplication and misguided competition for projects and survivor support.

International NGOs must consider their capacity to manage and lead large in-country teams in responding to disasters, the infrastructure and systems they have in place to respond at short notice to disasters and the preparation and support they provide to their deploying staff (or staff from the country affected).

Donors and NGOs must also take responsibility for building works they complete well after work is finished. It is necessary that concerns of sustainability are also applied to built infrastructure. Reconstruction efforts often concentrate on capital infrastructure without due regard for the on-going costs of operating these institutions (for example schools without teachers and resources, health clinics without nurses and medical supplies, houses without sewerage) These 'invisible' needs are just as great as the 'visible' needs.

These 11 lessons should be understood by host governments, local, national and international NGOs, as well as communities that are affected by natural disasters. When disasters do occur, it is vital that the response is immediate. However for the responses to be optimal it is necessary that there be thoughtful preparation. The lessons above can feed into this preparation.

References

AusAID (2009) *Budget 2009–10: Australia's Commitment to Overseas Aid*, www.ausaid.gov.au/publications/focus/jun09/01.pdf

Clarke, M. (2008) *Post-Kyoto: Designing the Next International Climate Change Protocol*, New York, Nova Science

Cornwall, A. (2008) 'Unpacking "Participation": models, meanings and practices', *Community Development Journal*, vol 43, no 3, July, pp269-283

Cosgrave, J. (2007) *Synthesis Report: Expanded Summary. Joint Evaluation of the international response to the Indian Ocean tsunami*, London, Tsunami Evaluation Coalition

Feeny, S. and Clarke, M. (2007), 'What Determines Australia's Responses to Emergencies and Natural Disasters', *Australian Economic Review*, vol 40, no 1, pp24–36

Fraser, N. (1989) *Unruly Practices: Power, Discourse and Gender in Contemporary Social Theory*, Minneapolis, University of Minnesota Press

International Panel on Climate Change (IPCC) (2007) *Climate Change 2007: Synthesis Report*, IPCC Fourth Assessment Report, Geneva, IPCC

Wisner, B., Blaikie, P, Cannon, T and Davis, I (2004) *At Risk Natural Hazards, people's vulnerability and disaster*, London, Routledge

Reconstructing the Invisible Landscape

Ismet Fanany

Once Indonesian President Susilo Bambang Yudhoyono officially announced the end of the emergency response phase on 26 March 2005, the reconstruction and rehabilitation phase began. Presidential Regulation no 30/2005 on the Master Plan for the Rehabilitation and Reconstruction of Aceh and Nias became law on 15 April 2005. The following day, the Agency for the Rehabilitation and Reconstruction for the Region and Community of Aceh and Nias (*Badan Rahabilitasi dan Rekonstruksi Wilayah dan Kehidupan Masyarakat Provinsi NAD-Nias*) was established by the Indonesian government. This agency eventually became known by its simplified Indonesian abbreviation, BRR (*Badan Rehabilitasi dan Rekonstruksi*). The organization was charged with coordinating the complex work of implementing the Master Plan.

The emphasis on physical reconstruction in the Master Plan is unmistakable and understandable. The destruction of houses, businesses, schools, offices, mosques, roads, bridges, cultivated fields, and hospitals and other health care centres was staggering in both scale and severity. A large part of the infrastructure of the affected area was destroyed completely or damaged beyond repair. The Master Plan offered an initial estimate of loss and quantified the destruction. This would guide rehabilitation and reconstruction work in Aceh. BRR and other agencies have largely reported the results of their work in quantifiable terms. On 18 April 2008, for example, a summary of progress in rehabilitation and reconstruction as of 29 February 2008 was posted on BRR's website. It found that 104,630 permanent houses had been built; 2045 survivors were still living in barrack; 757 healthcare facilities were constructed; 893 schools were built; 25,256 teachers were trained; 2475km of road were built; 254 bridges were built; 10 airstrips were built; 17 harbours were made; 101,848 small businesses had received support; 1620 places of worship were built or renovated; and 933 government buildings were erected or renovated.

In addition to the destruction of the physical landscape, loss of life was significant; the Indian Ocean tsunami was one of the largest natural disasters in history in this context. It immediately became clear that it would be as difficult to deal with several hundred thousand survivors as it would be to rebuild damaged infrastructure. These were the people who were supposed to benefit from the reconstruction, but even a complete and perfect restoration of the physical environment would be unable to completely eradicate the effects of the disaster from the lives of the survivors. The reason for this was that the tsunami inflicted another kind of serious damage on survivors, a destruction that was invisible to the eye but as potent as that to their environment. The wreckage of the physical aspects of people's lives lay all around where their homes and villages had once stood, but the wreckage of the psyche of the Acehnese lay inside each person, where it was not easily accessible and where it could not be perceived by the eye alone.

The focus on physical reconstruction was understandable, not just because of the scale and severity of the disaster, but also because it was so obvious. The 'destruction of the soul', referred to by Suaedy at the beginning of this volume, however, did not attract the attention of the people pouring into Aceh or move them as the physical destruction did. The destruction of the Acehnese psyche was invisible, and a deliberate effort was required to see that it was even there. It was a much larger undertaking to understand what its nature was, as well as its scale and severity. It is very difficult to measure this kind of damage. There is no unit of measurement for psychological distress that can be easily counted. Loss, depression, despair, hopelessness, fear of the future, sadness, and helplessness are not subject to easy enumeration. The way in which the survivors might come to terms with a disaster cannot be extrapolated by logic. The way in which they explain the disaster to themselves, which might affect them and affect their ability to recover their psychological equilibrium, might well be unpredictable, especially by observers from outside the survivors' culture.

To a significant degree, internal destruction to the psyche is related to loss of the physical environment. The loss of people and objects that normally populated the landscape is often a contributing cause to psychological damage. Studies have shown that buildings or villages or cities are more than just places to live or work – they are imbued with meaning. In addition to their practical functions, they also contain personal histories and shared memories of events and interpersonal relationships. These issues have been discussed by Rivlin (1987), Saegert and Winkel (1990), Altman (1993), Jacobs (1995), and Curtis and Rees Jones (1998). This is easily comprehensible and likely to be understood intuitively by those wishing to help. It is not surprising, then, that reconstruction of the missing houses, roads, businesses, hospitals, and so forth in Aceh was seen by the Acehnese as a necessary first step in reconstruction and rehabilitation of the region.

In the introduction to this volume, Ahmad Suaedy mentioned the silence and blank stares of the tsunami survivors immediately following the disaster. These were outward symptoms of damage to the psyche that was invisible to the eye. One means of understanding this internal damage is to interpret the silence and the blank looks. This can be done by encouraging the survivors to speak, and listening to what they say. Once the rehabilitation and reconstruction phase was well under way, the survivors did begin to speak. Their stories say a lot about their internal devastation, their feelings about the disaster, and the emotional strategies they might adopt to deal with the future. It is appropriate, then, that this discussion about the internal destruction suffered by the Acehnese should begin with one such story.

I remember, Halimah[1] began, two of my daughters and I were watching the local affiliate of the Indonesian state television broadcaster, TVRI (Televisi Republik Indonesian), on 24 December, Christmas Eve 2004. Something caught our attention. TVRI was screening a Christmas programme! We stopped talking and stared at the screen. It was unbelievable. The Aceh affiliate of TVRI was celebrating Christmas! Christmas songs were playing. There was a discussion about Christianity, the birth and life of Jesus, and the importance of Christmas and its celebration. Aceh, the most Muslim region of Indonesia, was celebrating Christmas!

We watched the programme with great interest, almost without blinking, but not because we were Christian. We looked at each other without speaking, but each of us knew what the others were thinking. That was the first time we had seen a Christmas show broadcast in Aceh. They might have done it in the past and we missed it for whatever reason, but this broadcast had a major impact on us.

At the end of the programme, I told the others what I was thinking. Oh, God, what had become of Aceh and the people of Aceh? Christianity was now really in Aceh! Our great Islamic tradition and culture was ending. Why, God, Why? Norma[2] and Indah,[3] my daughters, nodded in agreement. I told my children to raise their hands in prayer, and I did the same. I prayed out loud: 'God, if this is what our beloved land and its people have become, please bring an end to this world!' We said Amen together.

Norma, Indah and I were cleaning up after breakfast when the earthquake of 26 December 2004 struck. We were in the kitchen, dropped what we were doing, and looked at each other. The strength of the quake frightened us. It was so strong that we thought the house was going to collapse. In a split second, we remembered our prayer of two nights previous. I smiled at my children and then said: 'Thank you, God. You are answering our prayers!' My children nodded their agreement, smiling.

When the huge waves of the tsunami hit our house less than an hour later, I was upstairs with Norma. Indah was downstairs doing the regular house work, putting things away, sweeping, that kind of thing. The water quickly reached the second floor. Norma and I looked out the windows. We were amazed to see water all around us. Here and there, a few buildings that were more than one storey high were sticking out. Our house was more than 2km from the beach, and the water was up to our second floor and was still rising. There were not too many two-storey houses around us, and our neighbours had all disappeared! We both turned white. Almost at the same time, we screamed for Indah, but we knew we could not go downstairs because of the rising flood. We hugged each other as the water started to come in through the upstairs windows! The ocean had reached so far inland that we both felt certain the world was ending. 'God has indeed answered our prayer', I whispered.

We felt the water rising around our legs, and soon my daughter and I were floating towards the ceiling. We had no idea what had happened to Indah. We didn't know what had happened, but there was one thing we were sure about: the end of the world had come, and we were going to die soon! We praised God as the water approached near the ceiling.

Soon we could touch the ceiling. We knew that we would soon drown. When the water reached the ceiling, we would have no more air to breathe. Norma and I were clinging to each other. It was quite dark now as the dirty water did not reflect much light into the space between the ceiling and its surface. I could feel Norma shaking, even though we hadn't been under water for long, and the water was quite warm. I was shaking, too. We were terrified. The realization that we would die slowly in this way and that Indah might have died under equally frightening circumstances scared me in a way I had never felt before. I could tell my daughter felt this as well.

'God,' I whispered in the silence preceding death, 'please don't let us die this way. If this is what the end of the world is like, please abort it. We don't want to witness it.' I barely whispered, but my voice sounded clear and eerie in the small space. I heard Norma say amen at the end of my prayer.

By now our heads were touching the ceiling. All of a sudden, we realized the water had stopped rising! We did not know how long we were wedged against the ceiling before we felt the water start to recede. It felt like a lifetime. At that moment, we felt that our first life was over, and we were beginning a new life. God had answered our prayers in the most spectacular manner. It was nothing short of a miracle. He had brought an end to the world in Aceh, to the world we saw when we were watching the Christmas programme two nights before. Equally miraculous, He had spared our lives in the process!

Halimah ended her story with the comment that Indah had died in the tsunami. This was notable in that it lacked any emotion, even though Halimah was talking about her own daughter. Her expression did not change. In fact, she had shown no particular emotion at any time during the course of the story. It was hard to tell what she really felt. She hadn't really smiled but hadn't expressed any sadness either. She spoke in a monotone. She neither raised her voice nor had she lowered it. The only sign of emotion was in the moving of her hands. Every now and then she would adjust the headscarf wrapped fashionably around her face that matched her equally fashionable long-sleeved tunic. That seemed to be a nervous habit. She would run the tip of one or two fingers across her forehead under the edge of the scarf, for example. Or she would hold or touch one of her many pieces of jewellery.

The most likely emotion Halimah seemed to feel while telling the story, and perhaps in her life since the tsunami, was reconciliation. She appeared certain that God had sent the tsunami and everything that resulted from it, including the death of her own daughter. Not a shadow of doubt dimmed this realization for her. She also believed that God had answered her prayers a second time, saving her and Norma.

Halimah's story was a personal narrative. But it illuminates many of the invisible aspects of the tsunami's effects. In particular, the story illustrates, at least in part, the way the Acehnese view themselves and others and, in this context, the effects of the disaster on the emotions and feelings of those who survived. This self-conception is based on religion. The Acehnese see themselves primarily as Muslims, in contrast to others who are not. There may be other factors that contribute to their concept of self, but there is no doubt that this is a central feature of their identity that colours their perception of everything else.

This choice of a survivor's narrative was intentional. Religion is the most common theme when the Acehnese relate the story of the tsunami. In every personal story of destruction, there is always an element of the miraculous. Something worse could have happened, but didn't, because of God's intervention. The survivors seem to return to the security of God's blessing when they recall the tsunami's devastation. In addition, this religious perspective has significantly influenced the way survivors have viewed various aspects of the reconstruction process.

Within months of BRR's inception, Acehnese concerns about the effects of the rehabilitation and reconstruction work on their religion and religious life had become a national issue. They were concerned about the presence of non-Muslim organizations and NGOs, and were worried about using their money. They feared that these organizations were in Aceh to help with relief work but also to proselytize. Even before the rehabilitation and reconstruction phase officially began, rumours to this effect had become so serious that, in March 2005, Defence Minister Juwono Sudarsono asked some Christian groups to stop their relief work in Aceh and leave (Behn, 2005; Endonesia, 2005a), even though Coordinating Minister for Public Welfare Alwi Shihab later denied that the Indonesian government was going to instigate such a ban (Endonesia, 2005b).

Internationally, a number of issues faced by Christian organizations working in Aceh received a great deal of attention (see, for example, Powell, 2005; Gartland, 2005). These issues ranged from accusations of proselytizing, to threats against wearing Western-style swimsuits on the beach (*The Australian*, 2005) to fears that tsunami orphans would be placed in Christian homes (Cooperman, 2005). In short, rehabilitation and reconstruction work in Aceh was coloured by religion. One reason for this related to the way the Acehnese explained the reason for the disaster to themselves. This, in turn, influenced their views about how to live following the tsunami. The potential of conversion to Christianity or the possibility that the presence of Westerners in swimsuits on their beaches might undermine their religious values suggested to them that God might send an even greater disaster. Any such threat, therefore, had to be eliminated.

There were several effects of the tsunami on the internal landscape of Acehnese life. These include guilt about the past. Some Acehnese felt they had not been good enough Muslims. They are now determined to live in what they feel is a more righteous manner. Others felt suspicious of the present. They were suspicious about the way reconstruction had been carried out, and in particular distrusted the non-Muslim organizations. Finally, they feared the future. Many Acehnese were afraid that the future they were constructing, or more accurately was in large part being constructed for them, would not take a form that would support their Muslim identity.

Guilt about the past

It is highly unlikely that a majority of the public in Aceh thinks that the Christmas programme on the local TVRI affiliate on Christmas Eve 2004 caused the tsunami. Most probably, very few of them, if any at all, prayed for the end of the world that night. Nonetheless, it is very likely that most of the survivors, like Halimah, believe that God sent the tsunami to Aceh. In their mind, He did so for a reason, even though individuals may have different views on what this reason is. Some of them, like Halimah and her daughters, feel that they had allowed Islam to weaken in Aceh, and other religions to enter and become established. They feel that Christianity is spreading in Aceh, and they are partly to blame. The Acehnese often talk about their concern about the Christianization of the region, although this is not only in the context of the tsunami reconstruction effort. To these individuals, God sent the tsunami to check the weakening of Islam and halt the spread of Christianity in Aceh, either by bringing an end to the world as they knew it, or as a warning to the Acehnese that they must take action to repair the situation.

Others in Aceh believe that God sent the tsunami to punish them. Even though they believe that they are very devout Muslims, they feel that collectively they have behaved badly. Some members of the community drink alcohol. Others are involved in 'inappropriate' relationships, even when this amounted to no more than a couple alone together without doing anything. Many dress inappropriately, which is commonly taken to mean that women have not covered their whole body, showing only their faces and hands. These Acehnese believe that God has been angered by their bad behaviour and the tsunami was their punishment.

Still others are convinced that God used the tsunami to test the faith of the Acehnese. These people believe that the greater the test, the more God loves them. The tsunami, therefore, was good for Aceh but must result in a strengthening of their faith. They must not, for example, let their loss, no matter how serious, weaken their beliefs. They must not skip the required midday prayer on Fridays, even if their mosques were damaged and cannot be used. To these individuals, their failure to pass smaller tests from God, or the fact that they had not yet been sufficiently tested, was the cause of the tsunami.

Regardless of their exact interpretation, the majority of Acehnese interviewed for the writing of this chapter believe the tsunami was associated directly with them and their faith. They see their religious behaviour, as well as their devotion to and protection of Islamic culture and tradition in their region, as creating a need in God's eyes for the tsunami and resulting devastation. In some cases, they believe that their actions, while well-intentioned, were insufficient. In other cases, they feel their conduct has been inadequate and they have failed to protect, develop and value their Islamic heritage.

In this context, the importance of guilt and of the tsunami as a test might explain Halimah's lack of emotion. It was most striking that she showed no emotion when talking about the death of her daughter. She seemed to imply that the loss of a child was a small price to pay to make up for a dissolute past and any bad, inappropriate and inadequate actions she may have committed as well as for the things she should have done. This guilt has been evident in many of the personal narratives of the tsunami.

Suspicion of the present

While the Acehnese were most suspicious of the intentions of non-Muslim organizations in Aceh that they believed intended to convert survivors, this was not their only fear. Many expressed privately but explicitly that they did not trust many of the individuals and organizations involved in rehabilitation and reconstruction work in their area, and this applied to local, national and international agencies regardless of whether they were private or governmental. They believe that these organizations have their own self interest and agendas which, to varying degrees, are more important to them than the interests of the Acehnese.

The widespread idea that individuals and organizations involved in reconstruction largely operated in their own self interest was often supported by various allegations and cases of corruption associated with the rehabilitation and reconstruction effort. It is worth noting that this self-interest represents 'business as usual' in Indonesia and was not necessarily unexpected, at least on the part of Indonesian organizations. By October 2005, for example, the Anti Corruption Section of BRR in Aceh had received 85 allegations of corruptions from communities that were supposed to benefit from aid efforts (Tempointeraktif, 2005).

Even BRR itself was accused of corruption. Anti Corruption Movement (*Gerakan Anti Korupsi*), an NGO, alleged that, in 2006, an incidence of corruption took place in BRR in relation to a sum of Yen 14.6 billion provided by Japan for reconstruction (BRR, 2006). The endemic nature of Indonesian corruption has been widely discussed (see, for example, Harahap, 1999; Lindsey, 2002; Henderson and Kuncoro, 2004; and many others). The Acehnese, like most Indonesians, have lost the ability to react with outrage to corrupt behaviour (Shambazy, 2008). It is instead accepted as a given, even when resented. For this reason, the suspicions of the Acehnese in relation to the rehabilitation and reconstruction of their region are not entirely baseless.

The results of the reconstruction further confirmed the legitimacy of their suspicions. Some of the houses built for survivors could not be occupied because their quality was substandard (Perlez, 2006). Survivors, and individuals pretending to be survivors, themselves engaged in corrupt behaviour. In several locations, it is generally reported that individuals have claimed more than one house each. This was sometimes possible because of connections; in other cases, opportunistic survivors simply took advantage of the confusion and lack of records to obtain houses in several villages. There were even cases of individuals who did not lose a house in the disaster demanding compensation. Timber for the reconstruction effort was in short supply. This led to another form of corruption among aid organizations as well as survivors, namely the pillaging of protected jungle as a source of timber (James, 2006; Wade, 2006).

However, the greatest suspicions centred on religion. In this case, any Acehnese felt that the presence of organizations openly associated with a church, or whose operating principles referred to Christianity, was suspect. Many believed, without a doubt, that the real aim of these groups was to convert survivors, gain control of Muslim orphans so they could be raised as Christians, and build churches in the region. The assurances of the Indonesian government that this would not be permitted and the assertions of the aid providers themselves only suggested to many that this issue was, in fact, part of a conspiracy against the Acehnese (Powell, 2005; Cooperman, 2005; Gartland, 2005). A number of media outlets suggested that this suspicion was fanned by fundamentalist groups that were rushing to Aceh along with aid organizations with the self-proclaimed aim of ensuring religious purity in the region (see, for example, Harvey, 2005), and observations of these religious suspicions have been linked to what some see as an increasing tendency towards rigid orthodoxy in the region (see, for example, de Guzman, 2007).

Fear of the future

Many Acehnese fear the future when reconstruction is complete. Their trepidation centres on doubt whether the Islamic identity, culture and tradition of the region can be maintained following a prolonged period of interaction with outsiders, many of whom are supposed to possess ulterior motives for their presence in the area. This fear is perhaps best exemplified by the case of an American aid organization, WorldHelp, that was rumoured to be planning to place 300 Muslim orphans of the tsunami in a Christian orphanage (see Cooperman, 2005). Despite claims of misreporting and an outright denial by the organization that this was an attempt to do anything other than assist in the care of these children, many Acehnese could not believe that this issue resulted from a misunderstanding or possibly a misguided attempt to help. The attempts of the central government to ameliorate the situation did little to dispel Acehnese fears for the future.

This issue was so controversial because it intensified survivors' fears that they would lose control of themselves and their own destiny. If, for example, their desire to raise tsunami orphans as Muslims, ideally in Aceh, had been overruled, many would have taken it as an indication that the ability to make significant decisions had been taken away from them by experts and professionals who knew little about their way of life and culture but nonetheless felt qualified to advise and dictate. An interesting insight into the Acehnese psyche can be found in the apparent paradox that so many survivors believed themselves to be righteous and virtuous Muslims, whose religious beliefs had been validated by God in a variety of ways, but also believed that those religious values were so tenuous as to be easily erased by community exposure to Westerners and outside practices and religions. The source of this apparent internal conflict is not clear, but may stem from survivors' observations that un-Islamic behaviour was already becoming more common even before the tsunami. Such un-Islamic behaviour has been connected with an increase in HIV/AIDS infection, drug use, prostitution and the like (see, for example, Komisi Penanggulangan Aids, 2007; Harian Berita Sore, 2007; Harian Umum Pelita, 2007). This perhaps represents a source of cognitive dissonance that is disturbing to many Acehnese and has contributed to the psychic damage many suffer.

Reconstructing the invisible landscape

Compared with the internal landscape, the reconstruction of the physical environment following the tsunami in Aceh has been relatively straightforward, despite the problems in aid disbursement and utilization that have now been widely documented. The internal landscape, composed of the thoughts, feelings, and emotions of survivors, is not so easily restored however. This internal landscape in Aceh is coloured and formed by the religious views and beliefs of the community that shape identity, dictate behaviour, give meaning to culture and infuse tradition.

In Aceh, tsunami survivors will soon find themselves living in a more or less complete physical environment that can reasonably take the place of the houses, offices, hospitals, roads, bridges, schools, and so forth that were destroyed in the disaster. While these structures will not fully replicate those that were lost, they will be recognizable in purpose and serviceable in form. Many tsunami survivors are already occupying houses built for them and making use of infrastructure and public buildings. Nonetheless, the internal landscape that should lie behind the external and give it structure and meaning is still largely missing in the tsunami affected areas.

The means to repair the psyche of the Acehnese may not lie with aid, aid workers or experts of any kind. Instead, it is likely to come itself with time from the all encompassing religious framework through which they view the world and understand its content. This is a cognitive structure whose workings are largely indiscernible, even to other Indonesian Muslims, as it contains the basic elements of Islam as it is understood in Indonesia but also the overlay of Acehnese culture and language as have developed throughout the history of the region. This has been noted by some observers, but remains unaddressed in aid programmes (see, for example De Jong et al, 2005).

There is considerable literature on the value of strong religious beliefs in coping with and recovering from natural disaster (see, for example, Priya, 2002; de Silva, 2006; Trevino and Pargament, 2007). Generally, this research indicates that faith is an advantage in coping, but may also serve as a hindrance to recovery, especially when it suggests to survivors that the disaster was punishment of some kind and God is angry (Smith et al, 2000). It has even been suggested that this view indicates a need for mental help (Pargament et al, 1998). The majority of available research on this topic, however, has related to disasters in the West, where a majority of survivors were Christian. Gillard and Paton (1999) suggested that different religious beliefs and traditions may generate different psychological responses to disaster as well as different expectations for its resolution. The specific characteristics of the Acehnese culture and their internal and external environment may mean that survivors' reactions are different from those observed in Western communities, and the exact nature of a Muslim response to disaster (if one exists) has not been fully elucidated (see Basit, 2007).

In any case, there is now much evidence to suggest that a certain means to reconstruct the Acehnese psyche following the Indian Ocean tsunami remains elusive and may, in the end, be out of reach to aid providers, officials, community leaders and perhaps even to the survivors themselves. There is no doubt the rehabilitation of the internal environment of survivors will take much longer than the rebuilding of the external environment and is considered, at least by some aid providers, to be outside of their expertise. This was the conclusion of WHO in its 2005 recommendations for mental health provision in Aceh, which stated:

> *. . . Attempts from outside Aceh to 'train' various community leaders in how they might respond to widespread psychological distress at a community level, using western constructs of community reconstruction and development, might be misguided and will probably be unwelcome; the religious construction of meaning surrounding the disaster may mean that efforts to deal with psychological and social consequences of the disaster in ways that are not consonant with such religious and cultural values and beliefs (e.g. trauma-focused counseling, psychiatric approaches) will be both ineffective and unacceptable; . . . (WHO, 2005).*

This realization, made explicit by WHO but likely recognized by a number of others, seems to accurately summarize much of the psychological response of the Acehnese to various issues that seemed to threaten their identity, values, and mores. Perhaps, then, the reconstruction of the survivors' psyche and, with it, the refurbishment of their internal landscape in accord with their physical environment, should really be left to time and the Acehnese themselves to determine form, nature and specifics.

In this context, another survivor's narrative is telling. Where Halimah's story described a view of the past and present, Baharuddin's[4] story is one of the future. A local official, Baharuddin presides over a small community of survivors who have received newly built houses on the site of their former village:

> *Two months ago, we got the keys to all 700 houses in the new village, he said. But many of the houses are still empty. People are choosing to live together communally, rather than just one or two people alone in a big house. There is too much empty space where family members and friends used to be. Together, though, we can support each other and try to recreate the kind of life we had.*

> *I just got married. We intentionally had the wedding in the new house to give it some history and make sure it became part of our new life. It can't make up for all the births, deaths, and celebrations the old house had witnessed, but it's a start. Now, my wife is pregnant, so soon there will be a new baby and all the excitement of the birth to fill the space.*

> *Time passes, and you have to keep going,' he finished, smiling.*

The normalcy of the scene, and the optimism in Baharuddin's voice, suggest that the reconstruction of the survivors' internal landscape has begun in Aceh and, although it perhaps lags behind the reconstruction of the physical environment, indicates that a true recovery encompassing religion, values, custom, tradition and history old and new can eventually take place in Aceh.

References

Altman, I. (1993) Dialectics, Physical Environments, and Personal Relationship,' *Communication Monographs*, vol 60, pp26–34

Basit, A. (2007) 'An Islamic Perspective on Coping with Catastrophe,' *Southern Medical Journal*, vol 100, no 1, pp950–951

Behn, S. (2005) 'Indonesian Ousts Christian Groups,' *The Washington Times*, 17 March

BRR (2006) 'BRR Bantah Korupso Bantuan Jepang,' 6 November; www.e-aceh-nias.org/news/news.aspx?id=32

BRR (2008) Home page, www.e-aceh-nias.org/home/

Cooperman, A. (2005) 'Tsunami Orphans Won't Be Sent to Christian Home', *The Washington Post*, 14 January

Curtis, S. and Rees Jones, I. (1998) 'Is There a Place for Geography in the Analysis of Health Inequality?' in Bartley, M et al, eds, *The Sociology of Health Inequalities*, Oxford, Blackwell pp85–112

de Guzman, O. (2007) 'Indonesia After the Wave', *The Washington Post*, 27 June

De Jong, K. et al (2005) 'Addressing Psychosocial Needs in the Aftermath of the Tsunami', *PLOS Medicine*, vol 2, no 6, p179

De Silva, P. (2006) 'The Tsunami and Its Aftermath in Sri Lanka: Explorations of a Buddhist Perspective,' *International Review of Psychiatry*, 18: 281–287

Endonesia (2005a), 'Juwono: LSM Kristen Silakan Keluar dari Aceh;' www.endonesia.com/mod.php?mod=publisher&op=viewarticle&cid=27&artid=679

Endonesia (2005b), 'Alwi Bantah Akan Pulangkan LSM Kristen;' www.endonesia.com/mod.php?mod=publisher&op=viewarticle&cid=27&artid=681

Gartland, M. (2005) 'Banda Aceh Invites Christians' Aid, But Not Their Proselytizing', *The Post and Courier*, 26 December

Gillard, M. and Paton D. (1999) 'Disaster Stress Following a Hurricane: The Role of Religious Differences in the Fijian Islands', *Australian Journal of Disaster & Trauma Studies*, 1999, p2

Harahap, R. M. (1999) *Strategies for Preventing Corruption in Indonesia*, Asia Pacific School of Economics and Management Working Paper No GOV99-3, Canberra, Australian National University

Harian Berita Sore (2007) 'Pengguna Narkoba di Aceh Mulai Mengkhawatirkan, 25 June; http://beritasore.com/2007/06/25/pengguna-narkoba-di-aceh-mulai-mengkhawatirkan/

Harian Umum Pelita (2007) 'Kalangan Swasta Dominasi Kasus Narkoba di Aceh,' 5 December; www.hupelita.com/baca.php?id=40628

Harvey, R. (2005) 'Aceh Aid prompts Rival Aid,' BBC News Asia-Pacific; http://news.bbc.co.uk/2/hi/asia-pacific/4181521.stm

Henderson, J. V. and Kuncoro, A. (2004) *Corruption in Indonesia*, NBER Working Paper No 10674, Cambridge, MA, NBER

Jacobs, M. (1995) 'Sustainability and Community: Environment, Economic Nationalisam, and Sense of Place', *Australian Planner*, vol 32, no 2, pp109–115

James, E. (2006) *Clean or Corrupt: Tsunami Aid in Aceh*, Asia Pacific School of Economics and Governance Discussion Paper No 06-04, Canberra, Australian National University

Komisi Penanggulangan Aids (2007) 'Analisa: Pengidap HIV/AIDS di NAD Terus Bertambah'; www.aidsindonesia.or.id/index.php?Itemid=2&id=820&option=com _content&task=view

Lindsey, T. (2002) 'Anti-Corruption and NGOs in Indonesia,' in Holloway, R, ed, *Stealing from the People: 16 Studies on Corruption in Indonesia*, Jakarta, Partnership for Governance Reform, pp29–71

Pargament, K. I. et al (1998) 'Patterns of Positive and Negative Religious Coping with Major Life Stressors', *Journal for the Scientific Study of Religion*, vol 37, pp710–724

Perlez, J. (2006) 'Aid Groups Are Criticized Over Tsunami Reconstruction', *The New York Times*, 27 July

Powell, S. (2005) 'Christian Group 'Proselytising': Muslims', *The Australian*, 24 December

Priya, K. R. (2002) 'Suffering and Healing Among the Survivors of the Bhuj Earthquake,' *Psychological Studies*, vol 47, pp106–112

Rivlin, L. (1987) 'The Neighborhood, Personal Identity, and Group Affiliations,' in Altman, I. and Wandersman, A., eds, *Neighborhood and Community Environments*, New York, Plenum, pp1–34

Saegert, S. and Winkel, G. W. (1990) 'Environmental Psychology,' *Annual Review of Psychology*, vol 41, pp441–477

Shambazy, B. (2008) 'Geleng dan Angguk Kepala,' *Kompas*, 8 March 2008

Smith, B. W. et al (2000) 'Noah Revisited: Religious Coping by Church Members and the Impact of the 1993 Midwest Flood,' *Journal of Community Psychology*, vol 28, no 2, pp169–186

Tempointeraktif (2005) Satuan Anti Korupsi BRR Aceh-Nias Terima 85 Pengaduan, 19 October; www.tempointeraktif.com/hg/nasional/2005/10/19/brk,20051019-68228,id.html

The Australian (2005) 'Aid Groups Warned Against Preaching', 11 January

Trevino, K. M. and Pargament, K. I. (2007) 'Religious Coping with Terrorism and Natural Disaster,' *Southern Medical Journal*, vol 100, no 9, pp946–947

Wade, M. (2006) 'Corruption Undermines Aceh Tsunami Aid', *Sydney Morning Herald*, 27 February

WHO (2005) *WHO Recommendations for Mental Health in Aceh*, WHO, http://who.or.id/eng/contents/aceh/WHO_Recommendations_Mental_Health_Aceh.pdf

Notes

1   Halimah (not her real name) was a middle-aged widow with nine children, of whom two were living at home when the tsunami hit Banda Aceh. She was an educated woman and chair of the Aceh branch of an influential, national women's organization. She was wealthy and owned a large modern house on the outskirts of Banda Aceh. She told me this story during one of my visits to Banda Aceh in June 2007.
2   Not her real name.
3   Not her real name.
4   Not his real name.

Index